SURVIVING

AUTOCRACY

SURVIVING
AUTOCRACY

MASHA GESSEN

RANDOM HOUSE
LARGE PRINT

Published in the United States of America by Random House Large Print in association with Riverhead Books, an imprint of Penguin Random House LLC.

Portions of this book previously appeared, in different form, in **The New Yorker**, **The New York Times**, **The New York Review of Books**, and **Harper's**.

"Let America Be America Again" from **The Collected Poems of Langston Hughes** by Langston Hughes, edited by Arnold Rampersad with David Roessel, Associate Editor, copyright © 1994 by the Estate of Langston Hughes. Used by permission of Alfred A. Knopf, an imprint of the Knopf Doubleday Publishing Group, a division of Penguin Random House LLC, and Harold Ober Associates. All rights reserved.

Cover design by Jason Booher

The Library of Congress has established a Cataloging-in-Publication record for this title.

ISBN: 978-0-593-28600-5

www.penguinrandomhouse.com/large-print-format-books

FIRST LARGE PRINT EDITION

Printed in the United States of America

10 9 8 7 6 5 4 3 2 1

This Large Print edition published in accord with the standards of the N.A.V.H.

CONTENTS

PART TWO | KING OF REALITY

PART THREE | WHO IS "US"?

SURVIVING

AUTOCRACY

PROLOGUE

Donald Trump's entire repertoire had long been familiar to Americans by the time he decided to address the nation on the evening of March 11, 2020, about the pandemic of the novel coronavirus. We knew Trump's range: government by gesture; obfuscation and lying; self-praise; stoking fear and issuing threats. He had repeatedly dismissed the coronavirus as a minor flu and even a hoax; he had predicted that it would miraculously vanish. It had been two months since China, where the disease appeared first, had made the genetic code of the virus publicly available. The United States had wasted most of that time. Hospitals were not equipped to face the looming onslaught of patients. Protective equipment was in short supply. Essential information had been kept secret by the White House. Testing was not available. Now the virus was spreading in the country, it was too late for prevention, and no one had a plan for mitigation or suppression. Panic was starting to rise in Washington state, where the first American deaths occurred, in California, New York, and elsewhere. Trump finally appeared on television.

He performed his entire repertoire. He announced that he was banning travelers coming in from Europe—this was his grand gesture. He boasted of "responding with great speed and professionalism," promised widespread testing and effective antiviral therapies, and asserted that insurance companies would waive all copayments for treatments; this was the obfuscation and lying. These pledges blended seamlessly with self-praise, which included calling the American effort "the most aggressive and comprehensive," claiming to have handled the epidemic better than European countries had, and assuring his audience that the United States was well prepared. None of this was true. Finally, the fearmongering came when Trump called COVID-19 a "foreign virus," pointing the finger at Europe. Soon, he would home in on a better name—"the Chinese virus"—and hate crimes against Asian-Americans would spike.

Trump apparently read from a teleprompter that night. He sounded grave. This was, in other words, one of those times when Trump sounded presidential to some people, because he didn't sound entirely deranged. For example, former Ohio governor John Kasich, a Republican, defended Trump on CNN, saying that "he did fine," in part because he read from a script. But precisely because Trump was not at his worst—just his ordinary obfuscating and self-aggrandizing self—in the extraordinary situation of the pandemic, what we were witnessing was peak Trump.

Over the next few weeks, Trump would

shirk responsibility for the crisis, at one point saying literally, "No, I don't take responsibility at all," when he was asked about a lack of access to testing. He would tell governors to figure out their own ways of procuring supplies, and he would offer no guidance on policy. He would take the podium at the White House during almost daily briefings and issue bogus medical advice, such as extolling the virtues of untested drugs, which some people then rushed to use. He would resist calls to invoke the Defense Production Act, to compel companies to turn their facilities over to manufacturing essential equipment, evidently for fear of cutting into the profits of his corporate cronies. All along, he would praise his own intelligence and approach. The television networks would broadcast these sessions live; the newspapers would report on them, and Trump's other coronavirus-related pronouncements, as though they were the stuff of an intelligible presidency, with positions, principles, and a strategy. As a result, even as hospitals across the country buckled, people died, and the economy tanked, more than half of all Americans claimed to approve of Trump's response to the pandemic.

Some people compared the Trumpian response to COVID-19 to the Soviet government's response to the catastrophic accident at the Chernobyl power plant in 1986. For once, such a comparison was not far-fetched. The people most at risk were denied necessary, potentially lifesaving information, and this was the government's failure; there was rumor and fear on the one hand and dangerous oblivion on the other. And, of course, there was unconscionable, preventable tragedy. To be sure, Americans in 2020 had vastly more access to information than did Soviet citizens in 1986. But the Trump administration shared two key features with the Soviet government: utter disregard for human life and a monomaniacal focus on pleasing the leader, to make him appear unerring and all-powerful. These are the features of autocratic leadership. In the three years of his presidency, even before the coronavirus pandemic, Trump

PROLOGUE

had come closer to achieving autocratic rule than most people would have thought possible. This is a book about that transformation—and about the hope we may yet have for emerging from Trumpism.

Part One

AN AUTOCRATIC ATTEMPT

1.

WHAT DO WE CALL IT?

It could have been any week of the Trump presidency—a week when he kept contradicting the government's experts on the COVID-19 pandemic, or a week when he was railing against Supreme Court justices, or a week when he humiliated his own cabinet members in public. Take one week in October 2019, a month into the impeachment inquiry in Congress and just over a thousand days into the presidency. The acting ambassador to Ukraine, William B. Taylor, Jr., testified about waging a losing battle against Trump and his people to pursue a foreign agenda consistent with government policy and practice. House Republicans stormed a closed impeachment-inquiry hearing in a bizarre direct action of Congress members against congressional practice. Trump's personal attorney William Consovoy argued in court that his client was immune from any prosecution—including, hypothetically, for murdering someone in the middle of Fifth Avenue—as long as he was president. And on Friday morning, **The New York Times** website had two headlines stacked on the left side of the home page. The top one reported that the Justice Department had launched a criminal probe into its own investigation of Russian interference in the 2016 election. The headline directly below announced that the secretary of education, Betsy DeVos, had been found in contempt of court for continuing—in direct contravention of judicial decisions—to collect student-loan payments from former students of defunct for-profit colleges. The government seemed to be at war with itself on every front.

Trumpian news has a way of being shocking without being surprising. Every one of the events of that week was, in itself, staggering: an assault on the senses and the mental faculties. Together, they were just more of the same. Trump had beaten the government, the media, and the very concept of politics into a state beyond recognition. In part by habit and in part out of a sense of necessity, we continued to report the news and consume the news—this presidency produced more headlines per unit of time than any other—but at the end of each of his thousand days of presidency we seemed hardly closer to understanding what was happening to us.

The difficulty with absorbing the news lies, in part, in the words we use, which have a way of rendering the outrageous ordinary. The secretary of education was held in contempt, and this astounding event was narrated in normalizing newspaper prose: probably the strongest description called it an "exceedingly rare judicial rebuke of a Cabinet secretary." This could not begin to describe the drama of a cabinet member remaining unrepentant for her agency's seizure of assets from people whom it had been ordered by the courts to leave in peace—sixteen thousand people. And even when we could find the words to describe the exceptional, barely imaginable nature of Trumpian stories, that approach could not scale. How could we talk about a series of nearly inconceivable events that had become routine? How do we describe the confrontation of existing government institutions with a presidential apparatus that wants to destroy them?

I found some possible answers in the work of Hungarian sociologist Bálint Magyar. In struggling to define and describe what had happened in his country, Magyar had realized that the language of both the media and the academy was not up to the task. After the Eastern Bloc collapsed in 1989, both local and Western commentators adopted the language of liberal democracy to describe what was happening in the region. They talked about elections and legitimacy, rule of law and public opinion. Their language reflected their assumptions and their limitations:

they assumed that their countries would become liberal democracies—this seemed the inevitable outcome of the Cold War; and they had no other language at their disposal anyway. But if we use the wrong language, we cannot describe what we are seeing. If we use the language developed for describing fish, we cannot very well describe an elephant: words like "gills," "scales," and "fins" will not get us very far.

When some of the post-Soviet societies developed in unexpected ways, language impaired our ability to understand the process. We talked about whether they had a free press, for example, or free and fair elections. But noting that they did not, as Magyar has said, is akin to saying that the elephant cannot swim or fly: it doesn't tell us much about what the elephant **is**. Now the same thing was happening in the United States; we were using the language of political disagreement, judicial procedure, or partisan discussion to describe something that was crushing the system that such terminology was invented to describe.

Magyar spent about a decade devising a new model, and a new language, to describe what was happening in his country. He coined the term "mafia state," and described it as a specific, clan-like system in which one man distributes money and power to all other members. He then developed the concept of autocratic transformation, which proceeds in three stages: autocratic attempt, autocratic breakthrough, and autocratic consolidation. It occurred to me that these were words that American culture could now borrow, in an appropriate symbolic reversal of 1989: these terms appear to describe our reality better than any words in the standard American political lexicon. Magyar had analyzed the signs and circumstances of this process in post-Communist countries and proposed a detailed taxonomy. But how it might happen in the United States was uncharted territory.

2.

WAITING FOR THE REICHSTAG FIRE

Immediately following the November 2016 election, the defeated majority of Americans who had voted for Hillary Clinton seemed to split into two camps, distinguished by the degree to which they were panicked. One camp was exemplified by outgoing president Barack Obama, whose goal, in the days after the vote, seemed to be to reassure Americans that life would go on. On November 9, he gave a short, dignified talk in which he made three points—most memorably, that the sun had risen that morning.

Yesterday, before votes were tallied, I shot a video that some of you may have seen in which I said to the American people, regardless of which side you were on in the election, regardless of whether your candidate won or lost, the sun would come up in the morning.

And that is one bit of prognosticating that actually came true. The sun is up.

Obama acknowledged his "significant differences" with Trump but said that his phone conversation with the president-elect in the wee hours had reassured him that in the end, Democrats and Republicans, he and Trump, had shared goals.

We all want what's best for this country. That's what I heard in Mr. Trump's remarks last night. That's what I heard when I spoke to him directly. And I was heartened by that. That's what the country needs—a sense of unity, a sense of inclusion, a respect for our institutions, our way of life, rule of law, and respect for each other.

Obama finished on an optimistic note.

The point, though, is that we all go forward, with a presumption of good faith in our fellow citizens, because that presumption of good faith is essential to a vibrant and functioning democracy. That's how this country has moved forward for two hundred forty years. It's how we've pushed boundaries and promoted freedom around the world. That's how we've expanded the rights of our founding to reach all of our citizens. It's how we have come this far. And that's why I'm confident that this incredible journey that we're on, as Americans, will go on.

Every president is a storyteller-in-chief. The Obama story, which drew and built on the stories told by his predecessors, was that American society was on an inexorable march toward a better, freer, fairer world. It may stumble, the story goes, but it always rights itself. This was the meaning to which Obama adapted his favorite Martin Luther King, Jr., quote: "The arc of the moral universe is long, but it bends toward justice." This is also the premise on which the belief in American exceptionalism, or what the legal scholar Sanford Levinson has called the "American civil religion," is based: that the United States Constitution provides an all-but-perfect blueprint for politics, in perpetuity. In 2016, as Trump emerged the frontrunner in the race for the Republican nomination, many of us reassured ourselves and each other that American institutions were stronger than any one candidate or even any one president.

But after the election, this reassurance rang hollow. Writing in **The New York Review of Books** on the day Obama celebrated the sun's rising as scheduled, I warned readers, "Institutions will not save you." I was drawing on my experience reporting on Russia,

Hungary, and Israel—three countries that were very different from the United States, to be sure, but also different from one another. Their institutions had folded in remarkably similar ways. I couldn't know that American institutions would fail similarly, but I knew enough to say that absolute faith in institutions was misplaced. Many people shared this intuition. They were the more panicked camp. A common expectation took hold among them: the expectation of the Reichstag Fire.

The actual fire in the Reichstag—the German parliament building—burned on the evening of February 27, 1933. Adolf Hitler had been appointed chancellor four weeks earlier, and already he had begun placing restrictions on the press and expanding the powers of the police. But it is the fire, rather than Hitler's toxic first steps, that is remembered as the event after which things were never the same, in Germany or in the world. The day after the fire, the government issued a decree allowing the police to detain people without charges, on the grounds of prevention. Activists were rounded up by Hitler's paramilitary forces, the SA and the SS, and placed in camps. Less than a month later, the parliament passed an "enabling act," creating rule by decree and establishing a state of emergency that lasted as long as the Nazis were in power.

The Reichstag Fire was used to create a "state of exception," as Carl Schmitt, Hitler's favorite legal scholar, called it. In Schmitt's terms, a state of exception arises when an emergency, a singular event, shakes up the accepted order of things. This is when the sovereign steps forward and institutes new, extralegal rules. The emergency enables a quantum leap: Having amassed enough power to declare a state of exception, the sovereign then, by that declaration, acquires far greater, unchecked power. That is what makes the change irreversible, and the state of exception permanent.

Every galvanizing event of the past eighty years has been compared to the Reichstag Fire. On December 1, 1934, Sergei Kirov, the head of the Communist Party in Leningrad, was murdered by a lone gunman. The assassination is remembered as the pretext for creating a state of exception in Russia. Show trials and mass arrests followed, swelling the Gulag with people accused of being traitors, spies, and terrorist plotters. To handle the volume, the Kremlin created troikas—three-person panels that doled out a sentence without reviewing the case, much less hearing from the defense.

More recently, Vladimir Putin has relied on a succession of catastrophic events to create irreversible exceptions. In 1999, a series of apartment bombings in Moscow and cities in southern Russia killed hundreds. This allowed Putin to proclaim that he could summarily execute those deemed "terrorists"; it also became a pretext for a new war in Chechnya. In 2002, the three-day siege of a Moscow theater served as a demonstration of the principle of summary execution: Russian law enforcement pumped the theater full of sleeping gas, entered the building, and shot the hostage-takers as they lay unconscious. The Kremlin also used the theater siege as a pretext to ban the already cowed media from covering antiterrorist operations. Two years later, more than three hundred people, most of them children, died following an attack on a school in Beslan, in southern Russia. Putin used this catastrophic event to cancel the elections of local governors, effectively abolishing the country's federal structure.

The thinking that transforms tragedy into crackdown is not foreign to the United States. During the crisis that followed the Alien and Sedition Acts at the end of the eighteenth century, the ruling Federalists and the opposition Republicans accused each other of treason and a fatal lack of vigilance, of being Jacobin puppets. The courts, stacked with Federalist appointees, wasted no time shutting down opposition newspapers. Half a century later, President Abraham Lincoln suspended habeas corpus, the right not to be imprisoned without civilian judicial review. He did this to be able to indefinitely hold rebels whom he judged a danger to the Union—but whom, he said, "the courts, acting on ordinary rules, would discharge." It wasn't until 1866 that the Supreme Court ruled the practice unconstitutional.

The next major war was the First World War. Now speech perceived as critical of or detrimental to the American war effort was punished with prison sentences as long as ten years. Historian Geoffrey Stone has called Woodrow Wilson's Sedition Act of 1918 "the most repressive legislation in American history." Thousands of people were arrested—many without a warrant—and two hundred forty-nine anarchist and Communist activists were deported to Soviet Russia. It wasn't until later that Supreme Court Justices Oliver Wendell Holmes, Jr., and Louis Brandeis started on a dissenting streak that ultimately restored and clarified free-speech protections.

During the Great Depression, state courts, legislatures, and law enforcement acted in concert—and with the tacit agreement of the federal government—to denaturalize and deport hundreds of thousands of

Mexican Americans, a majority of whom were birthright citizens.

The Second World War brought another presidential assault on the Constitution: the internment of more than a hundred thousand Americans of Japanese descent. Then came the McCarthy era, when the government took up spying on the enemy within, and accusations of treason, whether or not they were supported by evidence, ruined life after life. The next generation of Americans lived through the secrecy, deceit, and paranoia of the Vietnam War years, which culminated in a president who had his opponents prosecuted and wiretapped.

In the twenty-first century, Congress granted sweeping surveillance powers to intelligence agencies and domestic law enforcement. George W. Bush's administration lied to the world in order to start a war in Iraq and created an elaborate legal mechanism to facilitate torture. Obama's administration continued to concentrate power in the executive branch, using executive orders and pushing the limits of policy-making by federal agencies on the one hand and suppressing whistleblowing and keeping the media at arm's length on the other.

In other words, every generation of Americans has seen the government claim exceptional powers to repressive, unjust ends. These intermittent states of exception rested on the fundamental structural state of exception that asserts the power of white men over all others. Trump emerged not as an exception to this history but as its logical consequence. He was building on a four-hundred-year history of white supremacy, and he was building on a fifteen-year-long mobilization of American society against Muslims, immigrants, and the Other. A future historian of the twenty-first century might point to September 11, 2001, as the Reichstag Fire of the United States.

For that matter, even the original Reichstag Fire was not the Reichstag Fire of our imagination—a singular event that changed the course of history once and for all. The Reichstag burned five years before the Anschluss, six years before the start of the

Second World War. Those years were filled with events big and small, each a step that made the darkest future possible. As tempting as it was to imagine that Trump would do us the favor of announcing the point of no return with a sweeping, unequivocal gesture (and even that upon this announcement we would all justifiably give up hope or, alternatively, become desperately heroic), his autocratic attempt, too, has been not one but a series of actions that change the nature of American government and politics step by step.

Magyar has described aspiring post-Communist leaders as building their autocracies by gradually undermining the divisions among branches of government, especially by packing the courts and taking over prosecutorial authority. Of course, his model cannot be simply transposed onto United States reality—not least because some of the formal divisions between branches of government have been weak here for some time. The Justice Department, for example—the wielder of ultimate prosecutorial authority—is a part of the executive branch, and its independent functioning is determined by tradition. A monopoly on political power, which Magyar identifies as a major risk factor, is not unusual in the United States: Trump enjoyed it for his first two years in office, when both houses of Congress were controlled by Republicans, but a number of his predecessors had benefited from the same condition. Still, it is clear that this presidency is different from ones that preceded it.

Americans tend to talk about institutions much more than we talk about another factor Obama mentioned in his reassuring post-election speech: the presumption of good faith. It is true that, despite a consistent history of injustice, an ever-increasing number of Americans, different kinds of Americans, have gained access to the rights and protections of citizenship. A long enough and generous enough view of American history affirms the narrative of continuous progress toward justice. The thoughtful design of our institutions is only one reason for this history of progress. The other is that American citizens and public officials have largely acted in good faith. Some of them have lied, many have cheated, many have bent the system to their ends, but they generally did so in accordance with sincerely held beliefs and a coherent system of values. Their abuses of power have usually been limited to discrete ideologically defined areas—and this meant that even when the system of checks and balances failed, a successive administration could address the damage (though it's worth noting that Obama did not succeed in closing the detention camp in Guantánamo Bay). No powerful political actor had set out to destroy the American political system itself—until, that is, Trump won the Republican nomination. He was probably the first major party nominee who ran not for president but for autocrat. And he won.

3.

THE STYROFOAM PRESIDENT

One of Trump's three rallying cries on the campaign trail—one of the three apparent components of making America great again—was "Drain the swamp" (the other two were "Lock her up" and "Build that wall"). It may have sounded like a call to battle against corruption, but it was in fact a declaration of war against the American system of government as currently constituted.

The Trump campaign ran on disdain: for immigrants, for women, for disabled people, for people of color, for Muslims— for anyone, in other words, who isn't an able-bodied white straight American-born male—and for the elites who have coddled the Other. Contempt for the government and its work is a component of the disdain for elites, and a rhetorical trope shared by the current crop of the world's antipolitical leaders, from Vladimir Putin to Brazil's Jair Bolsonaro. They campaign on voters' resentment of elites for ruining their lives, and they continue to traffic in this resentment even after they take office—as though someone else, someone sinister and apparently all-powerful, were still in charge, as though they were still insurgents. The very institutions of government—their own government now—are the enemy. As president, Trump went on to denigrate the intelligence services, rage against the Justice Department, and issue humiliating tweets about officials in his own administration.

For his cabinet, Trump chose people who were opposed to the work, and sometimes to the very existence, of the agencies they were appointed to lead. His pick for the Environmental Protection Agency, Scott Pruitt, had, as attorney general of

Oklahoma, sued the EPA fourteen times for what the state alleged was regulatory overreach. In his opening remarks at his Senate confirmation hearing on January 18, 2016, Pruitt claimed that the extent of the human impact on climate change—and our very ability to measure it—were still subject to debate. For Health and Human Services, Trump nominated Georgia congressman Tom Price, who said that he wanted to get rid of the Affordable Care Act and Medicaid. For attorney general, Trump's choice was Jeff Sessions, an Alabama senator who was once denied a judgeship and was an outspoken opponent of civil rights law. For labor secretary, Trump picked Andrew Puzder, a fast-food executive who was opposed to labor rights; when, in February 2017, Puzder withdrew his nomination because even Republican senators' support could not be assured (this, however, was because Puzder favored immigration reform with a focus on labor legalization), Trump nominated Alexander Acosta, a law school dean and former U.S. attorney for southern

Florida. In that capacity, Acosta had overseen a sweetheart deal with billionaire sex trafficker Jeffrey Epstein. But by the already established standards of the Trump era, in March 2017 the media generally covered Acosta as a "conventional candidate"—after all, he had government experience and some of it was even relevant to the job. For housing, Trump nominated Ben Carson, a retired neurosurgeon with no policy experience or expertise in housing or any other area of government. Trump's choice for energy secretary, former governor of Texas Rick Perry, had during the Republican primary race in 2011 promised to abolish the Department of Energy (along with Commerce and Education)—though he apparently didn't know what the Energy Department was (its main work is nuclear weapons, not, as Perry apparently believed, the regulation of the energy industry). Betsy DeVos, Trump's choice for secretary of education, was a consistent foe of public education. In her native state of Michigan, the billionaire activist had pushed reform that defunded public schools in favor of virtually unregulated charter schools and contributed heavily to the collapse of the public education system in Detroit. DeVos herself had never worked in education, and during her confirmation hearing betrayed an utter lack of familiarity with the field. Asked whether she thought that tests ought to focus on proficiency or progress, she fumbled, apparently unaware of the debate. Asked about guns in schools, she suggested that they might be used against "potential grizzlies."

Trump's cabinet picks lied and plagiarized their way through their confirmation hearings. Six weeks after Trump took office, the investigative-journalism foundation ProPublica compiled a list of lies told to the Senate by five of Trump's nominees: Pruitt, DeVos, Treasury pick Steve Mnuchin, Price, and Sessions. DeVos also appeared to have cribbed some of her written questionnaire responses from documents authored by other officials and available online.

Lying to Congress is a criminal offense. It would also, in other historical periods, be a disgrace. Why would the nominees to some of the nation's highest offices lie, and lie in ways that were easy enough to catch and document? Why wouldn't they? They weren't merely parroting the behaviors of their patron, who lied loudly, insistently, incessantly; they were demonstrating that they shared his contempt for government. They were lying to the swamp. They couldn't be bothered with the conventions of government because they found government itself contemptible.

A close cousin of contempt for government is disdain for excellence, also shared by a number of contemporary leaders—whose antipolitical politics are also distinctly anti-intellectual. As president-elect, Trump opted to take intelligence briefings just once a week—rather than daily or almost daily, as had been the custom. He explained why: "I'm, like, a smart person." Like a pouty eighth-grader, he added, "I don't have to be told the same thing in the same words every single day for the next eight years."

AN AUTOCRATIC ATTEMPT

If something should change in the world, he said, the intelligence chiefs could find their president and inform him. Trump was perhaps the first American president who seemed not at all impressed by the burden of responsibility of his office: he had no regard for his predecessors, or for the job, and its demands annoyed him.

Intelligence briefings were a small part of the journey from candidate to nominee to president, a component in the transformation that Trump was, at least nominally, undergoing. Much was said following the election about the probability of Trump—the buffoon, the vulgarian, the racist—becoming "presidential." The word certainly meant different things to different speakers, but the shared underlying assumption was that as president, Trump should develop some reverence for the office he would now hold, and for the system at the pinnacle of which the electoral college had placed him. This assumption—this misplaced hope—ran counter to the essence of the Trumpian project. On January 20, 2017, the nation saw that it was inaugurating a president like no president before him: a president who viewed the government with contempt.

A study of modern autocrats may show us that a Reichstag Fire is never quite the singular and signal event that changes the course of history, but it will also expose a truth behind the single-event narrative: autocrats declare their intentions early on. We disbelieve or ignore them at our peril. Putin, for example, had made his plans apparent by the end of his first day in office: a series of spare statements and legislative initiatives, along with a police raid, showed that he was going to focus on remilitarizing Russia, that he would dismantle its electoral institutions, and that he would crack down on the media. His autocratic attempt— the buildup to actually wielding autocratic power, throwing opponents into jail, controlling media, and eviscerating any political power outside his office—took three or four years, but he had made his objectives clear from the start.* Trump was also broadcasting his intentions—during the campaign and again on the first day of his presidency.

For twenty-four hours, Trump not only trampled on some of the most hallowed public rituals of American power; he made a spectacle of doing so. He defiled the inauguration with a speech that was mean and meaningless and also badly written, pitched to the basest level of emotion and intelligence. "We've made other countries rich while the wealth, strength, and confidence of our country has disappeared over the horizon" was how he summed up the American foreign policy legacy: a zero-sum game in which a penny spent—whether on an ill-conceived war or on the Marshall Plan—is a penny lost. "For too long, a small group in our nation's capital has reaped the

---

*Milestones for Putin's establishment of autocracy might include the arrest of Russia's richest man, Mikhail Khodorkovsky, in October 2003—three years into the Putin presidency—and the abolition of gubernatorial elections in September 2004.

rewards of government while the people have borne the cost" is how he summed up the work of all the men and women who had come before him, in effect the entire political history of the country, which he now declared to be over: "This American carnage stops right here and stops right now." Having dismissed the political past, he offered, by way of a vision for the future, a fortress under siege: a walled country that puts itself first, convention and consideration for others be damned.

In his small-mindedness and lack of aspiration, Trump curiously resembled Putin, though the origins of the two men's stubborn mediocrity could not be more different. Aspiration should not be confused with ambition—both men want to be ever more powerful and wealthy, but neither wants to be, or even to appear to be, better. Putin, for example, continuously reasserts his lack of aspiration by making crude jokes at the most inappropriate times—as when, during a joint appearance with German chancellor

Angela Merkel in 2013, he compared EU monetary policy to a wedding night: "No matter what you do, the result will be the same," he quipped, his way of lightly covering up the "you get fucked" punch line. (The German chancellor was captured cringing on video.)

Trump marked his first moments in office by wielding power vengefully: the head of the D.C. National Guard lost his job at noon, as did all U.S. ambassadors around the world—just because they all serve at the pleasure of the president, and the incoming president liked firing people. Between festivities, Trump signed an executive order to begin undoing his predecessor's singular achievement, the Affordable Care Act. He had the White House website swept clean of substantive content on climate policy, civil rights, health care, and LGBT rights, took down the Spanish-language site, and added a biography of his wife that advertised her mail-order jewelry line. At the same time, as the new president moved through the day, he repeatedly turned his back on his wife. He immediately degraded the look of the Oval Office by hanging gold drapes.

American political pageantry is aspirational. The extended ritual of the inauguration conveys an understanding of the importance of the office of president and awe and pride in the miracle of the repeated peaceful transfer of power. The ceremony, the concert, the lunch, the parade, the balls, and more—all of this serves to create a nationwide mood of celebration and self-congratulation. It is like a giant wedding designed to make even the most curmudgeonly of relations tear up. It is a moment for all to shine—the celebrants in their magnanimity and the less fortunate in its reflected glow. As the day progresses and the new first couple accept the honor and the responsibility bestowed on them, they transition into a different state of being: as the country watches, they acquire the quality of being presidential, or such is the expectation.

Trump had no use for any of it: the magnanimity, the glow, the awe (unless inspired by him personally), the pride (except his own), the aspiration. Indeed, the single quality he displayed repeatedly was his lack of aspiration. Take his speech. Better yet, take the cake. At one of the inaugural balls, Trump and Vice President Mike Pence cut a great white cake with a sword. The cake, as it turned out, was a knockoff of President Obama's 2013 inaugural-ball cake. Obama's was created by celebrity chef Duff Goldman. Trump's was commissioned from a decidedly more modest Washington bakery than Goldman's, and the transition-team representative who put in the order explicitly asked for an exact copy of Goldman's design—even when the baker suggested creating a variation on the theme. Only a small portion of Trump's cake was edible; the rest was Styrofoam (Obama's was cake all the way through). The cake may have been the best symbol yet of the incoming administration: much of what little it brought was plagiarized, and most of it was unusable for the purpose for which presidential administrations are usually intended. Not only did it not achieve excellence: it rejected the idea that excellence is desirable. As if to underscore the point, DeVos tweeted that she was "honored to witness this historical inauguration"—using the word "historical" where "historic" should have been. She later deleted the tweet and blamed her staff for the mistake.

Three years to the day after the inauguration, the first person in the United States, a man in Washington state, was diagnosed with the novel coronavirus, starting the symbolic clock on the Trump administration's inaction in the face of a deadly pandemic. While all American presidents wield the power to save and destroy lives, only in times of peril—during wars, natural disasters, and epidemics—is that power wielded so immediately, and with such devastating effects.

Trump maintained his disdain for government and his contempt for expertise. He ignored intelligence briefings in which he was warned about the threat of mass deaths. He ignored the public pleas of epidemiologists, including his own former top officials writing in **The Wall Street Journal**. On television and on Twitter, he dismissed fears about the coronavirus as a "hoax" and promised, "It's going to be just fine." In the first half of March, when the looming disaster was coming into focus, Trump visited the Centers for Disease Control, wearing a red "Keep America Great" cap, and bragged, "I like this stuff, I really get it. People are surprised that I understand it. Every one of these doctors said, 'How do you know so much about this?' Maybe I have a natural ability. Maybe I should have done that instead of running for president." Standing in a lab, facing the cameras, Trump claimed that anyone in the United States who needed to be tested for COVID-19 would be able to get the test. Everything he said was a lie.

He lavished praise on himself for acting decisively, but he resisted taking action such as invoking the Defense Production Act, which could have displeased the heads of large corporations. Instead, he trafficked in false hopes and even the promise of fake remedies. This left experts either to try to correct Trump in real time, as Dr. Anthony Fauci, the director of the National Institute of Allergy and Infectious Diseases, tried to do, at great personal risk, or to neutralize him, as the coordinator of his coronavirus task force, Dr. Deborah Birx, tried to do, at great cost to her reputation as a public health specialist. As the death toll climbed, Trump's lack of aspiration took on grotesque dimensions. He did not seem cowed by catastrophe, or scared by it: he could barely be bothered to notice it. At moments, he would seem grave, even referring to himself as a "wartime president," but almost immediately he would be distracted by his real and permanent concerns: adulation and money. Nothing and no one else mattered.

4.

WE COULD CALL IT A KAKISTOCRACY

Trump's disdain for excellence is neither a personal quirk nor an anomaly among autocrats present and past. It is logical: they see the work of government as worthy only of mockery, and so they continue to mock it when they have power. It is also integral to their overall stance: these are men who intentionally, openly call out to the worst that humans have to offer. Trump's contempt for excellence is of a piece with his public mockery of a disabled journalist, just as Putin's contempt is expressed in his deployment of gutter humor. Trump's project is the government of the worst: a kakistocracy.

On the day Trump assumed office, less than half of his cabinet had been confirmed; his predecessors had started the job with most or, in the case of Bill Clinton, all of the cabinet posts filled. Four weeks after the inauguration, only thirty-four out of seven hundred jobs that needed Senate confirmation even had a candidate. With Republicans in control of both houses of Congress, Trump should have faced little opposition to his nominees—if only he had had the names to propose. The assumption on Capitol Hill was that the president-elect had been caught unprepared, surprised by his own victory. But Trump also evidently lacked interest in the job of filling the cabinet—much of which, he seemed convinced, shouldn't exist at all.

Trump's attention to the presidency comes in exceptional flashes and glimmers. Unlike the government as a whole, the military clearly attracted Trump—he had even reportedly hoped that a military parade might accompany the inauguration—so his earliest nominees were generals: Mike Flynn as national security advisor, John Kelly to head the Department of Homeland Security, James Mattis for secretary of defense, and retired army captain Mike Pompeo for the CIA. Trump was also apparently interested in the public spectacle of choosing his staff, so for secretary of state he put on a performance reminiscent of his reality TV show: he interviewed former electoral rival Mitt Romney and floated the idea of appointing former New York City mayor Rudy Giuliani before finally announcing that he had settled on Exxon CEO Rex Tillerson—one in a string of very wealthy individuals with no government experience. Tillerson's qualifications boiled down to having conducted successful business negotiations with some of the world's most repressive regimes, such as those of Russia and Saudi Arabia.

In his first weeks in office, Trump signed a slate of executive orders corresponding to his campaign promises: to build a wall on the southern border; to increase deportations of immigrants; to ban entry to the United States to travelers from predominantly Muslim countries; and to abolish the health insurance system created by the Affordable Care Act. The orders were messily drafted, and it was unclear what, if any, consequences they could have: funding for the wall could not be conjured by executive order, nor could the Affordable Care Act be repealed by one. **The New York Times** was reporting that the new president's team was skeletal—a half-dozen advisers disoriented in the White House, where they could not figure out how to operate the light switches—while Trump himself was disengaged or, rather, engaged only with what he saw on his television screen. The presidential workday, such as it was, ended at six thirty p.m., the **Times** reported. After Trump retired to his bedroom, he would proceed to fire off tweets spurred by "random inputs," as the paper put it.

Trump had campaigned on insulting the

government, and he himself was an insult to the presidency. But could someone so absurd, so evidently incompetent, be a true danger? In the early months of the Trump presidency, the hope that Trump would become "presidential" was gradually replaced by the hope that he was too bad at the job to do true lasting damage. We could have imagined, but we could not have predicted, that a pandemic would render his arrogant ignorance lethal.

We imagine the villains of history as masterminds of horror. This happens because we learn about them from history books, which weave narratives that retrospectively imbue events with logic, making them seem predetermined. Historians and their readers bring an unavoidable perception bias to the story: if a historical event caused shocking destruction, then the person behind this event must have been a correspondingly giant monster. Terrifying as it is to contemplate the catastrophes of the twentieth century, it would be even more frightening to imagine that humanity had stumbled unthinkingly into its darkest moments. But a reading of contemporaneous accounts will show that both Hitler and Stalin struck many of their countrymen as men of limited ability, education, and imagination—and, indeed, as being incompetent in government and military leadership. Contrary to popular wisdom, they were not political savants, possessed of one extraordinary talent that brought them to power. It was, rather, the blunt instrument of reassuring ignorance that propelled their rise in a frighteningly complex world.

Contemporary strongmen, because we watch their ascent in real time, retain their more human outlines. We witnessed the greed and vanity of Silvio Berlusconi, who ran Italy's economy into the ground. We recognize the desperate desire of Putin to be admired or at least feared—usually literally at his country's expense. Still, physical distance makes villains seem bigger than they are in real life. Just as the full absurdity of Trump was sinking in, crushing any hope that he would turn "presidential," Putin, in the American imagination, was turning into a brilliant strategist, a skilled secret agent who was plotting the end of the Western world. In fact, Putin was and remains a poorly educated, underinformed, incurious man whose ambition is vastly out of proportion to his understanding of the world. To the extent that he has any interest in the business of governing, it is solely his own role—on the world stage or on Russian television—that concerns him. Whether he is attending a summit, piloting a plane, or hang gliding with Siberian cranes, it is the spectacle of power that interests him. In this, he and Trump are alike: to them, power is the beginning and the end of government, the presidency, politics—and public politics is only the performance of power.

Trump was instituting government by tweet but also, more broadly, government by gesture—whether that gesture was a phone call to Carrier, the air-conditioner manufacturer whose plan to move jobs from Indiana to Mexico Trump ostensibly quashed (in fact, at best his phone call delayed some layoffs by a few months), or the announcement of banning travel from Europe in response to the spread of the coronavirus. Trump's campaign ran in part on his apparent belief that the presidency should be a job of simple decisions and clear gestures. In public, he chanted single-phrase solutions, and in private he reportedly asked a foreign policy adviser repeatedly why the United States couldn't use nuclear weapons "if we have them." In the third month of his presidency, he authorized a bombing in Syria. Buoyed by positive television coverage of the event, he ordered a giant explosive device known as the "mother of all bombs" to be used in Afghanistan, and then bragged of giving the military "total authorization"—because why complicate things by restraining the generals? The following month, Trump announced that the United States would pull out of the complex, sprawling, painstakingly negotiated Paris climate accord, which he apparently had made no effort to understand: the complexity of the agreement was itself an offense, and the simplicity of pulling out was itself the solution.

In an April 2017 interview, Trump admitted that being president was proving harder than he had expected. He did not appear to be humbled by this discovery. In keeping with his understanding of politics, he was resentful that his opponents—his predecessor, the elites, the establishment—had made things so complicated. If they had not, things would be as he thought they should be: One man would give orders, and they would be carried out. He would not have to deal with recalcitrant legislators or, worse, meddlesome investigators. One nation, with the biggest bombs in the world, would dominate every other country and would not have to concern itself with the intricate relationships among and between all those other countries. The United States would run like a business, an old-fashioned top-down company, the kind managed through the sheer exertion of power.

Trump's incompetence is militant. It is not a factor that might mitigate the threat he poses: it is the threat itself. The mechanics of the war of militant incompetence against expertise were laid bare during the impeachment hearings in 2019 and again a few months later, during the COVID-19 pandemic. In one instance, the government's own public health experts worked to contain the pandemic and educate the public while the president denigrated such efforts and repeatedly dismissed the risks in the smug manner of a man proud of his ignorance. In the other, Trump, his personal lawyer Rudy Giuliani, and a small crew of amateurs and swindlers pursued what passed for foreign-policy objectives (but what was more accurately described by witness Fiona Hill as a "domestic political errand") in relations with Ukraine, consistent with Trump's conspiratorial and vengeful worldview. A group of career foreign service officials tried to resist and maintain policies consistent with norms, laws, logic, and the national interest.

Some of it sounded comical. "We had all kinds of officials from Europe . . . literally appearing at the gates of the White House, calling on our personal phones, which are actually in lock boxes, so it was kind of difficult to get hold of them," testified Hill, one of the country's most experienced Russia experts, who served on the National Security Council from April 2017 until July 2019. "I'd find endless messages from irate officials who'd been told they were supposed to meet with me by Ambassador Sondland." Gordon Sondland was a megadonor, a hotelier with no government or policy experience, whom Trump had appointed his ambassador to the European Union—and then added Ukraine (which is not a member of the EU) to his portfolio. Sondland spent several months trying to broker an arrangement whereby the Ukrainian president, Volodymyr Zelensky, would publicly state that he was pursuing an investigation into alleged corruption on the part of Hunter Biden, son of former vice president and Democratic presidential contender Joe Biden, and in exchange would receive a meeting with Trump at the White House—and the release of nearly four hundred million dollars in military aid. Hill testified that she had tried to get someone to explain to Sondland that this was not how things were done—among other things, that foreign policy could not be conducted by personal unsecured cell phone with people Sondland knew nothing about, on issues in which he wasn't versed: "It's like basically driving along with no guardrails and no GPS on an unfamiliar territory." The acting ambassador to Ukraine, William B. Taylor, a career diplomat, threatened to quit. Sondland pressed on: this was how things were done now. His team of incompetents was stronger than the institutionalists, who either lost their jobs or folded. National Security Advisor John Bolton either quit or was fired; Hill quit; the ambassador to Ukraine, Marie Yovanovitch, was re-called, but not before suffering character assassination by rumor and Trumpian tweet. Meanwhile, career diplomat Kurt Volker, the special envoy to Ukraine, was roped into the game of diplomacy-by-racket, and John Eisenberg, the senior lawyer at the

National Security Council, helped cover up the effort by placing the record of an incriminating Trump-Zelensky phone call on a secure server. Both men, it seems, were trying to alleviate the damage Trump was doing to government—and both became enablers of the damage.

When the pandemic came, the vacuum Trump had willfully created at the top of the federal government translated into deadly inaction. In three years, the government had been partly dismantled, partly corrupted, and partly—in the areas that had not drawn Trump's attention—allowed to churn along. But in a crisis, the government cannot function without a leader—or at least its proper functioning is severely delayed. For several crucial weeks, the workings of the Centers for Disease Control, state labs, and other public health agencies resembled the contradictory and confusing processes described by diplomats during the impeachment hearings. A diagnostic test that was crucial to fighting the epidemic was delayed by human error, but more than that, it was held up by rules that had unintended consequences; by a reluctance to make decisions; and most of all, by a system's essentially Trumpian inability to recognize its own failures. For all his antibureaucratic rhetoric, Trump had engendered a colossal chain of bureaucratic failings. Hannah Arendt called bureaucracy "the rule of Nobody." Trump was this Nobody now. He did not even know what he was not doing.

5.

WE COULD CALL IT CORRUPTION

Two weeks after winning the election, Trump sat down for a forty-five-minute interview with **New York Times** editors, reporters, and columnists. Still evidently shell-shocked, the journalists seemed to struggle to balance the expression of respect for the office of president—and the man who would now occupy it—with the jarring substance of the questions they had to ask. Several of the journalists had a peculiarly hard time getting to the point of their questions, as though they were embarrassed by having to ask them.

White House correspondent Michael D.

Shear finally asked about "your sort of mixing of your global business interests and the presidency. There's already, even just in the ten, two weeks you've been president-elect, instances where you've met with your Indian business partners . . ."

"Sure," said Trump.

Shear continued, "You've talked about the impact of the wind farms on your golf course [during a meeting with British politician Nigel Farage]. People, experts who are lawyers and ethics experts, say that all of that is totally inappropriate . . ." What was the new president going to do to separate his presidency from his business?

"The law is totally on my side," Trump answered. "The president can't have a conflict of interest."

Trump said that "in theory I can be president and run my business a hundred percent, sign checks for my business . . . I could run my business perfectly and then run the country perfectly." He rambled. He implied that if he were to draw a hard line between the presidency and his business, he would have to forgo seeing his adult children, all of whom were involved in the Trump business empire. "I'd never ever see my daughter Ivanka."

An unidentified participant—probably a **Times** journalist—interjected, "That means you'd have to make Ivanka deputy president, you know." According to the transcript, everyone laughed.

Soon Ivanka took an office in the East Wing of the White House—the traditional domain of the First Lady—and after a few months moved to the West Wing, where policy is made. She joined her father in a meeting with Japanese prime minister Shinzō Abe, then a meeting with German chancellor Angela Merkel, then took her father's seat at a meeting of G20 leaders in Hamburg. Because Ivanka was not drawing a salary, her father claimed that normal ethics rules did not apply to her. The Office of Government Ethics disagreed, and this changed nothing.

In January, a week before the inauguration, Trump held a press conference to announce that he was turning over the management—but not the ownership—of the Trump Organization to his sons Don and Eric. If this was true, it still did not resolve conflict-of-interest issues, since Trump would continue to profit from the businesses bearing his name—his name was indeed his business. But it was also probably not true. Trump made the announcement from a lectern stationed next to a desk that was covered with stacks of manila folders, but he didn't allow reporters to look at any of the documents the folders contained—if, in fact, they contained any documents.

In July 2017, one day short of the six-month anniversary of Trump's inauguration, the head of the Office of Government Ethics, Walter Shaub, stepped down in subdued indignation. In an interview on MSNBC, he called the ethics program of the Trump White House "a very serious disappointment." The administration, he said, claimed to have negotiated ethics agreements with staff, but the office was cut out of the process. "We've received very little information about what the individuals in the White House do on a day-to-day basis for a living," he said. The institution Shaub had headed since 2013 had proved helpless against a president acting in bad faith. Compliance with ethics rules was optional because Trump said it was optional. Then he opted not to comply.

The president and his family were not exactly hiding their sources of income—they just refused to act accountable for them. In February 2017, when the department store chain Nordstrom dropped Ivanka's footwear line, possibly in response to a boycott that had driven down sales, the president tweeted, "My daughter Ivanka has been treated so unfairly by @Nordstrom . . . Terrible." The following day, Kellyanne Conway, a top adviser to the president, spoke to Fox News from the White House briefing room to advertise the first daughter's merchandise. "Go buy Ivanka's stuff is what I would say," she said. "I'm going to give a free commercial here: Go buy it today, everybody. You can find it online." This administration believed that Ivanka's newly powerful position should help her profits—as should the presidency help every member of the family make money. The same assumption was made explicit in a complaint Melania Trump's lawyers filed against the British tabloid **Daily Mail** in February 2017, alleging financial damage to the First Lady: "The plaintiff had the unique, once-in-a-lifetime opportunity, as an extremely famous and well-known person as well as a former professional model, brand spokesperson and successful businesswoman, to launch a broad-based commercial brand in multiple product categories, each of which could have garnered multimillion-dollar business relationships for a multi-year term during which plaintiff is one of the most photographed women in the world." Melania got a settlement—one of the highest ever to go through the British courts (the exact amount was not disclosed).

As for Ivanka's shoe line, whatever money the first daughter was making from it was a drop in the giant bucket of revenue coming to her and her husband, Jared Kushner. At the end of March, the Office of Government Ethics released documents showing that the couple remained beneficiaries of a business empire worth an estimated seven hundred forty million dollars. This empire included investment and real estate businesses, among them the Trump International Hotel in Washington, DC. The hotel, which arrived in the capital just months ahead of its namesake, was doing business in synergy with the presidency. The Republican National Committee held its Christmas party there. Lobbyists for the Saudi Arabian government were booking blocks of rooms, paying for roughly five hundred nights in the months following the election. In 2017, the hotel generated more than forty million dollars in revenue, while the Trump Organization as a whole brought in five hundred million. By July 2019, when Trump had the phone call with Ukrainian president Zelensky that would eventually launch the impeachment inquiry, it seemed that anyone who got on the phone with Trump knew to mention being a loyal customer. Zelensky said that during his last visit to New York (before he was president) he had stayed at the Trump Hotel.

Trump's cabinet—the wealthiest in history—produced more allegations of conflicts of interest than an army of journalists could track, or that, crucially, any media audience could absorb. DeVos was an investor in a debt-collection company and a charter-school operator, among other businesses. Commerce Secretary Wilbur Ross, an investor in gas and steel companies, helped formulate tariff policy for those industries before selling off some—but not all—of his investments. Mick Mulvaney received tens of thousands of dollars in campaign contributions from payday lenders and then served as acting head of the Bureau of Consumer Protection, where he proposed loosening regulations on the lending industry. In May 2017, while Tillerson was in Saudi Arabia, that country signed a major deal with his former company, Exxon Mobil. That same month, Kushner personally brokered a deal between the Saudi government and the aerospace and defense company Lockheed Martin. Being a member of the administration carried more-direct benefits too: Pruitt, Interior Secretary Ryan Zinke, Mnuchin, Health and Human Services Secretary Tom Price, and Veterans Affairs Secretary David Shulkin each were accused of spending millions of taxpayer dollars on travel. Ben Carson attempted to order a thirty-one-thousand-dollar dining set for his Washington office (the spending limit for decoration was five thousand).

Corruption would not be the right word to apply to the Trump administration. The term implies deception—it assumes that the public official understands that they should not benefit from the public trust, but, duplicitously, they do it anyway. The opposite of **corruption** in political discourse is **transparency**—indeed, the global anticorruption organization calls itself Transparency International. Trump, his family, and his officials are not duplicitous: they appear to act in accordance with the belief that political power should produce personal wealth, and in this, if not in the specifics of their business arrangements, they are transparent.

When the coronavirus came, the Trump administration followed the logic of competition, and profit. Officials tried to persuade a German company working on a potential vaccine to sell it first—and perhaps exclusively—to the United States. Rather than coordinate the production and distribution of ventilators, the federal government created a system whereby states bid against one another and the federal government. Trump gave Jared Kushner broad authority to organize a private-sector response to the pandemic, working in parallel with or around the government effort. In other words, Trump acted in ways that would be unthinkable for a political leader, a man entrusted with the welfare of millions of people—but his administration uses a different calculus and makes no secret of it.

Trumpism builds on weaknesses and opportunities inherent in the logic of the system. The American system of government has never separated money from political power, and in the two decades before Trump's election, the role of money in American politics had grown manifold. Elections are decided by money: unlike in many other democracies, where electoral campaigns last from several weeks to a few months, are financed by government grants and/or subjected to strict spending limits—in the United States, it is contributions from the private sector that allow campaigns to exist in the first place. National and state party machines reinforce this system by apportioning access to public debates on the basis of the amount of money a candidate has secured. Access to media, which is to say, access to voters, also costs money: where in many democracies media are bound by obligations to provide airtime to candidates, in America the primary vehicle for addressing voters is through paid advertisements. No one in the political mainstream seemed to think anything was wrong with the marriage of money and politics. Former elected officials went to work as lobbyists. Using campaign contributions and lobbying to create (or kill) laws was normal. Power begat more money, and money begat more power. We could call the system that preceded and precipitated Trump's rise an oligarchy, and we would be right.

When Trump claimed that the president could not have a conflict of interest, he was not lying, for once. The issue had not been visited in nearly forty years, since the Justice Department and Congress codified the understanding that the powers of the presidency were so broad that no set of rules could be devised to prevent conflict of interest: the president just had to act in good faith. Lyndon Johnson, Jimmy Carter, Ronald Reagan, both of the George Bushes, and Bill Clinton had placed their assets in blind trusts, voluntarily. Obama did not, because he had no direct business investments. Trump did not, because he didn't think he should. One might say that Trump grasped the essence of the system, which turned money into power and power into money but, until Trump came along, did it politely, tastefully, and by group agreement. Or one might say that Trump acted at once the emperor and the boy who said that the emperor has no clothes, ripping the illusory cover of decency off the system, forcing everyone to stare at its obscene nature. Unlike the emperor in the fairy tale, though, Trump felt no shame and so was not transformed by the exposure—rather, he transformed the system, once again stripping away the moral aspiration of politics.

The lessons of post-Communist states can help us to think through some of the difficulty of describing the corruption—or whatever it ought to be called—of the Trump administration. Soviet Bloc countries, with their one-party systems and command economies, fostered a symbiotic relationship between power and wealth (though wealth was not measured in money). In fact, the only way to accumulate wealth was to become a part of the party hierarchy—and at the top of the party pyramid, people could achieve fantastic wealth.

These systems served as the foundations for the mafia states of Hungary and Russia, where the party was replaced with a political clan centered on a patron who distributes money and power. Western analysts use the word **corruption** to describe these systems, but this can be misleading: here corruption does not describe bureaucrats soliciting bribes for small acts of civil service (though this happens too); it describes the people in charge using the instruments of government in order to amass wealth, but also using their wealth to perpetuate power. This corruption is integral to the system. The system cannot exist without corruption because corruption is its fuel, its social glue, and its instrument of control. Anyone who enters the system becomes complicit in the corruption, which means everyone is always in some way or another outside the law—and therefore punishable. Autocracies love to smear their opponents with accusations of corruption, jail them on corruption charges, and even execute them, as does China.

Trump inherited a very different political

system and culture. In the United States, proximity to political power is certainly not the only way to become rich. But political power does translate into wealth, and vice versa, and this is the feature of the system most salient to Trump and Trumpism. Trump's flaunting of the expectations of decency on the one hand and his denial of his blatant self-dealing on the other moved the American government a giant step closer to the mafia states. Like those autocracies, Trumpism smears everyone: its friends because they become complicit in the corruption, and its enemies because they are accused of corruption.

It was Trump's attempt to smear, with the accusation of corruption, former Vice President Joe Biden, who he feared would be his Democratic opponent in the 2020 election, that ultimately led to the impeachment inquiry. (And it was the very normal American system of marrying money and political power that made this move possible, when Biden's son Hunter was hired as a highly paid consultant to a Ukrainian energy company.) Perhaps Trump intuited the potential of corruption-as-cudgel, or perhaps his personal lawyer Rudy Giuliani's Soviet-émigré associates suggested it. Either way, Trump was deploying both edges of the corruption sword: he was using the power of his office to his personal political ends, and he was wielding the accusation of corruption in the way an autocrat wields it. When Republicans in Congress defended his actions, by asserting that he was concerned about corruption in Ukraine, they became accomplices in his autocratic attempt—and the American government grew more corrupted, in the sense of the word that denotes a transformation beyond recognition.

6.

WE COULD CALL IT ASPIRATIONAL AUTOCRACY

The best description of Trump's relationship to autocrats belongs to historian Timothy Snyder, who observed, in April 2016, "It is not hard to see why Trump might choose Putin as his fantasy friend. Putin is the real world version of the person Trump pretends to be on television." Trump admired Putin's grip on power, his 82 percent popularity rating, and praised him for being "a leader far more than our president [Obama] has been a leader." Trump's love for Putin has drawn a lot of public attention, but in fact candidate Trump and, later, President Trump spread the love evenly among the world's autocrats.

Trump praised the mastery with which Kim Jong-un had solidified power in North Korea: "He goes in, he takes over, and he's the boss." Later, preparing for an in-person meeting with Kim, Trump claimed, "We fell in love."

Trump invited Philippine dictator Rodrigo Duterte to the White House and lauded him for his war against drugs, a campaign of extrajudicial executions that had killed thousands.

For his first trip abroad, Trump chose Saudi Arabia, where he received an honorary gold collar from the king. A year and a half later, dissident Saudi journalist Jamal Khashoggi, who had been living and working in exile, was murdered inside the Saudi embassy in Istanbul, on orders from and with the knowledge of Saudi Prince Mohammed bin Salman. Trump's statement in response to the murder was titled "America First!"

and reaffirmed his friendship with the Saudi royal.

Trump's second foreign trip was to Israel, where he was greeted on arrival at the Tel Aviv airport by Prime Minister Benjamin Netanyahu. They addressed each other as Donald and Bibi. Before the year was out, Trump issued a proclamation recognizing Jerusalem as the capital of Israel and ordering that the embassy be relocated there—in contravention of international law and policy consensus. In 2019, the United States took another step, effectively declaring that international law did not apply to the Israeli-occupied West Bank.

Early in the presidency, Trump hosted Chinese dictator Xi Jinping at Mar-a-Lago. Over dessert—"the most beautiful piece of chocolate cake that you have ever seen," according to Trump—he told Xi that the United States had just bombed Syria. Fox News put up a split screen: Trump recalling the conversation on the left, missiles exploding in the night sky on the right.

It was the perfect pictorial encapsulation of Trump's understanding of power: raw, brutal, unitary, and performative. Trump is always playing an exaggerated idea of himself on TV.

Congressional Republicans and the grown men (and a couple of women) of the administration proved willing to join the Trump show. When Trump scored his first legislative victory by passing a tax-reform bill—it did not come until December 2017, because legislation is peripheral to Trump's understanding of power—he celebrated by making the Republican Party genuflect. Trump had the press stay in the room at the beginning of a cabinet meeting, and he asked Carson to start off by leading the room in prayer. "Our kind Father in Heaven," Carson began, "we are so thankful for the opportunities and the freedom that you've granted us in this country. We thank you for a president and for cabinet members who are courageous, who are willing to face the winds of controversy in order to provide a better future for those who come behind us." Trump, his eyes closed and hands clasped, appeared to be following along, as though he had heard this prayer many times before. Carson continued, "We're thankful for the unity in Congress that has presented an opportunity for our economy to expand so that we can fight the corrosive debt that has been destroying our future." (Not a single Democrat, in either chamber of Congress, had voted in favor of the bill, which, it appeared, was more likely than not to increase the federal deficit.) After the prayer, Trump called on his vice president the way a teacher might cold-call on a pupil. For a full two minutes, Pence offered thanks for the president's "middle-class miracle"; he said that he was "deeply humbled, as your vice president, to be able to be here." Trump looked stern as he listened, nodding slightly, his arms crossed below his chest.

Later in the day, the Republican leaders of both houses of Congress, the vice president, and other Republican politicians gathered at the White House to offer praise to their leader. Senate Majority Leader Mitch

McConnell, House Speaker Paul Ryan, and others hailed Trump for his accomplishments. Representative Diane Black, of Tennessee, thanked Trump "for allowing us to have you as our President." Orrin Hatch, of Utah, who has been in the Senate for forty years, predicted that the Trump presidency will be "the greatest presidency we have seen not only in generations but maybe ever." Pence addressed Trump: "**You** will make America great again."

In less than a year, the performance, on demand, of loyalty and adulation for the leader had become normalized, at least among Republicans. Then Trump began demanding it of Democrats. Following his first State of the Union address in February 2018, Trump, aggrieved by Democrats who had sat motionless and stone-faced for most of his talk, accused them of being traitors. Speaking at a rally in Ohio, he said, "You're up there, you've got half the room going totally crazy—wild, they loved everything, they want to do something great for our country. And you have the other side—even on positive news, really positive news like that [low rate of unemployment for African Americans]—they were like death. And un-American. Un-American. Somebody said, 'treasonous.' I mean, yeah, I guess, why not? Can we call that treason? Why not! I mean they certainly didn't seem to love our country very much."

In the first year of his presidency, Trump had effected a remarkable shift in American politics—a shift of political audiences. In a representative democracy, a politician's primary audience is their voters, the residents of their district, state, or country who will decide whether to bring them back to office in the next election cycle. In an autocracy, the politician's primary audience is the autocrat himself, because he is the patron who apportions power and influence. In Trump's America, Republican politicians perform for Trump—he is their primary audience—but **his** audience is his base, the people who come to his rallies and absorb his tweets. He distributes power by mobilizing these voters. As long as the Democrats are performing for the audience of their voters rather than for Trump, there is hope of reversing the autocratic attempt—but even now half of the country in which we are living is functioning, in the public space, like an autocracy.

When congressional Democrats initiated an impeachment inquiry in September 2019, Trump, the administration, and the Republican Party effectively made the argument that Trump was an autocrat. His lawyer claimed absolute immunity and impunity; the White House ordered administration employees not to testify. Washington split into two camps, one that inhabited a representative democracy and one that lived in an autocracy. Some administration employees crossed the line, drawing Trump's Twitter ire and death threats from his followers; at least one person had to consider protective custody. Unusually for the Trump era, the argument in the hearings was not about the facts—the facts were known and uncontested—but about the nature of political power in America. One side was arguing that political power was provisionally granted by voters and limited by law, rules, norms, expectations, policy legacy, and the system of checks and balances. The other side was arguing that power wants to be absolute and is limited only by what the president can get away with.

On the first day of public impeachment hearings, Trump received the Turkish president, Recep Tayyip Erdoğan, at the White House. Erdoğan is one of Trump's autocrat crushes: Trump had called to congratulate Erdoğan on winning a referendum that solidified his autocratic rule, invited him to the White House soon after, and lauded him as an ally. The day of that visit, protesters who came to the Turkish embassy in Washington were beaten, several of them severely, by a group that reportedly included members of Erdoğan's security team. The White House had no comment. For decades, Washington was the last-resort option for dissidents from around the world: if peaceful protest was no longer possible in their own countries, or if they had been forced into exile, they could at least protest at their embassy in the United States. But the regime in America had, evidently, changed. Now, in November 2019, a smiling Trump stood next to Erdoğan, who had jailed several thousand dissidents and more than a hundred journalists, and said he was "a big fan" of the Turkish president. A month earlier, Trump had pulled almost all U.S. troops out of Syria, opening the way for a Turkish invasion and the massacre of thousands of Kurds.

Analysts who like to think that events have strategic meaning had suggested that Trump pulled out of Syria to enable Putin to strengthen Russia's positions there—perhaps even that he did this to compensate for U.S. military aid to Ukraine, released as the scandal that would spark impeachment was brewing—or that, as many people had thought for years, Putin had dirt on Trump and was blackmailing him. But Trump's actions are emotional, consistent with his understanding of himself in the world. When he talks about love, admiration, and being a fan of autocrats, he means it: he wants to be not merely their friend but one of them. He naturally wants to please them, and pleasing them comes naturally to him.

7.

WE COULD PRETEND HE IS AN ALIEN, OR CALL IT THE GOVERNMENT OF DESTRUCTION

Of all the autocrats who attract Trump's affections, only Putin has captured the American imagination. Rather, he has become a crutch for the American imagination. Putin and his alleged plot to install Trump in the White House promise not only to explain how Trump could have happened to America but also to create hope. When the Kremlin conspiracy behind Trump was finally exposed, surely the national nightmare would end. For nearly two years, the most popular political talk show in the country—MSNBC's **The Rachel Maddow Show**—and the country's most important newspaper, **The New York Times**, devoted the bulk of their political-reporting resources to the excruciatingly slow, tantalizingly complicated, deliciously dirty story of Russian interference in the 2016 election and the alleged collusion between the Trump campaign and the Kremlin.

The conspiracy theory was not baseless. A covert Russian effort to influence the American election was well documented. But the actual existence of a conspiracy barely makes conspiracy thinking less damaging. Conspiracy thinking focuses attention on the hidden, the implied, and the imagined, and draws it away from reality in plain view.

In plain view, Trump was flaunting, ignoring, and destroying all institutions of accountability. In plain view, he was degrading political speech. In plain view, he was using his office to enrich himself. In plain view, he was courting dictator after dictator. In plain view, he was promoting xenophobic conspiracy theories, now claiming that millions of immigrants voting illegally had cost him the popular vote; now insisting, repeatedly, that Obama had had him wiretapped. All of this, though plainly visible, was unfathomable, as Trump's election itself had been. The more Trump assaulted the sense of the possible and the acceptable, the louder became talk of a sinister, all-powerful, all-knowing, world-dominating Russia. Finally, our search for the magic bullet that would rid us of a xenophobic conspiracy theorist in the White House landed us on a xenophobic conspiracy theory: the president was a Russian puppet.

Meanwhile, Trump boasted that he had repealed more regulations in his first year than had any other president in his entire tenure, including, "in one instance, sixteen years." Everything in this boast was a lie. But it's true that his was the first administration focused on destruction. Trump appointees started deregulating by reversing or suspending Obama-era rules, from protecting transgender students' rights to public-school accountability metrics, protecting streams from mining, and restricting the sale of firearms to people with mental disabilities. Trump appointees attacked government institutions themselves. In the winter of 2017, for example, most of the senior staff in the State Department either left or were fired. The State Department building in Washington became a ghost town. Where there had once been long lines to go through security on the way in, guards now waited around, idling between visitors. Inside, remaining staff struggled to understand what was going on: the programs they worked on were still funded—many of them, they assumed, only until a new budget went into effect—but they no longer had a line of communication to the top of the agency or, in some cases, to country specialists. Daily State Department briefings were suspended (occasional briefings were reinstituted when Mike Pompeo replaced Tillerson as secretary of state)—as were the Pentagon's briefings; eventually, the White House effectively discontinued briefings too.

Trump issued an executive order requiring that for every new rule introduced, two existing rules be scrapped. The Environmental Protection Agency exceeded this goal. In 2017, the EPA had repealed sixteen rules and introduced one; in 2018 it scrapped ten and created three.

Advisory groups resigned or were disbanded, starting with the White House Council of Economic Advisers; scientific knowledge was being sidelined or literally erased, as when information on climate change disappeared, first from the White House and then from the EPA websites. Most of the absences created in the administration, including the absence of expertise, were invisible to most people most of the time. Sometimes a disconcerting example would emerge, though. During a hearing in May 2019, when Representative Katie Porter, a law professor and former California bank-oversight official, asked Ben Carson about REOs—a common abbreviation for "real estate owned," meaning foreclosed properties—Carson thought Porter was talking about Oreo cookies. He had been HUD secretary for more than two years.

Carson had come to Congress that day to defend a proposed cut of more than 16 percent from his agency's budget. Every draft budget proposed by the Trump administration cut funding for every agency outside of Defense, Homeland Security, and Veterans Affairs (in 2018, NASA, Energy, Commerce, and Health and Human Services were added to the "plus" column, but by 2019, only Commerce, with a 7 percent increase, remained). Each of the proposed budgets would have cut State Department funding by between 24 and 33 percent, EPA funding by between 25 and 31 percent, and HUD funding by between 13 and 19 percent. The heads of the agencies did not object, leaving it up to Congress to continue funding an administration that wished to disinvest in itself.

Amid all this destruction, one area stands apart: the federal courts. It turns out that Magyar's description of the mechanics of autocratic attempts in post-Communist countries is useful in analyzing what is happening in the United States after all. Magyar talks about capturing the institutions of the state, obliterating distinctions among branches of government, and packing the courts. In Trump's case, the takeover of state institutions has consisted of two parts: using them for personal gain and handicapping their service to the public. Obliterating divisions among branches of government has taken the shape of subjugating the Republican Party. And packing the courts is packing the courts. By November 2019, Trump had set a record for the number of judges appointed. His appointees made up a quarter of all judges in the courts of appeal. He had flipped courts that could make key decisions connected to the impeachment process. And he had appointed two Supreme Court justices.

Trump's appointments are not just ideologically far right: antichoice, dismissive of civil rights protections, opposed to LGBT rights, and in favor of deregulation. Several are also notably inexperienced. Like only one other recent president, George W. Bush, Trump has chosen to bypass the American Bar Association's vetting process. With time, his picks have become more ideologically extreme and less qualified—more and more reflective of the administration itself. Some of the confirmation hearings have constituted an attack on politics not dissimilar to a Trump rally or press conference: they make one ashamed to see and hear.

8.

THE DEATH OF DIGNITY

Trumpism has waged daily assaults on American political culture, but a few events seem destined to stay in our collective memory—not, perhaps, because of their own disproportionate impact, but because they illuminated what had already been lost. One such event is the confirmation hearings on Brett Kavanaugh's nomination to the Supreme Court. Trump's second court nominee, Kavanaugh, was worse than his first, Neil Gorsuch. The Gorsuch nomination and confirmation hearing came after the Republican-controlled Senate had refused, for eleven months, to consider Obama's last

Supreme Court nominee. That Gorsuch could now be nominated and confirmed was an affront to politics. But Gorsuch himself seemed to be the kind of conservative judge whom any recent Republican president might have appointed. To the Supreme Court, an organism that runs—or at least appears to run—on civility and considered respect for a variety of opinions, Gorsuch was not a foreign body. During the confirmation process he even distanced himself from Trump's attacks on judges.

By the measures of judicial philosophy and political opinion, Kavanaugh was not more extreme than Gorsuch. In his first session on the court he voted with the majority more often than any other judge (Gorsuch was one of two judges least likely to vote with the majority). But his nomination hearing was the spectacle of the death of dignity in politics.

There are at least two ways in which the concept of dignity is key to our understanding of politics. There is the dignity that participation in the political process affords each citizen. Having a voice, being heard, and exercising political agency are component parts of this form of dignity. There is also the dignity of political performance, with its reliance on honorifics, procedure, particular modes of dress, and a codified use of language. People have long understood that this performance can signal and even precede the content of politics. Of course, the public spectacle of politics can and has been used to exclude those who don't look or speak the right way. That underscores the interplay of the two kinds of political dignity: the dignity of participation and the dignity of performance. The challenge of democracy is to create procedures that sustain the dignity of performance while they continuously expand the range of inclusion. Trumpism attacks both sorts of dignity, by degrading the performance of politics and by restricting participation in it.

On September 27, 2018, the Senate Judiciary Committee heard testimony by Christine Blasey Ford, a fifty-one-year-old psychology professor who said that at the age of fifteen she had been sexually assaulted by Kavanaugh, who was three years older. Blasey Ford detailed the indignity of the assault. She talked about the sound of her assailants' laughter that had stayed with her ever since. "I was underneath one of them while the two laughed, two friends having a really good time with one another," she said. Blasey Ford's testimony was measured, thoughtfully narrated, and occasionally apologetic—in other words, she performed respect for the political body and procedure in which she was appearing. In her opening, she said, "I am here today because I believe it is my civic duty to tell you what happened to me while Brett Kavanaugh and I were in high school." Kavanaugh's performance, on the other hand, was Trumpian.

In advance of the hearing, Kavanaugh denied the allegations in an interview on Fox, where he appeared with his wife, and in written testimony submitted to the Senate committee. In the interview, he was as measured and apparently humble as his accuser would be, and he too expressed respect for procedure. "I am looking for a fair process, a process where I can defend my integrity and clear my name," he said. "All I'm asking for is fairness, and that I be heard."

In his written statement, Kavanaugh acknowledged the gravity of the accusations and again expressed respect for process: "Sexual assault is horrific. It is morally wrong. It is illegal. It is contrary to my religious faith. And it contradicts the core promise of this Nation that all people are created equal and entitled to be treated with dignity and respect. Allegations of sexual assault must be taken seriously. Those who make allegations deserve to be heard. The subject of allegations also deserves to be heard. Due process is a foundation of the American rule of law." He concluded, "I am not questioning that Dr. Ford may have been sexually assaulted by some person in some place at some time. But I have never done that to her or to anyone. I am innocent of this charge."

On the morning of the hearing, CNN reported that Trump had called Kavanaugh the evening before and urged him to be forceful in his denials. "Will the belligerent style Trump has employed to refute similar allegations work for Kavanaugh today?" asked the report. "Stay tuned."

Kavanaugh started shouting as soon as he took the stand. He shouted that he had written his statement himself. He shouted that no one had seen his statement. He shouted, "My family and my name have been totally and permanently destroyed by vicious and false additional accusations." He shouted, "This confirmation process has become a national disgrace . . . You have replaced 'advise and consent' with 'search and destroy.'" He shouted that the Left was willing to do anything to derail his nomination and called the accusations against him "revenge of the Clintons."

The Kavanaugh hearing was the first

congressional hearing in which people inhabiting the two non-overlapping American realities—one an autocracy, the other a representative democracy—were addressing two different audiences while speaking in the same room. Blasey Ford was addressing the Senate Judiciary Committee and a broader public. Kavanaugh, who deployed Trump's favorite tone—aggrieved and aggressive—and one of his favorite tropes—a Clintonian plot—was speaking to Trump. The president enjoyed the show. "Judge Kavanaugh showed America exactly why I nominated him," he tweeted. "His testimony was powerful, honest, and riveting. Democrats' search and destroy strategy is disgraceful and this process has been a total sham and effort to delay, obstruct, and resist."

While Blasey Ford was addressing the committee, its Republican members refused to engage with her. Bizarrely, they had invited a prosecutor from Arizona, Rachel Mitchell, to question Blasey Ford instead.

Majority Leader Mitch McConnell referred to Mitchell as a "female assistant." Kavanaugh maintained a hectoring tone in response to questions posed by Mitchell, Democratic senators, and Republican senators. He told all of them over and over that he liked beer. Everyone in the room but the Democrats and Blasey Ford was performing for Trump that day. The spectacle required trampling the dignity of politics—both the dignity of performance, instead of which there was shouting and the discussion of beer, and the dignity of participation, which was denied to Blasey Ford, who was speaking to a room most of which refused to hear her.

During the confirmation process, eighty-three different complaints were filed in the Tenth Circuit against Kavanaugh, alleging that his testimony was untruthful and his behavior during the hearing was disrespectful of the judiciary. In August 2019, all of those complaints were dismissed by a nationwide committee of federal judges because Kavanaugh, as a Supreme Court justice, was no longer under their jurisdiction. Like Trump, who was not subject to conflict-of-interest rules because he was president, Kavanaugh had advanced beyond the reach of the rules that used to govern American politics.

9.

MUELLER DID
NOT SAVE US

It has been a time of strange bedfellows. The more Trump trampled public politics, the more the opposition cathected onto the former FBI director, Special Counsel Robert Mueller. Fawning profiles—or, rather, what journalists call "write-arounds," pieces reported without the participation of the principal subject—projected an unexamined nostalgia for pre-Trump normality. **The Washington Post** contrasted Mueller's old-money roots with Trump's scrappy, immigrant ones. **Politico** called him "America's straightest arrow." Everyone wrote about Mueller's clothing style: off-the-rack Brooks

Brothers suits, white shirts, and foulard ties in blue or red—which the menswear blog **Die, Workwear** praised as "the other end of the spectrum from Trump's oversized Brioni suits and shiny satin ties." The blog added that "Mueller is the real deal. He learned his sense of dress through his privileged WASP upbringing, not style blogs such as this one." A **GQ** profile called Mueller, admiringly, "a throwback to an earlier regime, when, the story goes, Ivy League patricians entered government for the sake of service, not self-enrichment." Most writers noted, too, that Mueller's wristwatch was a thirty-five-dollar Casio, worn with the face on the inside of the wrist, military style. Even Mueller's extraordinarily long tenure at the helm of the FBI—twelve years, which had required a special dispensation for reappointment, a term second in length only to the reign of J. Edgar Hoover—became fawn fodder.

Mueller's leadership of the FBI, which began on September 4, 2001, was in fact both a symptom and a cause of the processes that had made Trumpism possible:

the rise of the politics of conspiracy, the unprecedented concentration of power in the executive branch, the transformation of the FBI from a criminal-police organization into a domestic spy agency. In September 2013, as Mueller's second, special term as FBI director was ending, the American Civil Liberties Union published a sixty-nine-page report on the FBI under Mueller. It was called "Unleashed and Unaccountable: The FBI's Unchecked Abuse of Authority." The report concluded that "the FBI is repeating mistakes of the past and is again unfairly targeting immigrants, racial and religious minorities, and political dissidents for surveillance, infiltration, and 'disruption strategies.'" But this time around, the report's authors continued, the FBI had far more powerful tools at its disposal: "Modern technological innovations have significantly increased the threat to American liberty." The report detailed several instances when agents of Mueller's FBI engaged in torture—a word that did not appear in any of the laudatory profiles. The **Post**, instead, claimed that "although more terrorist attacks were feared, Mueller was intent on protecting civil liberties"—a statement that should have earned the paper a Pinocchio or two from its own fact-checking department. To support this fanciful claim, the paper quoted former Attorney General Eric Holder as saying, "He didn't allow FBI agents in the post-9/11 era to engage in interrogation techniques that he thought were inconsistent with American law and tradition"—a carefully crafted statement that said nothing.

So fervent was the hope that Mueller could rid us of Trump that no one seemed to consider the implications of being delivered from the nightmare by the author of the contemporary American surveillance state. But then the deliverance didn't happen.

After twenty-two long months, Mueller's 448-page report dropped. Under a single cover, it provided the most comprehensive portrait of Trumpism to date.

The first half of the report attempted to tell the story of Russian interference and the relationship the Trump campaign had had to it. The opposition's great hope had been that the investigation would connect the dots evident in earlier indictments and subpoenas, and lay out the story of a conspiracy that would fatally discredit the Trump presidency. But the Mueller report didn't tie anything together in the end. Rather than tell the story of a single crime masterminded by a single actor or entity, it detailed many hustles, most of them unsuccessful. If anything, the lack of coordination among them was striking, as was the scrappy, almost petty nature of many. The hustlers were Russians and Americans and Russian-Americans, shady lawyers, shadier entrepreneurs, and the shadiest political consultants, and each was out to swindle everyone else. Everyone exaggerated what they knew and could deliver. Everyone lied, and almost no one got what they wanted.

By the time the report was released, Trump's former campaign manager Paul Manafort and Trump's personal lawyer Michael Cohen were both in prison, sentenced to seven and a half and three years, respectively. But such was the nature of Trumpism that the president's closest associates could be in prison and he could be unaffected by this—in part because we already knew that his was an administration of swindlers and conmen, and in effect we had come to accept it.

Volume II, which was just a few pages shorter than the Russia part of the Mueller report, detailed the president's behavior during the investigation. Here, in addition to events and actions that could be surmised from the president's public outbursts—such as his attempts to force Attorney General Sessions to quash the Russia probe—there were new facts. The most important revelation was that Trump had instructed White House Counsel Don McGahn to get Mueller removed (McGahn ignored the request) and then tried to get McGahn to write a statement denying that this had ever happened. To a lay person, these revelations would have looked like clear evidence of obstruction of justice. But Mueller wrote that he did not make a determination on whether the president was guilty of obstructing justice. The report stated,

> Finally, we concluded that in the rare case in which a criminal investigation of the President's conduct is justified, inquiries to determine whether the President acted for a corrupt motive should not impermissibly chill his performance of his constitutionally assigned duties. The conclusion that Congress may apply the obstruction laws to the President's corrupt exercise of the powers of office accords with our constitutional system of checks and balances and the principle that no person is above the law. . . . Because we determined not to make a traditional prosecutorial judgment, we did not draw ultimate conclusions about the President's conduct.

In other words, Mueller believed that an indictment by him would have paralyzed the presidency—a risk he was unwilling to take.

But he was signaling that he had collected the evidence that would enable Congress to take the next step.

The Mueller report was a manifesto of institutional restraint, consistent with the Mueller persona conjured by the media over the nearly two years of anticipation. Unlike the Mueller FBI, the Mueller investigation stayed pointedly inside the borders of its authority, as drawn on the most conservative possible map. Mueller opted not to question Trump in the course of the investigation. Most important, he opted not to make a determination on the matter of obstruction of justice. But in the dry language of his report, he was exhorting Congress to act, to pick up where he left off.

Before the report could reach Congress, however, it landed on the desk of Mueller's boss, Attorney General William Barr, who had been on the job all of five weeks. Barr had served as attorney general in the George H. W. Bush administration, from 1991 to 1993. For most of the quarter century since, he had been a corporate lawyer and a prolific Republican donor. He had also been an outspoken defender of Trump's most controversial actions, including the travel ban and the president's decision to fire FBI director James Comey. On both subjects, Barr had published op-ed pieces in **The Washington Post**. After Barr defended the Comey firing, Trump asked him to serve as his defense attorney. Barr turned the offer down, but in June 2018 he wrote an apparently unsolicited memo to the Justice Department, with the subject line "Mueller's 'Obstruction' Theory." The memo argued, in essence, that the president had all the legal authority to do whatever he wanted—the same grounds on which he had defended the travel ban. Barr was laying the legal case for autocratic power.

Barr, the first person outside of Mueller's team to read the report, informed Congress and the public:

The evidence developed during the Special Counsel's investigation is not sufficient to establish that the president committed an obstruction-of-justice offense. Our determination was made without regard to and is not based on the constitutional considerations that surround the indictment and criminal prosecution of a sitting president.

Here was the biggest institutional crisis, to date, of the Trump presidency, contained in the contradiction between Mueller's conclusion, which called on Congress to step in and act on the evidence collected, and Barr's reinterpretation of the report, which told Congress that there was nothing more for it to do. Mueller wrote to Barr to object:

The summary letter the Department sent to Congress and released to the public late in the afternoon on March 24 did not fully capture the context, nature, and substance of this Office's work and conclusions. . . . There is now public confusion about critical aspects of the results of our investigation. This threatens to undermine a central purpose for which the Department appointed the Special Counsel: to assure full public confidence in the outcome of the investigations.

This letter did not become public until May 1, 2019. By this time, Barr had released the report. It was a redacted version, but it contained Mueller's conclusion. By now, though, the product of Mueller's fact-finding mission was obscured by a battle of interpretations. Most Americans—indeed, most members of Congress—did not read the report, but they were aware that Barr and Mueller, or the president and the Democrats, were arguing about its conclusions. Depending on one's party affiliation or cable-news affinity, one could choose one side's position over the other—as though the president's actions were indeed a matter of opinion rather than fact.

The report landed in Congress on April 18, 2019. It was not an explosion. It was not, discernibly, the end or the beginning of anything. It was a dull thud. House Speaker Nancy Pelosi, wary of waging a battle only to lose it in the Republican-controlled Senate, opted not to open impeachment proceedings. It fell to junior Democrats to call for impeachment. Over the course of the spring and summer, the number of supporters of impeachment grew slowly, a dozen or two dozen representatives a month. Having a president who instructed his counsel to lie to Congress, a president who lied to the public himself, a president who was a con man, was, apparently, not an emergency—or at least American political institutions were not equipped to treat it as one.

10.

INSTITUTIONS HAVE NOT SAVED US

In July, Mueller testified before Congress. He restated the conclusions of his report. Somehow, in person his reserve became blandness. The story of the United States president ordering a White House lawyer to lie to Congress—the story of the president's obstruction of justice—sounded ordinary. In fact, it was ordinary. The president had been lying to the public daily for two and a half years. It no longer sounded like an emergency, a high crime. Hopes for impeachment were deflated.

The following day, Trump got on the phone with the Ukrainian president and asked him to dig up dirt on the Bidens in exchange for continued American military support. A CIA analyst detailed to the White House started writing a report that he would submit to the inspector general for the intelligence services, that the Trump administration would block, that would become known and would finally launch an official impeachment probe in Congress. In September, Pelosi declared that Trump had finally gone too far. "The President must be held accountable," she said. "No one is above the law."

But, of course, Trump had placed himself above the law. He fully believed that he was above the law and for nearly three years he had been getting away with acting as though he was above the law. The event that finally got Pelosi to draw the line was a proverbial straw: an incident that resembled a succession of other incidents when Trump had used his office for personal gain and sabotaged the system of checks and balances. His attempt to use four hundred million dollars of congressionally approved military aid for his own benefit fell in the same category as his and his children's foreign business deals, brokered on the back of American diplomacy; his use of the presidency to attract lobbyists, dignitaries, and perhaps entire summits as paying guests to his properties; and his use of taxpayer funds for incessant leisure travel. Trump's attempt to quash the whistleblower's report was similar to his attempt to pressure FBI Director Comey to stop the investigation of National Security Advisor Michael Flynn, or his attempt to get the White House counsel to lie to the public.

As witnesses testified in the course of the impeachment inquiry, they unspooled the story of abuse of power to which dozens of experienced officials had borne witness. Some of them had been fired, and left quietly. Some of them had quit, also quietly. Some tried to run interference on the inside. Only one person chose to use an existing legal procedure to sound an alarm. This avenue had been available to anyone who worked in or with the administration—yet it had taken two and a half years of the Trump presidency for someone finally to act.*

This act of whistleblowing was not like other acts of whistleblowing. Historically, whistleblowers reveal abuse of power that is surprising and shocking to the public. The Trump-Ukraine story was shocking but in no way surprising: it was in character, and in keeping with a pattern of actions. The incident that the whistleblower chose to report was not the worst thing that Trump had done. Installing his daughter and her

---

*Reading the whistleblower's report, one might surmise that it was a collective effort: it appears that a number of officials might have agreed that one of them would compile testimony and use the official whistleblowing channel on behalf of a self-selected group. The whistleblower, in other words, does not appear to have acted alone. This does not, however, detract from the fact that it took two and a half years of the presidency for someone in the administration to sound the alarm, or the fact that at least some of the people who shared the whistleblower's concerns continued to work for the administration.

husband in the White House was worse. Inciting violence was worse. Unleashing war on immigrants was worse. Enabling murderous dictators the world over was worse.

The two realities of Trump's America—democratic and autocratic—collided daily in the impeachment hearings. In one reality, Congress was following due process to investigate and potentially remove from office a president who had abused power. In the other reality, the proceedings were a challenge to Trump's legitimate autocratic power. The realities clashed but still did not overlap: to any participant or viewer on one side of the divide, anything the other side said only reaffirmed their reality. The realities were also asymmetrical: an autocratic attempt is a crisis, but the logic and language of impeachment proceedings is the logic and language of normal politics, of vote counting and procedure. If it had succeeded in removing Trump from office, it would have constituted a triumph of institutions over the autocratic attempt. It did not. The impeachment proceedings became merely a part of the historical record, a record of only a small part of the abuse that is Trumpism.

Still, there will come a day when the Trump era is over. In the best-case scenario, it is ended by the voters at the ballot box. In the worst-case scenario, it lasts more than four years. In either case, the first three years have shown that an autocratic attempt in the United States has a credible chance of succeeding. Worse than that, they have shown that an autocratic attempt builds logically on the structures and norms of American government: on the concentration of power in the executive branch, and on the marriage of money and politics. Recovery from Trumpism—a process that will be necessary whenever Trumpism ends—will not be a process of returning to government as it used to be, a fictional state of pre-Trump normalcy. Recovery will be possible only as reinvention: of institutions, of what politics means to us, and of what it means to be a democracy, if that is indeed what we choose to be.

Part Two

KING OF
REALITY

11.

WORDS HAVE MEANING, OR THEY OUGHT TO

Trump's autocratic attempt began with a war on words. As with other things he has done, in his attack on language Trump has resembled, or perhaps emulated, twentieth-century totalitarian leaders and twenty-first-century autocrats like Putin and Hungary's Viktor Orbán. Totalitarian regimes use words to mean their opposite. In **1984**, George Orwell imagined the Party dictating its slogans: "War is peace. Freedom is slavery. Ignorance is strength." Real-life totalitarian regimes do not grant their subjects the clarity of juxtaposing a word with its antonym—they enforce order by applying words in ways that invert meaning. The Soviet Union, for example, had something that it called "elections," usually referred to, as though more descriptively, as the "free expression of citizen will." The process, which was mandatory, involved showing up at the so-called polling place, receiving a pre-filled ballot—each office had one name matched to it—and depositing it in the ballot box, out in the open. The "free expression of citizen will" was not at all free, it did not constitute expression, and it had no relationship to citizenship or will. Calling this ritual either an "election" or the "free expression of citizen will" had a dual effect: it eviscerated the words "election," "free," "expression," "citizen," and "will," and it also left the thing itself undescribed. When something cannot be described, it does not become a fact of shared reality. Hundreds of millions of Soviet citizens had an experience of the thing that could not be described, but they did not consciously share that experience, because they had no language for doing so. At the same time, an experience that could be accurately described as, say, an "election," or "free," had been preemptively discredited because those words had been used to denote something entirely different.

In the early 1990s, after the Soviet regime collapsed, Russian journalists faced the challenge of reinventing journalism, which had been a vehicle for propaganda, not information. Now language stood in the way. The language of politics had been pillaged, as had the language of values and even the language of feelings, because after decades of performing revolutionary passion on command, people had become weary of the very idea of passion. The new Russian journalists opted for language that was descriptive in the most immediate way: they tried to stick to verbs and nouns, and only to things that could be directly observed. In a bid to regain trust, they resorted to a drastically reduced vocabulary. They spoke only of what was in front of their eyes, had a shape that could be clearly defined, and a weight that could be accurately measured. They stayed away from matters of the mind and heart, because they knew that no one believed them enough to enable them to venture into the unseen. Writing in Russian was like navigating a minefield: one misstep could discredit the entire enterprise.

Then things got worse. When Putin rose to power in 1999, a new kind of damage to language commenced. Putin declared a "dictatorship of the law." His main ideologue, Vladislav Surkov, advanced the idea of "managed democracy." Dmitry Medvedev, who kept Putin's chair warm between Putin's second and third terms, declared, "Freedom is better than unfreedom." These were no longer words used to mean their opposite. These were words used simply to mean nothing. The phrase "dictatorship of the law" is so incoherent as to render both "dictatorship" and "law" meaningless.

Similarly, when Orbán's party obliterated the divisions between Hungary's branches of government, the resulting regime was dubbed the "system of national cooperation." Proclaiming the successful completion of this system in a 2018 speech, Orbán said, "It represents an honorable goal when one considers that what we have had throughout Hungarian history has been more a system of national compliance." He went on to talk, at length, about censorship in Europe outside of Hungary— a country where nongovernment-allied media had become nearly extinct. He was invoking the specter of "political correctness," the word "censorship" to mean its opposite—to refer to a social consensus he disliked rather than to government controls on speech—but the words "compliance" and "cooperation" became, in his speech, hazy signifiers. In the absence of agency (stripping branches of government of their agency had been the project), what was cooperation if not compliance? Then why were the two words used in opposition? Who had been "compliant" in earlier periods but had the chance to "cooperate" now? The more one dug for meaning, the less one found.

Trump has an instinct, perhaps even a talent, for mangling language in both ways: using words to mean their opposite and stripping them of meaning. His knack is for inverting words and phrases that deal with power relationships. In November 2017, for example, less than two weeks after the election, Vice President–elect Pence went to see **Hamilton**, the immensely popular Broadway hip-hop musical about the Founding Fathers. Part of the audience booed Pence when he walked in. At curtain call, actor Brandon Victor Dixon, who played Aaron Burr, stepped forward to read a statement from the cast apparently drafted in the course of the show.

> You know, we have a guest in the audience this evening. And Vice President–elect Pence, I see you walking out, but I hope you will hear us just a few more moments. There's nothing to boo here, ladies and gentlemen. There's nothing to boo here. We're all here sharing a story of love. We have a

message for you, sir. We hope that you will hear us out.

And I encourage everybody to pull out your phones and tweet and post, because this message needs to be spread far and wide, okay?

Vice President–elect Pence, we welcome you and we truly thank you for joining us at **Hamilton: An American Musical.** We really do.

We, sir, are the diverse America who are alarmed and anxious that your new administration will not protect us, our planet, our children, our parents—or defend us and uphold our inalienable rights, sir.

But we truly hope that this show has inspired you to uphold our American values and work on behalf of **all** of us. All of us.

We truly thank you for sharing this show—this wonderful American story told by a diverse group of men, women of different colors, creeds, and orientations.

Dixon was addressing Pence in the standard language of American politics, which assumes the possibility of sharing reality across difference. It assumes that the phrases "inalienable rights" and "American values" have clear meaning even if politicians need to be reminded that these phrases apply to all people who live in the United States. It also assumes that politicians will accept the obligation at least to hear out all of their constituents. Pence, a supporter of the Tea Party movement who as governor of Indiana promoted anti-LGBT and anti-immigrant policies, nonetheless recognized the idiom in which he was being addressed. Asked for comment, he said, "This is what freedom sounds like."

But Trump's sensibilities were offended. "Our wonderful future V.P. Mike Pence was harassed last night at the theater by the cast of Hamilton," he tweeted. A few minutes later, he added, "The Theater must always be a safe and special place. The cast of Hamilton was very rude last night to a very good man, Mike Pence. Apologize!"

The tweets summed up Trump's understanding of power. His election victory entitled him—and, by extension, those whom he saw as his people—to adulation. Criticism, confrontation, and even the simple acknowledgment of political difference amount, in his view, to disrespect. Being disrespected makes him feel victimized—and he claims his imagined victimhood with glee. This claim turns the reality of power upside down, enabling Trump to come out on top by placing himself at the bottom.

The phrase "safe space" was coined to describe a place where people who usually feel unsafe and powerless would feel exceptionally safe. Claiming that the second most powerful man in the world should be granted a "safe space" **in public** turned the concept precisely on its head. Trump performed the same trick on the phrase "witch hunt," which he repeatedly claimed was being carried out by Democrats to avenge their electoral loss by launching the Russia investigation. Witch hunts cannot actually be carried out by losers, big or small: the agent of a witch hunt must have power.

Trump seized and flipped the term "fake news" in much the same way. Until roughly late fall 2016, "fake news" referred to false stories proffered by the likes of Breitbart, Russian internet trolls, or Macedonian teenagers who made a killing off gullible Americans by posting made-up tales on social networks. The term was unfortunate—something is either "fake" or "news," not both—but briefly it was widely understood. Then Trump began applying it to news outlets he felt were too critical of him, especially **The New York Times** and CNN. The flip served a dual function: the classic one of a liar, caught red-handed, screaming "Liar!" at his accusers, and of positioning Trump as the victim. The president complains about "fake news" as though the legacy media outlets were more powerful than he is—powerful enough to treat him unfairly.

Trump's other gift is for using words to make them mean nothing. Everyone he has ever mentioned while he was feeling disposed toward them is "great" or "wonderful," and everything is "tremendous." But any word can be given or taken away. In a January 2017 interview, Trump called NATO "obsolete." In April, when NATO Secretary General Jens Stoltenberg came to the White House, Trump said that the alliance was "no longer obsolete." These statements rendered the word "obsolete" meaningless—or, if one assumed that Trump was actually using "obsolete" to mean "obsolete," they challenged one's experience of time, which would have to run in reverse to render something "no longer" obsolete. They also created the conditions under which some commentators discussed the U.S. relationship to NATO as a going concern—as in, not obsolete—while others continued to debate whether NATO was obsolete or maintain that it was. Shared political reality kept shrinking.

A trademark Trumpian approach to attacking language is to take words and throw them into a pile that means nothing.

In April 2017, he gave several media interviews to discuss his first hundred days in office. The AP published one that was almost all word salad.

> Number one, there's great responsibility. When it came time to, as an example, send out the fifty-nine missiles, the Tomahawks in Syria. I'm saying to myself, "You know, this is more than just like, seventy-nine [sic] missiles. This is death that's involved," because people could have been killed. This is risk that's involved, because if the missile goes off and goes in a city or goes in a civilian area—you know, the boats were hundreds of miles away—and if this missile goes off and lands in the middle of a town or a hamlet. . . . every decision is much harder than you'd normally make. [unintelligible] . . . This is involving death and life and so many things. . . . So it's far more responsibility. [unintelligible] . . . The financial cost of everything is so massive, every

agency. This is thousands of times bigger, the United States, than the biggest company in the world.

A partial list of words that lost their meaning in this passage is: "responsibility," the number "fifty-nine" and the number "seventy-nine," "death," "people," "risk," "city," "civilian," "hamlet," "decision," "hard," "normal," "life," "the United States." Even the word "unintelligible," inserted by the journalist, became suspect here. While it is of course possible that an interviewee mutters something a journalist cannot make out, the convention of interviews with heads of state, whose words have real-life consequences, is to back up and clarify any word or passage. But the convention assumes that an interview is an interview and not a rant. The role of the journalist was rendered meaningless, too, in the most basic way: the interviewer was compelled to participate, interrupting this incomprehensible monologue with follow-up questions or words like "right," which only served to further the fiction that there was a narrative or a train of thought being laid out that the journalist (and hence a reader) could follow, that something was indeed "right" or could be "right" about what Trump was saying—when in fact he was saying nothing and everything at the same time, and this could not be right.

Trump's word piles fill public space with static, the way pollutants in an industrial city can saturate the air, making it toxic and creating a state of constant haze. The haze can be so dense that objects become visible only up close, but never in their entirety and never really in focus. In Trump's America, every once in a while a journalist or a politician makes a statement clear enough to capture a fragment of shared reality—but it is only ever a fragment, and it is inevitably soon obscured by more language used to mean nothing or the opposite of itself.

In the second half of the twentieth century, many philosophers and writers questioned the ability of words to reflect facts, and the existence of objective facts themselves. Was this not the Trumpian view, too? In 2018, former **New York Times** book critic Michiko Kakutani published a book called **The Death of Truth**, in which she argued that postmodern thinkers enabled the Trumpian moment.

Broadly speaking, postmodernist arguments deny an objective reality existing independently from human perception, contending that knowledge is filtered through the prisms of class, race, gender, and other variables. In rejecting the possibility of an objective reality and substituting the notions of perspective and positioning for the idea of truth, postmodernism enshrined the principle of subjectivity. Language is seen as unreliable and unstable (part of the unbridgeable gap between what is said and what is meant), and even the notion of people acting as fully rational, autonomous individuals is discounted, as each of us is shaped, consciously or unconsciously, by a particular time and culture.

Kakutani, though, was conflating the intentions of postmodernist thinkers and Trumpian post-truth, post-language propagandists like Kellyanne Conway, Sean Spicer, and the president himself. When writers and academics question the limits of language, it is invariably an exercise that grows from a desire to bring more light into the public space, to arrive at a shared reality that is more nuanced than it was before the conversation began: to focus ever more tightly on the shape, weight, and function of any thing that can be named, or to find names for things that have not, in the past, been observed or been seen as deserving of description. A shared language is essential to this exercise, and observing the limits of this language is an attempt to compensate for them. As Hannah Arendt argued, the awareness of one's subjectivity is essential to political conversation:

We know from experience that no one can adequately grasp the objective world in its full reality all on his own, because the world always shows and reveals itself to him from only one perspective, which corresponds to his standpoint in the world and is determined by it. If someone wants to see and experience the world as it "really" is, he can do so only by understanding it as something that is shared by many people, lies between them, separates and links them, showing itself differently to each and comprehensible only to the extent that many people can talk **about** it and exchange their opinions and perspectives with one another, over against one another. Only in the freedom of our speaking with one another does the world, as that about which we speak, emerge in its objectivity and visibility from all sides.

The "freedom of our speaking with one another" depends on a shared language.

Trump's attack on language is an attack on freedom itself. In his philosophy of the "rectification of names," Confucius warned: "If language is not correct, then . . . morals and art will deteriorate; if justice goes astray, the people will stand about in helpless confusion. Hence there must be no arbitrariness in what is said. This matters above everything." Trump's lies and his word piles both are exercises in arbitrariness, continued assertions of the power to say what he wants, when he wants, to usurp language itself, and with it, our ability to speak and act with others—in other words, our ability to engage in politics. The assault on language may be harder to define and describe than his attacks on institutions, but it is essential to his autocratic attempt, the ultimate objective of which is to obliterate politics.

What can journalists, writers, and everyday speakers of American language do to resist the assault or to recover from the damage once it's done? The Russian poet Sergey Gandlevsky once said that in the depth of the Soviet era he was taken with the language of hardware stores. He mentioned "secateurs" (garden shears). It was a specific word; it had weight, dimensions, shape. When a person said "secateurs," they could only possibly mean the distinct object the word indisputably described. The language of politics is less specific and more mutable than the language of hardware stores, even under the best of circumstances, but we can and should be more intentional when using it. The vocabulary of American political conversation is vague. "Authoritarian" is used to mean any regime or approach to governance that's not democratic. The Trump era saw a surge in the use of such words as "fascism," "coup," and "treason," often deployed less in reference to specific events or actions than to signal that American politicians were acting in ways American politicians ought not act. "Democracy" stands for everything we miss about the way politics used to be. But all of these words have clear, if sometimes multiple, definitions in political science, history, and law. If politicians, journalists, and even kitchen-table debaters adopted the habit of defining their terms, we would understand each other better—and begin the process of restoring language.

The damage done to American language is not yet nearly as profound as the century-long decimation of Russian under totalitarianism and Putinism, but the lessons of Russian journalists hold. Some words ought to be retired: "tremendous" can take a hiatus, for example. Essential words, in the debasement of which journalists have often been complicit, have to be rehabilitated before it's too late. The word "politics," or "political," is an example. It ought to refer to the vital project of negotiating how we live together as a city, a state, or a country; of working across difference; of acting collectively. Instead, it is used to denote emptiness: hollow procedure, inflated rhetoric, tactical positioning are dismissed as "just politics." But to use the word "politics," or indeed any other word, and be believed, journalists will have to understand the words as meaningful and consequential. That, in turn, requires a reckoning not only with the damage Trumpism has inflicted on the public sphere but also with the conditions that made him so effective.

12.

THE POWER LIE

Why would someone lie about the weather? Weather is directly observable. Everyone is an expert on the weather, and, generally speaking, we can easily reach consensus on the weather. It's what makes the weather the perfect place to retreat in conversation, away from more charged subjects. We may look at conflict and disagree on who is the aggressor. We may watch movies and have opposite interpretations of the plot. But when we see bright sunshine, feel strong wind, or get soaked by the rain, we usually agree. The weather is a simple, safe basis of shared reality. To lie about the weather, one would have to be a strange kind of liar.

Trump lies about the weather.

The presidency began on a rainy day. Standing under a gray sky, Trump continued his years-long assault on Washington.

> For too long, a small group in our nation's capital has reaped the rewards of government while the people have borne the cost.
>
> Washington flourished—but the people did not share in its wealth. Politicians prospered—but the jobs left, and the factories closed.
>
> The establishment protected itself but not the citizens of our country. . . .
>
> That all changes—starting right here, and right now, because this moment is your moment: it belongs to you.

The camera panned to former presidents—Obama, George W. Bush, Bill Clinton, and Jimmy Carter were there—listening. Hillary Clinton's face was partially obscured by a clear-plastic umbrella. It was raining. On either side of the new president, just behind him, one could glimpse clear-plastic raincoats. When the camera panned the crowd, there were raincoats of all shades, some pulled over red MAGA trucker hats, some worn without hoods, leaving the hats more visible.

The inauguration is remembered less for the speech—aggressive, vulgar, a striking downgrade of American political language—than for the battle of realities that followed. There was the issue of crowd size. A reporter for **The New York Times** tweeted two images side by side: aerial photographs of the 2009 and 2017 inaugurations showing a sea of bodies at the Obama event and white spaces at the Trump one. The official Twitter account of the National Park Service retweeted the images, along with another tweet, of an **Esquire** magazine item noting that civil rights, climate change, and health care content had disappeared from the White House website. Trump took time away from the festivities to call Mike Reynolds, acting chief of the National Park Service. The Interior Department suspended all its social-media accounts.

The following day, Trump made his first public appearance. He went to CIA headquarters, stood in front of a wall of stars—a memorial to fallen agents—and lied. He attacked the television networks for reporting on the comparatively low turnout. He claimed that he had drawn a million and a half people (the best available estimate was two hundred and fifty thousand). And he lied about the weather. He said, "God looked down and he said, we're not going to let it rain on your speech." A couple of drops fell when he began to speak, Trump said, but "the truth is that it stopped immediately. It was amazing. And then it became really sunny. And then I walked off and it poured right after I left. It poured." In fact, it had been raining during Trump's speech, and the sun never came out that day.

The same day, Trump's press secretary, Sean Spicer, held his first meeting with reporters. It was Saturday and the first official press briefing was not scheduled until Monday, but Spicer urgently met with journalists in order to accuse them, falsely, of "deliberately false reporting." He marshaled evidence, some of it falsified and the rest misrepresented, to support his claim that "this was the largest audience to ever witness an inauguration—period."

The journalists in the room had observed Trump's campaign, and many of them had reported on it firsthand. It was hardly news to them that Trump was a habitual liar. But Spicer's first meeting with journalists served as an announcement that the staff and rituals of the presidential administration would now be deployed to enforce Trumpian reality. This was news, and journalists looked for ways to report it. On CBS, anchor DeMarco Morgan said, "We want to play for you a press briefing by the new White House press secretary, Sean Spicer. . . . It was very unusual." CNN, breaking with tradition, declined to air the press conference live. NBC's **Meet the Press** host Chuck Todd tried to confront Trump counselor Conway.

"Why put him out there for the very first time in front of that podium to utter a provable falsehood?" he asked. "It's a small thing—but the first time he confronts the public, it's a falsehood?"

"Chuck," Conway said, "I mean, if we are going to keep referring to our press secretary in those types of terms, I think that we are going to have to rethink our relationship here." In other words, it was acceptable for the White House press secretary to lie, but it was not acceptable to call his lie a lie.

"It undermines the credibility of the entire White House press office on Day One!" Todd said.

"No, it doesn't," said Conway.

"On Day One," said Todd.

"Don't be so overly dramatic about it, Chuck. What—You're saying it's a falsehood. And they're giving Sean Spicer, our press secretary, gave alternative facts to that. But the point remains—"

"Wait a minute!" Todd exclaimed. "'Alternative facts'?"

"Alternative facts" was not a phrase concocted to justify or whitewash a lie—it was a declaration that the new administration reserved the right to lie. Conway spoke to

Todd from the position of power, threatening him from the first with the prospect of losing access. The two of them were having two different conversations: Todd was trying to cover a major news story, which was that the new White House press secretary had lied to the public; Conway was setting the new terms of the conversation between the administration and the media.

"You sent the press secretary out there to utter a falsehood on the smallest, pettiest thing," Todd said.

"I don't think that anybody can prove the—"

"And I don't understand why you did it," he persisted.

"Look, I actually don't think that—maybe this is me as a pollster, Chuck," Conway said. "And you know data well. I don't think you can prove those numbers one way or the other. There's no way to really quantify crowds. We all know that. You can laugh at me all you want. But I'm very glad—"

"I'm not laughing," Todd said. "I'm just . . . befuddled. . . . What was the motive to have this ridiculous litigation of crowd size?"

"Your job is not to call things ridiculous that are said by our press secretary and our president," Conway responded. "That's not your job. You're supposed to be a news person. You're not an opinion columnist."

"Can you please answer the question? Why did he do this? You have not answered it."

"I'll answer—"

"It's only one question."

"—it this way. I'll answer it this way. Think about what you just said to your viewers. That's why we feel compelled to go out and clear the air and put alternative—"

"So it's a political tactic?"

"—facts out there."

Todd was trying to engage Conway in a conversation about trust. His show, the work he had done as a journalist in the past, and, more broadly, mainstream American media were built on the premise that people value trust. Politicians and journalists need the public to trust them; both can earn public trust, and each can lose it easily. Everybody lies, but no one wants to be caught lying—or so Todd thought. Conway was defending a liar's right to lie. There were no facts in her universe, and no issue of trust. There was power. Power demanded respect. Power conferred the right to speak and not be challenged. Being right was a question of power, not evidence. Conway was outraged that Todd would violate this compact by calling the president's statements ridiculous. Alternatively, perhaps she was not so much outraged as performing outrage as a way of putting the media on notice. That her outrage may or may not have been heartfelt was a message too: nothing could be taken at face value anymore.

Lies can serve a number of functions. People lie to deflect, to avoid embarrassment or evade punishment by creating doubt, to escape confrontation or lighten the blow, to make themselves appear better, to get others to do or give something, and even to entertain. However unskilled a person may be at lying, they usually hope that the lie will be convincing. Executives want shareholders to think that they have devised a foolproof path to profits. Defendants want juries to believe that there is a chance that someone else committed the crime. People in relationships want their partners to think that they have never even considered cheating. Guests want the host to think that they like their fish overcooked. Nigerian e-mail scammers want their correspondents to believe that they are crown princes with vast inheritances. Single people on dating apps want others to think that they are better-looking, younger, and better adjusted than they are. Students want their teachers to believe that the dog ate their homework. These lies can be annoying or amusing, but they are surmountable. They collapse in the face of facts. Truth is an effective defense against these lies because they exist along the same set of coordinates as the truth.

The Trumpian lie is different. It is the power lie, or the bully lie. It is the lie of the bigger kid who took your hat and is wearing it—while denying that he took it. There is no defense against this lie because the point of the lie is to assert power, to show "I can say what I want when I want to." The power lie conjures a different reality and demands that you choose between your experience and the bully's demands: Are you going to insist that you are wet from the rain or give in and say that the sun is shining?

Trump's lies are outlandish because they are not amendments or embellishments to the shared reality of Americans—they have nothing to do with it. When Trump claimed that millions of people voting illegally cost him the popular vote, he was not making easily disprovable factual claims: he was asserting control over reality itself. When he insisted that the Obama administration had had him wiretapped, and continued to insist on this even after FBI Director James Comey said that it wasn't true, Trump was splitting the country into those who agreed to live in his reality and those who resisted and became his enemies by insisting on facts. When, in the fall of 2019, he lied that he had traveled to Alabama to aid in preparing for Hurricane Dorian, which, in fact, was never expected to hit Alabama, and when he then insisted that the National Weather Service had predicted that Dorian would hit Alabama—lying about the weather again—Trump was making a reality claim by way of a power claim. When, in the winter and spring of 2020, Trump claimed that the United States was prepared for the coronavirus pandemic, when he promised quickly to triumph over the virus, when he said that hospitals had the necessary equipment and people had access to tests, when he promised health and wealth to people facing illness and precarity, he was claiming the power to lie to people about their own experience. His right to make such claims was the substance of Conway's conflict with Todd: Todd was arguing that the president had a responsibility to the public to tell the truth; she was asserting that the president can say whatever he wants **because** he is president. At the only solo press conference Trump held as president, on February 16, 2017, he raged against CNN: "I mean it's story after story after story is bad. I won. I won." His victory should have made him immune to challenge, he thought. By the time he was lying about Hurricane Dorian, he was not merely criticizing those who contradict him; he was trying to bring the weight of the White House to bear on people who choose facts over Trump. The National Oceanic and Atmospheric Administration, which reports to the executive branch, rebuked Alabama forecasters for contradicting the president. The existence of alternative facts had become policy.

Unmoored from lived reality, the autocrat has no need to be consistent. In fact, the ability to change his story at will is a demonstration of power. Putin, for example, claimed that there were no Russian troops in newly annexed Crimea, then a month later affirmed that Russians had been on the ground, then spent more than a year denying that Russian troops were in Eastern Ukraine, then breezily acknowledged that they were there. His shifts from lies to truthful statements were not admissions: they were proud, even boastful affirmatives delivered at his convenience. He communicated that his power enables him to say what he wants, when he wants, regardless of the facts. He is president of his country and king of reality.

Trump re-created Putin's script in the spring of 2017, when he fired FBI director Comey. The original cover story was that Deputy Attorney General Rod Rosenstein had brought to Trump's attention Comey's handling of the investigation of Hillary Clinton's use of a private e-mail server when she was secretary of state and this was why Trump fired Comey. It was an obvious lie, but Spicer and Conway were dispatched to disseminate it, and Rosenstein's memo, to the media. But then Trump spoke to NBC anchor Lester Holt and told him that the decision to fire Comey had been entirely his own, made before he asked for Rosenstein's memo. In his word-salad way, Trump was clear about why he wanted Comey gone: it was to quash the Russia investigation.

When I decided to just do it, I said to myself, I said, you know, this Russia thing with Trump and Russia is a made-up story. It's an excuse by the Democrats for having lost an election that they should have won. . . . So everybody was thinking, they should have won the election. This was an excuse for having lost an election.

Trump confirmed what everyone had known all along but the media were not allowed to say until the president said it. He was demonstrating the power to say what he wanted when he wanted and the power to force the media to cover the story they were fed. Trump reversed himself on the coronavirus repeatedly. He dismissed the threat and later asserted that he "felt it was a pandemic long before it was called a pandemic." He promised to "reopen the economy," then changed his mind. He used his extraordinary power to create an ever-shifting reality, to keep the country riveted. Americans had no choice but to pay constant attention: so much in our lives depended on words that meant so little to the man who said them.

Trump demands that the media recognize his domain over reality—this was the substance of Conway's argument with Todd. This was also the heart of Trump's rant during his one press conference before he started holding daily briefings in March 2020. He had captured the term "fake news." He said, "The press—the public doesn't believe you people anymore. Now, maybe I had something to do with that. I don't know. But they don't believe you." He was saying that he had given the American people a choice between two realities and they had chosen his.

Are you going to believe your own eyes or the headlines? This is the dilemma of people who live in totalitarian societies. Trusting one's own perceptions is a lonely lot; believing one's own eyes and being vocal about it is dangerous. Believing the propaganda—or, rather, accepting the propaganda as one's reality—carries the promise of a less anxious existence, in harmony with the majority of one's fellow citizens. The path to peace of mind lies in giving one's mind over to the regime. Bizarrely, the experience of living in the United States during the Trump presidency reproduces this dilemma. Being an engaged citizen of Trump's America means living in a constant state of cognitive tension. One cannot put the president and his lies out of one's mind, because he is the president. Accepting that the president continuously tweets or says things that are not true, are known not to be true, are intended to be heard or read as power lies, and will continue to be broadcast—on Twitter and by the media—after they have been repeatedly disproven means accepting a constant challenge to fact-based reality. In effect, it means that the two realities—Trumpian and fact-based—come to exist side by side, on equal ground. The tension is draining. The need to pay constant attention to the lies is exhausting, and it is compounded by the feeling of helplessness in the face of the ridiculous and repeated lies. Most Americans in the age of Trump are not, like the subjects of a totalitarian regime, subjected to state terror. But even before the coronavirus, they were subjected to constant, sometimes debilitating anxiety. One way out of that anxiety is to relieve the mind of stress by accepting Trumpian reality. Another—and this too is an option often exercised by people living under totalitarianism—is to stop paying attention, disengage, and retreat to one's private sphere. Both approaches are victories for Trump in his attack on politics.

13.

THE TWEET TRAP

The lying president is an existential threat to journalism. In New York University media scholar Jay Rosen's definition, journalism is a report on "what's going on" in the community with which one identifies but outside the scope of individual experience: what happens in a place where you are not, at a time when you are doing something else. Journalists report on people who are unlike the people you know personally but whom you still consider your countrymen; on the proceedings and decisions of your government; on plays, movies, books, and music that you have not necessarily experienced firsthand but that form the culture in which you live. Journalism is essential to democracy because it creates a sense of shared reality across a city, a state, a nation. Without this shared reality, a public sphere—the term philosopher Jürgen Habermas uses to describe the space where public opinion takes shape—cannot exist.

Around the time of the 2016 election, a trope emerged and took hold: that Americans now lived in "media silos," one Trumpian and one not, each with its own encapsulated version of reality. According to this vision, the public sphere was dead because Americans were divided into two equal groups with no common ground. In actuality, things were bad, but not as bad as that. The boundary divided Americans into two unequal groups. The larger group consumed legacy media—they read **The New York Times** and **The Washington Post**, listened to National Public Radio, watched CNN—while a smaller group read Breitbart and watched Fox News. Members of the larger group were regularly exposed to opinions that they did not share. The range of opinion represented by **Times** columnists, from Farhad Manjoo and Michelle Goldberg to Bret Stephens and Bari Weiss, is broad enough that no one reader could possibly agree with all or even most of what they collectively express. But even more important, a large-scale study commissioned by **Columbia Journalism Review** found that consumers of legacy media read and watched and were exposed on social media to a large variety of stories and opinions, while Breitbart sat at the center of a closed media ecosystem. In other words, a slight majority of Americans inhabit a fairly healthy public sphere without realizing it. Equating this space with the Trumpian media universe is not merely factually wrong, it is also giving Trump exactly what he wants: the erasure of distinction between truth and lies. It has the further effect of devaluing journalism and demoralizing journalists when they are facing the impossible dilemma of the lying president.

What the lying president says is going on is not in fact what's going on. But, in the sense in which Rosen uses the phrase,

Trump's saying that something is going on is "what's going on," because he is president and he said it, even though it's not what's actually going on. Reality bifurcates: "what's going on" at any given time consists of actual events on the one hand and what Trump said on the other, and often no bridge exists between the two.

Journalists have looked for strategies for doing their job in this extraordinary situation. Several years before the 2016 election, fact-checking had advanced from back-office operation to journalistic genre. For a minute, it seemed like a brilliant invention because it gave journalists the option of covering the statements of public figures as statements rather than as statements of fact. But then the election itself precipitated a crisis of faith within the profession. It wasn't just that so much of the legacy media had failed to imagine the possibility of a Trump victory—this, after all, was a mistake, and mistakes can be corrected. Much more damning was the fact that many media outlets had delivered sterling fact-based reporting on Trump—the malfeasance of his businesses and charities, the credible allegations that he had assaulted women, his racist statements and racist behavior in the past, as a New York real-estate developer, and in the present, on the campaign trail, his habitual dishonesty—and it seemed to matter not at all. One might say that Trump voters were not the audience for this reporting by **The Washington Post**, **The New York Times**, ProPublica, BuzzFeed, and others, but this could hardly be a comfort to the journalists who felt that the very meaning of their profession had been thrown into question.

On closer examination, things looked even worse. **The Washington Post**'s "Fact Checker" column tracked Trump's lies at the rate of nearly thirteen for every day of his presidency. With time, the lying speeded up: after Trump crossed the ten-thousand-lie mark on April 26, 2019, he was averaging twenty "fishy claims," as the **Post** put it, a day. The president is in the habit of repeating his lies, some for a few days or weeks and some continuously. Some of his top counterfactual claims—ones that he has reiterated every few days throughout his presidency—are that the border wall is being built; that the U.S. economy is the best it has ever been; and that he passed the biggest tax cut in history. The reiteration highlights the problem with fact-checking as an antidote to the lying: while the lying is repeated, fact-checking is administered only once. The lie dominates in the public sphere. Worse, the fact-checking articles themselves, appearing soon after the lie is uttered in public or on Twitter, serve as a gateway for the lie's entrance into public consciousness. Worse still, this particular gateway has a way of placing the lie and the truth side by side, as though the facts were a matter of debate. Then one of the sides of the debate drops the conversation while the other continues pounding the subject. Arguments are often lost this way.

The presidential tweet poses a similar circular problem. At the beginning of the Trump presidency, it seemed that tweets might be a distraction or a sideline, a deletable part of the record. Some journalists advocated not covering the tweets at all. Rachel Maddow proclaimed that she would ignore the tweets and generally cover the White House "like a silent movie."

But tweets have consequences. This was evident long before the election: journalists got fired, as did professors, for things posted on personal Twitter accounts. It would be absurd to argue that the tweets of the most powerful man in the world have less weight than those of ordinary professionals. The tweets of @realDonaldTrump express what the president of the United States is thinking, and that alone makes them newsworthy. On top of that, Trump clearly believes that he can govern by tweet—and he is not wrong.

In July 2017, after Trump tweeted a ban on transgender people in the military, the country learned that the commander in chief can give commands in any manner he chooses, including by tweet, and the military is compelled to obey. Trump is unwilling, or unable, to consider that all of

American society doesn't function like the military. So, if a tweet fails to produce consequences, the president escalates, groping in the ether for levers to exert the power of his displeasure. In August 2019, for example, in a series of late-night tweets, Trump raged against Chinese trade policy and arrived at, "Our great American companies are hereby ordered to immediately start looking for an alternative to China, including bringing . . . your companies HOME and making your products in the USA." When the media fact-checked his assumption that he can order companies to pull out of a country, he insisted that a 1977 law gave him the power to do so. More fact-checking followed: it appeared that, while the president could not actually order companies to do anything, he had the power to pressure them severely and initiate action that could indeed compel them to divest from a country. All the back-and-forth validated the premise that Trump's desire to order companies out of China was a legitimate topic of political discussion.

In the fall of 2017, Trump used Twitter

to rage against National Football League players who were kneeling in protest during the national anthem. He issued angry tweets at first, then progressed to threats of using an actual instrument of federal government: "Why is the NFL getting massive tax breaks while at the same time disrespecting our Anthem, Flag and Country? Change tax law!" Less than twenty-four hours later, he noted that the NFL commissioner, Roger Goodell, had sent out a letter urging all players to stand for the anthem: "It is about time." Perhaps Trump's tax threat worked.

Trump has also searched, a hundred and forty characters at a time, for instruments of power available to him in his conflicts with the media. He repeatedly suggested prosecuting leakers. Then he wanted the Senate Intelligence Committee to go after journalists, "to see why so much of our news is just made up-FAKE!" Then, in October 2017: "With all of the Fake News coming out of NBC and the Networks, at what point is it appropriate to challenge their License? Bad for country!"

The Federal Communications Commission is not the military, and Trump could not tell it what to do, by tweet or by any other means. Nor does NBC itself hold a broadcast license: its local affiliate stations do. But battles over licenses in local markets are conceivable, and Trump's tweet could be interpreted as a call to wage those battles. **The New York Times** reminded its readers that such a call was not without precedent in presidential history: Richard Nixon encouraged a business associate to challenge a license held by a **Washington Post**–owned television station in Florida, and Nixon's Justice Department went after the three major networks on antitrust grounds.

Deploying laws and institutions designed for liberal democracy to restrict media freedom is essential to autocratic attempts. Putin has used economic instruments, from hostile takeovers of media companies to libel suits that have bankrupted journalists and entire news outlets. Silvio Berlusconi proposed one restrictive bill after another— most did not pass, but they served to intimidate the media—and he also called for boycotts of media outlets that were critical of him. Viktor Orbán has done all that while also weaponizing friendly tabloids to harass and discredit political opponents. Trump's Justice Department scuttled a merger deal between AT&T and Time Warner, in apparent retaliation for Time Warner–owned CNN's coverage of Trump. And, by the force of his tweet, Trump took America into the previously unimaginable territory of discussing whether the president can shut down a television network.

At least one way out of the tweet trap and the fact-check trap has emerged, and it came into existence even before the election. This solution lies in covering Trumpism not as news but as a system. Two examples of this approach are the podcasts **Trumpcast**, which then-head of the Slate Group, Jacob Weisberg, launched in 2016, and **Trump, Inc.**, a joint production of ProPublica and WNYC, the New York Public Radio station. These podcasts treat Trumpism as a phenomenon that is distinct from both our experience and our expectations of politics. They avoid using the old familiar vocabulary of government and policy to cover Trump. Instead, they practice what the Russian literary scholar Viktor Shklovsky called "estrangement." **Trump, Inc.** calls itself "an open investigation"—it examines Trump's and the Trump Organization's business practices, which include his and his family's profiting from the presidency. **Trumpcast** is more like an anthropological inquiry: scholars, journalists, writers, politicians, and former administration officials discuss the nature of Trump and Trumpism. Both shows make ample use of Trump's tweets and lies, but they treat them as symptoms and clues rather than news in themselves. It's probably no accident that this approach has been successful in the conversational, engaged format of a podcast; the traditional, neutral tone and current-moment focus of a legacy newspaper is more easily bent by an actor like Trump.

14.

NORMALIZATION IS (ALMOST) UNAVOIDABLE

When ridiculous pronouncements have grave real-life consequences, the world feels topsy-turvy. How can we balance an appreciation for the ludicrousness of Trump's subliterate, ignorant, absurd tweets and the power his words and actions wield? The stakes demand respect; the president does not deserve it—but his office does. The discrepancy of scale is crippling.

In the early days of the administration, journalists longed to find a way to see the president as fitting his role. The first occasion presented itself on February 28, 2017, when Trump addressed a joint session of Congress for the first time. One of his invited guests was Carryn Owens, widow of William "Ryan" Owens, a Navy SEAL who died in a raid in Yemen in late January.

When Trump introduced her, everyone but the widow rose to their feet and began applauding. Carryn Owens cried, looking up at the ceiling. "And Ryan is looking down right now, you know that, and he's very happy because I think he just broke a record," Trump said, apparently referring to the duration of the applause. "For as the Bible teaches us, there is no greater act of love than to lay down one's life for one's friends. Ryan laid down his life for his friends, for his country, and for our freedom—and we will never forget Ryan."

CNN commentator Van Jones said:

He became president of the United States in that moment, period . . . For people who had been hoping that he would become unifying, hoping that he would find some way to become presidential, they should be happy with that moment. For people who have been hoping that maybe he would remain a divisive cartoon, which he often finds a way to do, they should begin to become a little bit worried tonight. Because that thing you just saw him do—if he finds a way to do that over and over again, he's going to be there for eight years. Now, there is a lot that he said in that speech that was counterfactual, that was not right, that I oppose and will oppose—but he did something there tonight that you cannot take away from him. He became president of the United States.

The orchestrated applause, the comment that the dead soldier was "happy" because he had set a record in adulation constituted the coming together of the pabulum-patriotic style of American politics and the reality-TV lens through which the new president viewed the universe. The president refused to be a normal president, but Jones was still struggling to be a normal journalist. He tried to create oppositions, a standard device of objective-style journalism: on the one hand, there were people who hoped Trump would become presidential, and on the other hand, there were people who hoped he would remain a cartoon; on the one hand, there were "counterfactual" statements in the speech, and on the other, there was what Jones called "one of the most extraordinary moments you have ever seen in American politics." These false equivalencies suggested that in the new architecture of American politics, Trump was in the middle—the point of normalcy—and on either side of him were people with different but equally valid views of his presidency. They also suggested that a moment of looking "presidential" carried the same weight as "a lot" of "counterfactual" statements. Meanwhile, **The Washington Post**'s "Fact Checker" column called the speech "filled with inaccuracies," of which it chose to highlight just thirteen, most of which, in turn, were "old favorites that he trots out on a regular, almost daily basis."

The word "presidential" came to mean moments when Trump acted in a way that a journalist could imagine an American president—a normal American president—acting. In April 2017, after the bombing of Syria, another prominent CNN voice, Fareed Zakaria, lauded Trump for briefly not acting like a deranged clown. "I think Donald Trump became president of the United States last night," Zakaria said. "I think this was actually a big moment . . . For the first time really as president, he talked about international norms, international rules, about America's role in enforcing justice in the world." Trump had acted and spoken the way a president might, and this was news. Less than three months into the presidency, his being unhinged and uninformed had become normalized because it was, in fact, now the norm, the everyday reality of American life.

"Normalization," as a word of caution, the description of a state to avoid, entered the vocabulary immediately after the 2016 election. But American journalists, who shared a strong belief in reporting "what's going on" neutrally, by which they usually mean **without assigning value or providing more than the immediate context**, were ill-equipped to problematize the normalization of what had indeed become the norm. The standard tools and approaches of American journalism translate into enforced restraint in language and tone—many journalists believe that these are the hallmarks of objectivity.

During the presidential campaign, National Public Radio took the position that it would not call Trump a liar or call his statements lies. In a letter published on the network's website, Senior Vice President Michael Oreskes explained:

We want everyone to listen to us and read us. We want our reporting to reach

173

as many people as possible. It is a well-established piece of social science research that if you start out with an angry tone and say something a listener disagrees with, they will tune out the facts. But if you present the facts calmly and without a tone of editorializing you substantially increase the chance that people will hear you out and weigh the facts. That is why the tone of journalism matters so much. We need potential listeners and readers to believe we are presenting the facts honestly, and not to confirm our opinions. . . .

It is not overly sweeping a thought to say this is a nation built on a faith in facts. At NPR we still hold that faith in facts. . . . We doubt that you, our audience, needs us to characterize people, least of all presidential candidates. . . . The more we inflame our tone, the less people will listen. What we need these days as a network, and as a country, is for people to listen more.

Oreskes was making an explicitly political judgment without acknowledging or perhaps even recognizing that it was political. After the election, NPR reiterated its position on the word "lie," though this time the reasoning was different. Reporter Mary Louise Kelly went on the air to explain why she chose not to use the word in her story on Trump's post-inauguration appearance at the CIA headquarters. She said that she checked the definition in the **Oxford English Dictionary**. "A false statement made with intent to deceive," she said. "Intent being the key word there. Without the ability to peer into Donald Trump's head, I can't tell you what his intent was. I can tell you what he said and how that squares, or doesn't, with facts." Oreskes agreed and reiterated that he saw the word "lie" as an expression of opinion. "Our job as journalists is to report, to find facts, and establish their authenticity and share them with everybody," he said. "It's really important that people understand that these aren't our opinions. . . . These are things we've established through

175

our journalism, through our reporting . . . and I think the minute you start branding things with a word like 'lie,' you push people away from you." Over the following several months, Oreskes was forced to leave NPR over accusations of sexual harassment, but the policy of not calling Trump's lies "lies" survived its disgraced author.

Both ways of framing the policy—whether by stressing that calling something a lie goes beyond fact and becomes opinion, or by focusing on internal, unknowable intent—place artificial limits on a journalist's ability to observe reality. In order to assume that Trump was not aware that he was lying when he said that millions of immigrants had voted illegally, or that Obama had him wiretapped, or that his tax cut was the biggest in history, or that the economy was better than ever, or that he was building a wall and this wall would keep out drugs and crime, one had to ignore the very act of repetition. Trump repeats his false statements after they have been fact-checked by the media and, in many cases, contradicted by officials in his own administration—and it is this repetition that gives Trumpian lies much of their power. A journalist who assumes that Trump's intention is unknowable, that repeated false statements—when the truth is indeed knowable—do not, factually, constitute lying, is abdicating the responsibility to tell the story, to provide the context of what happened a year ago, yesterday, or even in parallel with the lying. The journalist becomes complicit in creating the bizarre sense of ahistoricism of the Trump era, which seems to exist only, ever, in the current moment.

NPR and many other media outlets practice the same self-enforced amnesia in a recurrent argument about whether to call Trump a racist—or even whether to call his statements racist. It took NPR until July 2019 to apply the word "racist" to a Trump uttering; the network took the step after Trump tweeted that four Democratic Congress members, all of them women of color, should "go back" to where they came from. NPR's public editor, Elizabeth Jensen, stressed, "To be clear: NPR used the word 'racist' to describe the tweets, not the man who wrote them." The dichotomy, characteristic of virtually all media discussions of Trump, creates two counterintuitive assumptions: that a person can systematically say racist things but still not be a racist—and that there is a meaningful distinction between making racist statements and being a racist. This is a dichotomy reserved for behavior that society claims to condemn but in fact tolerates, behavior that may not sully the actor's reputation. One cannot steal and not be a thief, commit murder but not be a murderer, drive drunk and not be a drunk driver—but one can establish a pattern of racist statements over decades and still not be a racist. Reluctance to label the statements themselves "racist" suggested that the judgment of whether a statement was racist or not was far more complicated than most people experienced it as being. This, in turn, reinforced the Trumpian sense of mushy reality, the growing feeling that nothing was knowable. The shared reality of many Americans is that they are hearing the president engage in racist speech; when journalists refuse to affirm this shared reality, it thins even more.

If Trump's tweets and bizarre pronouncements make policy, then policy is Trump's tweets and bizarre pronouncements. In September 2017, Trump brought the United States and North Korea to the brink of a nuclear confrontation when he started taunting Kim Jong-un, calling him "Little Rocket Man" and threatening his country with annihilation. In January 2018, Trump tweeted, "I too have a Nuclear Button, but it is a much bigger & more powerful one than his, and my Button works!" But soon, he was talking about a summit with the North Korean leader and claiming that he ought to get the Nobel Peace Prize for these negotiations. The media covered his insane Nobel fantasies in a tone of extreme restraint, which made the fantasies sound not entirely insane. In the lead-up to the summit, North Korea released three American citizens who had been held there on espionage or insurgency charges. Trump went to Andrews Air Force Base in the middle of the night to greet the returning men in front of television cameras and immediately claimed that he had broken "the all-time-in-history television rating for three o'clock in the morning." The White House then issued a press release titled "What You Need To Know About The President's Victory For The World By Freeing Three Brave Americans." (Similarly, during his coronavirus briefings, Trump bragged about his television ratings and about being "number one on Facebook.")

Then Trump decided to cancel the summit. The White House released a letter to Kim that read, in part:

> Based on the tremendous anger and open hostility displayed in your most recent statement, I feel it is inappropriate, at this time, to have this long-planned meeting. . . . You talk about nuclear capabilities, but ours are so massive and powerful that I pray to God they will never have to

be used. . . . If you change your mind having to do with this most important summit, please do not hesitate to call me or write. . . . This missed opportunity is a truly sad moment in history.

The tone of the letter was a mix of a first-grader taking his toys and going home and a forlorn seventh-grader hoping that his love interest will come running after him. But the survival of the known world was hanging in the balance. The legacy media, once again, covered the letter with restraint. **The New York Times**'s morning podcast, **The Daily,** offered a thoughtful analysis of Trump's summit-canceling missive, which it called "strikingly personal." But no sooner was the podcast posted than Trump told the media that he might hold the summit after all.

Trump's temper tantrums and television stunts now had the power to change the course of history, so the media covered them as though they **were** diplomacy. In August 2019, **The Wall Street Journal** reported that

Trump had become preoccupied with the idea of buying Greenland from Denmark; the headline was "President Trump Eyes a New Real-Estate Purchase." In short order Trump confirmed his interest and tweeted an image of a giant golden Trump tower looming over Greenland, with the caption "I promise not to do this to Greenland!" The image read as satire on several levels—a comment on the nature of Trump's interest in the world; an illustration of the negligible value of his promises—but it was, in fact, a public statement by the president of the United States. The Danish prime minister, Mette Frederiksen, explained that Greenland was not for sale and made the most genuinely diplomatic statement possible under the circumstances: "I strongly hope that this is not meant seriously." Trump took offense and canceled a planned visit to Denmark.

If observing Trump's schoolboy act in relationship to North Korea felt like watching a disaster movie, then witnessing his Greenland bid and subsequent tantrum was more like seeing a guest at a fancy dinner party blow his nose in an embroidered napkin and proceed to use a silver fork to scratch his foot under the table. But not only did most journalists cover the debacle with restraint—many also provided historical and political context. Explanations of the strategic and economic importance of the Arctic proliferated; many media outlets noted that President Harry S Truman had also wanted to buy Greenland. **Washington Post** columnist Anne Applebaum, a consistent Trump critic, tried the opposite approach and wrote a piece explaining why the United States needs a tiny country like Denmark to be its ally. The media were doing what media should do—providing context, organizing relevant information, creating narrative—and this too had a normalizing effect, simply by helping media consumers to absorb the unabsorbable. It was as though the other dinner guests had carried on with their polite conversation and even handed the disruptive, deranged visitor a clean fork so that he wouldn't have to eat dessert with the utensil he had stuck in his shoe.

As the Trump presidency marches on to the rhythm of near-daily Twitter rants, daily outrages, and weekly embarrassments, it remains unimaginable—even if it is observable. To think that a madman could be running the world's most powerful country, to think that the commander in chief would use Twitter to mouth off about whose nuclear button is bigger or to call himself a "very stable genius," verges on the impossible. **This can't be happening. This is happening**—the thought pattern of nightmares and real-life disasters has become the constant routine of tens of millions of people. Every Trump tweet, televised statement, and headline causes a form of this reaction. If the word "unthinkable" had a literal meaning, this would be it: thinking about it makes the mind misfire; it makes one want to stop thinking. It brings to mind the psychiatrist Judith Herman's definition of a related word: "Certain violations of the social compact are too terrible to utter aloud," she once wrote. "This is the meaning of the word **unspeakable**." The Trump era is unimaginable, unthinkable, unspeakable. It is waging a daily assault on the public's sense of sanity, decency, and cohesion. It makes us feel crazy, and the restrained tone of the media compounds this feeling by failing to acknowledge it.

Early in the Trump era especially, we found relief in sitting down at the end of the day in front of the screen and watching the hosts of the major late-night talk shows state the obvious in their opening monologues: they imagined the unimaginable, thought the unthinkable, and spoke the unspeakable. There was nothing funny about it, but the audience laughed with relief. Not being bound by the conventions of respect and restraint, comedians could free us from the nagging sense that we were crazy. None of this was normal. It wasn't us, it was him. The laughter became hysterical.

Survivors of totalitarian regimes have often written about the role of laughter.

SURVIVING AUTOCRACY

Croatian author Slavenka Drakulić has said that laughter was essential to surviving communism; others have argued that laughter could subvert terror and help foment dissent. But Trump is not a totalitarian leader who rules by terror, and the late-night jokes don't expose the ridiculousness that hides beneath a veneer of strength and power: Trump is ridiculous on the face of it. **Saturday Night Live** routines and late-night talk-show hosts got laughs simply by repeating statements made by Trump, Spicer, Conway, and other members of the administration. No exaggeration was necessary or even possible. On closer examination, political satire was acting as a substitute for news journalism rather than a parody of it.

15.

RESISTING TRUMP'S WAR ON THE MEDIA

Autocracy is incompatible with free and open media because autocracy does not brook transparency and accountability. Bálint Magyar suggests that where totalitarian regimes of the past sought to control media, today's autocracies seek to dominate it; and where a totalitarian regime sought to suppress media rights, the autocrat seeks to neutralize them. The end result is not a controlled communications sphere where reality is dictated from above, but a weak one, where nothing can be known, no reality is tangible. As in other areas, Trump has exploited existing problems and weaknesses: dwindling trust in journalism, profit-driven media's reluctance to engage with substantive politics, and a tradition of extreme restraint in covering politics.

For decades, journalists had taken daily televised White House press briefings for granted. These were not always substantive—the relationship between White House reporters and presidential spokespeople was often too cordial, and the administration was not always the best source of information about itself—but they created an assumption of accountability. Trump began by overturning this assumption. His administration floated the idea of moving press briefings from the West Wing to the Old Executive Building, a physically separate part of the White House complex, then dropped the idea, but Trump articulated the underlying message on his favorite Fox News program, **Fox & Friends**. He said, "Some people in the press will not be able to get in." This was one of the many ways in which he signaled his intention to dominate the media.

In the first week of the presidency, Trump's chief strategist, Steve Bannon, cofounder of the alt-right, alternative-reality site Breitbart, who didn't usually speak to journalists, gave an interview to **The New York Times**, specifically to explain the new rules of the game. "I want you to quote this," he said. "The media here is the opposition party. They don't understand this country. They still do not understand why Donald Trump is the president of the United States." His counsel to journalists was that they "should shut up and listen for a while." Trump seized the phrase "the opposition party" and later upgraded it to the Stalinist "the enemy of the American people."

After his first press conference, Trump did not hold another formal solo press conference. He appeared jointly with world leaders following meetings (and once with Mitch McConnell), he sometimes wandered into the briefing room, and on a number of occasions he took questions from reporters as he was leaving the White House, but, for his three years as president before the coronavirus pandemic, he discontinued the practice of press conferences that are announced in advance, ensuring that experienced journalists are present and allowing journalists to prepare. Here was a norm that seemed inviolate to journalists—all other presidents in recorded history of White House coverage had held press conferences—but was elementary for Trump to dismiss. The same was true for dropping the so-called protective pool, a small group of journalists from the White House pool who shadow the president at all times. Other executive-branch agencies also shut out the press: Tillerson discontinued the tradition of traveling with a pool as well as the practice of press briefings; the Pentagon stopped holding briefings. The White House press briefing became extinct in stages. In the first months of the administration, Spicer stopped allowing television cameras into every daily briefing. Then the briefings ceased being daily. Then weeks began to pass between briefings, and then months. By the time Trump's third spokesperson, Stephanie Grisham, started the job in the summer of 2019, there was no longer an expectation of any briefings at all. When the COVID-19 pandemic hit the United States, there had not been a briefing in one year. And when, in March 2020, Trump began taking the podium daily to talk about the coronavirus crisis, it was not to be accountable to the public by speaking to the media. Whenever he sensed that a question was based on the premise of accountability, Trump lashed out at the reporter who asked it. "Why don't you act in a little more positive?" he barked at one of his frequent targets, Yamiche Alcindor of the PBS **NewsHour**. "It's always get ya, get ya, get ya." He was not there to answer the tough questions: he was there to show who was in charge.

Before routine White House briefings vanished, their tone had changed. While many previous administrations—including Obama's—had been criticized, fairly, for being less transparent than they ought to

have been, all had at least acknowledged
that the media served as an essential bridge
between the American people and the government they had put into office. Trump's
official stand was that the media were an
enemy, and his people had to demonstra-
tively treat them as such. Spicer, during
his six-month tenure as press secretary, was
belligerent and openly hostile; he lied often.
His successor, Sarah Sanders, lied too, but
she delivered her lies in an even, bored tone
that seemed to indicate that she resented
having to answer anything, or to anyone.
Sanders's tenure was just short of two years.
Grisham gave her first media interview—to
America This Week on the conservative
Sinclair network—a month and a half after
starting the job.

If Spicer broadcast Trump's bluster,
Sanders channeled his inner bully. She
treated the White House press corps the
way a sadistic teenager would treat a group
of third-graders. In November 2017, during
the last press briefing before Thanksgiving,
Sanders began by saying that she was

thankful for all the reporters in the room. "That goes without saying," she added, in a tone that made it clear that the White House press secretary really did not like the White House press corps. There was slight, uncomfortable laughter in the room. Then Sanders listed the people and things for which she was actually grateful: her family, her faith, the military, the police, the firemen, and the first responders. Then, without changing her tone—she generally spoke in an impenetrable monotone—Sanders said, "If you want to ask a question, I think it's only fair, since I've shared what I'm thankful for, that you start off with what you're thankful for."

It is the job of reporters to ask questions, and it was Sanders's job to answer them. That was why they were all gathered there: to do their jobs of asking and answering. Of course, this was merely a matter of convention; there was no law or rule to prevent Sanders from rejecting questions or from setting conditions for their asking. Reporters in the room might have argued that they had the power because they served as representatives of the voting public. But Sanders was reminding them that this administration interpreted the relationship differently—that she had the power.

"Anybody want to be first on what they are thankful for?" she asked. Her tone was menacing, the voice of a bully asking for a volunteer to be humiliated in front of the room. She called on April Ryan, of American Urban Radio Networks. Ryan was one of the few African American reporters in the room, and her questions had clearly annoyed Sanders in the past. Ryan had tried, unsuccessfully, to ask a question during an earlier part of the briefing, when Secretary of State Rex Tillerson spoke about North Korea.

"April, you've been **sooo** eager," Sanders said. There was laughter.

"I'm thankful for life," Ryan said, going along with the rule proposed by Sanders. "I'm thankful for my children. I'm thankful for twenty years in this job. I'm thankful to be able to talk to you and question you every single day." Ryan ended on a big, insincere smile.

"I feel the gratefulness here," Sanders responded, with her own angry smile. There was a smattering of laughter.

As a person responding to a bully, Ryan had held her own: she had complied with the terms dictated, but she had not let herself be humiliated. But as a reporter in the White House briefing room, she had just been co-opted into a hypocritical ritual. She was no longer an observer of the Trump administration's habit of lying; she had become complicit. She had also participated in the spectacle of denigrating her profession. Ryan's question was about North Korea and the apparent lack of reliable information on that country's nuclear arsenal. But she had helped Sanders make that seem unimportant, compared with the petty power struggle in the room. When Ryan tried to ask a follow-up question about Trump's continued Twitter war with North Korea, Sanders said, "April, I'm starting to regret calling on you first." Then she moved on to the next questioner.

The next reporter, Francesca Chambers,

of the **Daily Mail**, responded enthusi-
astically. "I will follow your lead," she
said, and expressed thanks for service members and the police, noting that her brother
was a service member and her father a police-
man. She asked an easily deflected question
about the Alabama senatorial race.

Jon Decker, of Fox News, was thankful
for his health, his family, his faith, and the
fact that he lived "in the best country on
the face of the Earth."

"See, isn't this nice?" Sanders asked.

"And I'm thankful, of course, that you
address us every day here," Decker continued. He asked if the president would be
happy to see Roy Moore, credibly accused
of rape, win his bid for a Senate seat from
Alabama. Sanders avoided answering this
question.

Blake Burman, of Fox Business Network,
was thankful for his family, his parents, and
his wife, who was pregnant with the couple's
second child. Cecilia Vega, of ABC News,
was grateful for the First Amendment.
Steven Herman, of Voice of America, was

grateful for surviving the trip to Asia that Trump had recently taken. Jenna Johnson, of **The Washington Post**, neglected to offer thanks. Instead, she asked two questions: Had the president talked to the senatorial candidate Roy Moore since allegations that he had sexually abused several young women first surfaced a week and a half earlier? Sanders said that he had not. What had the president meant, earlier that day, when he said that welfare reform was "desperately needed in this country"? Sanders answered that specifics would be forthcoming—her way of saying that it was anybody's guess what Trump had meant.

Zeke Miller, from the Associated Press, launched straight into a question as well, asking about the lack of diversity among Trump's judicial nominees. Sanders called him out, though: "You did break the rule," she said, demonstrating that power grows if the rules are enforced selectively. Miller quickly said that he was grateful for her question, and pressed on with his own, which Sanders, again, deflected. Margaret

Brennan, of CBS News, was thankful for the First Amendment, "and for this exercise." Kristin Fisher, from Fox News, was grateful for the opportunity to attend the briefing, and for the fact that she had only one month to go until her pregnancy was over. She happened to have a relevant question: it concerned gratitude. The president had used the word "ungrateful" to describe three UCLA freshmen who returned home after being detained in China on suspicion of shoplifting. Sanders deflected this question, but then Matthew Nussbaum, of **Politico**, asked why the president had tweeted that he "should have left them in jail."

"Look, it was a rhetorical response," Sanders said, asserting, in effect, that the president's words have no meaning.

Finally, John Gizzi, of Newsmax, was thankful "for the position I have and the colleagues who are my friends. I'm thankful for my father, ninety-six years old and going strong, and to my wife, my heroine, thankful to her for saying yes on the fourth request." There was laughter. "My question is about Zimbabwe." That country appeared to be undergoing a change of regime. Much more laughter.

"That's the best pivot I've ever seen," Sanders said, as though questions about actual coups in actual countries, and the actual American position on them, were extraneous to the White House briefing—as though the briefing existed only as a spectacle of power, a (no longer daily) battle for dominance between the journalists and the press secretary. "I don't have any announcements on our relationship with Zimbabwe at this time, but certainly we'll make sure and keep you guys posted," she said. "Again, want to wish everybody a happy Thanksgiving and thank you for participating in this very fun exercise."

The exercise had established that the White House press pool consisted primarily of straight, pious white men. The press secretary had enlisted the reporters' help in mocking the purpose of the briefing; no information was conveyed from the White House to the public. She had shown who was boss: she could hold journalists to an arbitrary rule by making them offer thanks before asking a question, which diminished the journalists' ability to hold her to the task of answering their questions. She reaffirmed that both the president and she herself lied easily and blatantly—as he did when he issued a "rhetorical response" on the UCLA students, and as she did at the beginning of the briefing, when she claimed to be thankful for the reporters in the room. By making them laugh when she said that, and when she mocked April Ryan, and when she called the forced ritual a "fun exercise," she gave them a role in debasing the job of reporting on the White House and their profession as a whole. Few media outlets reported on this small episode in the diminishment of journalism. It was just one of many minor steps in the rapid deterioration of the media's ability to hold American power to account, but a striking example of the ways in which old assumptions no longer obtained. The journalists in the room had conflicting motivations: they were there to act as representatives of the public, but they also wanted to get to ask a question, get their question answered, avoid burning bridges so they would get to ask questions in the future, avoid being humiliated in front of their colleagues, on television, and avoid confrontation that would break the veneer of neutrality. Sanders had only one task: to assert power. She won.

In November 2018, the White House suspended the "hard pass" of Jim Acosta, a CNN reporter whom Sanders falsely accused of assaulting an intern who was trying to take away the microphone he had used to ask Trump a question in the briefing room. This was the most consequential of possible humiliations of the White House press room. The hard pass allows a journalist to enter the working areas of the White House anytime. One can be a reporter without a

hard pass, but this requires a daily bureaucratic security procedure.*

Some journalists argued for a boycott:
"The entire White House press corps should
walk out," wrote Jane Merrick, a British

---

*Acosta's hard pass was eventually restored by a judge
who ruled that the White House had revoked it arbi-
trarily: there were no rules for journalistic conduct in the
White House, or for granting or revoking hard passes. In
response to the ruling, the administration began instituting rules that would allow it to revoke the passes, making
it a regular practice. The key new rule called for hold-
ers of hard passes to be physically present in the White
House for at least half of any hundred-and-eighty-day
period. It was a brilliant ploy: on the one hand, the
administration worked to disincentivize reporters from
actually being in the White House, where weeks could
now go by without an opportunity to ask a question on
the record; on the other, it punished them for not being
in the White House. The rule implicitly offered an agreement: **We don't want you here, and you don't want to
be here, so why don't we just go our separate ways?** For
those who declined the agreement, the new rules would
be applied selectively: for example, in May 2019, most
Washington Post reporters who had passes but had not
spent three months camping out in the White House
were granted exemptions, but columnist Dana Milbank,
who had been particularly critical of Trump, was not.

reporter. "Deny him coverage. Take him off the air. Cancel his series. Leave him to rage into Twitter's echo chamber, which is all he deserves."

There were solid arguments in favor of a boycott. It would have felt good and righteous to stop rebroadcasting the messages of a corrupt, lying, hateful administration. A walkout would have served as a clear demonstration of professional solidarity, and solidarity is an absolute value. Reducing the amount of Trump on the air and in print would also probably have been a good thing. But there was a counterargument. There was no way to boycott merely the briefing room: there were hardly any briefings anymore anyway. As for the rest of the White House, it was a lousy source of information about itself, but it was also the best available source. Walking away would have given the White House exactly what it wanted: less contact with the media, less visibility, ever less transparency and accountability. Walking away would have felt good, but it would ultimately have been a loss. Would the loss in information have been greater than the gain in solidarity? The answer depended on the still-unsettled question of how journalists should behave in the age of Trump.

Should journalists fight to protect the status quo ante—the norms of regulated but regular access, as well as the restrained neutrality of American journalism? This may be called the stand-your-ground approach. From this point of view, a boycott would seem like a terrible idea: one shouldn't walk out if one is standing one's ground. Alternatively, should journalists treat the Trump presidency as an emergency and a call to action, and reinvent their approach to covering politics? If one accepted that American journalism was ripe for reinvention, then the answer became less clear.

There was no consensus on what a reinvention might entail. Some media theorists suggested ignoring Trump's declaration of war, or accepting it—either way, upending the old norms of covering the presidency. Jay Rosen pioneered the hashtag #sendtheinterns—by which he meant, literally, that the major media organizations should send only their most junior staff to the White House briefing room while more experienced reporters spent their time reporting "from the outside in."

Look: they can't visit culture war upon you if they don't know where you are. The press has to become less predictable. It has to stop functioning as a hate object. This means giving something up. The dream of the White House briefing room and the Presidential press conference is that accountability can be transacted in dramatic and televisable moments: the perfect question that puts the President or his designate on the spot, and lets the public see—as if in a flash—who they are led by. This was always an illusion. Crumbling for decades, it has become comically unsustainable under Trump.

Todd Gitlin, a media scholar at Columbia University, called on **The New York Times,** as the leader of American media, to be more definitive in its coverage—and critique—of Trump. Writing in March 2017, Gitlin analyzed a **Times** story on Trump's proposal to vastly increase the defense budget. Gitlin divided the article into "sharp" or "straightforward" and "blurry" parts. "In the blur category is this: '. . . it is difficult to know what problem Mr. Trump is trying to address by adding 100 fighter aircraft.' **Difficult** to know? How about impossible?" Gitlin wrote. In the "sharp" category were statements like "They don't know exactly what they want to do, except that they want a bigger military" or "Mr. Trump has not articulated a new mission that would require a military spending increase. This has left analysts wondering what goals he has in mind. Erin M. Simpson, a national security consultant, called Mr. Trump's plans 'a budget in search of a strategy.'" Gitlin called on the **Times** to become unapologetically sharp: "As long as you are going to be damned as 'the opposition party,' get on with it."

The problem, however, was that the "sharp" statements were uttered by other people or were anchored by quotes from people interviewed for the story while the "blurry" statements were written by **Times** reporters. Journalists are trained to avoid decisive pronouncements. Superlatives are a classic: one usually cannot prove that something is the first, the largest ever, or the best, so one opts for "one of" the first, largest, or best. The same is true for any definitive assertion. How could one really say that it was **impossible** to know what problem Trump's one hundred new fighter planes would address? What if the problem was just very, very elusive? It seemed more prudent to say that it was **difficult** to locate the problem. And—this was a corollary of the problems with saying that Trump was a liar or a racist—what if members of the administration really did know what they wanted to do but were for some reason terrible at explaining it? How could a journalist claim to have observed the vacuums in their minds? The pedantic insistence on only ever reporting empirically proven facts, and staying away from facts for which only logical, intellectual evidence can be summoned, creates the blurry style of American journalism. By using noncommittal statements, the blurry style in effect aids the Trumpian project of neutralizing the most important of media rights—the public's right to know.

Anodyne headlines and noncommittal writing become an automatic way of normalizing Trump, to be sure, but also a way of reassuring journalists and editors that they can continue to work in the way they were taught. In August 2019, this kind of automatic writing produced a headline that created a crisis at the **Times**. Following a weekend in which thirty people died in two mass shootings, at least one of them perpetrated by a Trump supporter who had posted a white supremacist manifesto online, the printed edition of the paper carried the headline "Trump Urges Unity vs. Racism" over the story on Trump's reaction. The headline was terrible in several ways. It misrepresented the substance of the story, which was that the president had failed to address gun control. It ignored context, which was that one of the shooters had been a Trump supporter, that most of his victims were Mexican Americans—a group Trump had systematically villainized—and that Trump, a documented racist, had no business calling for "unity vs. racism." It lent legitimacy to a statement that had none.

Executive editor Dean Baquet later explained the problem, in part, by saying that physical-paper headlines were now written by junior editorial staff, late at night, as an afterthought to whatever was happening online, where most of the **Times** readership was. That explanation emphasized, though, that the headline was an accurate reflection of institutional culture, which privileges neutrality over all else, including substance. The headline, and an unrelated ill-advised series of tweets posted by a **Times** editor, created a crisis that Baquet addressed with an all-staff town meeting. It began by revisiting the use of the words "lie" and "racist." Unlike NPR, the **Times** did not have an outright ban on the use of these words—rather, the paper used them with extreme restraint. "I used the word **lie** once during the presidential campaign, used it a couple times after that," said Baquet. "And it was pretty clear it was a lie, and we were the first ones to use it. But I fear that if we used it twenty times, ten times, first, it would lose its power. And secondly, I thought we would find ourselves in the uncomfortable position of deciding which comment by which politician fit the word **lie**. I feel the same way about the word **racist**." In other words, the **Times** has a policy of not calling every racist remark "racist" and every lie a "lie" but reserving these words for only the biggest lies and the most racist of statements. This, of course, has the effect of establishing a new and fairly consistent standard for both lies and racist comments: one now has to work hard to sink that low.

One staff member brought a letter from another staff member, a writer who apparently did not want to be identified. It read, in part,

I am concerned that the **Times** is failing to rise to the challenge of a historical moment. What I have heard from top leadership is a conservative approach that I don't think honors the **Times**' powerful history of adversarial journalism. I think that the NYT's leadership, perhaps in an effort to preserve the institution of the **Times**, is allowing itself to be boxed in and hamstrung. This obviously applies to the race coverage. The headline represented utter denial, unawareness of what we can all observe with our eyes and ears. It was pure face value. I think this actually ends up doing the opposite of what the leadership claims it does. A headline like that simply amplifies without critique the desired narrative of the most powerful figure in the country. If the **Times**' mission is now to take at face value and simply repeat the claims of the powerful, that's news to me. I'm not sure the **Times**' leadership appreciates the damage it does to our reputation and standing when we fail to call things like they are.

Baquet did not directly address the comment during the town hall, but later, a **Times** employee who spoke to another journalist summed up the issue and the paper's position: "We have to remember we are not advocates for the left. We are not fucking part of the resistance." Here were two possibilities of viewing the relationship between the nation's leading newspaper and the president: as adversaries; or as, explicitly, **not** adversaries. By choosing to act as though in the war on reality it was possible not to choose sides, the **Times**—and with it, the American media mainstream—became, reluctantly though not unwittingly, the president's accomplices.

The **Times'** approach to covering Trump's lies remained unchanged during the coronavirus crisis. The paper did extraordinary reporting uncovering the hidden truths of the pandemic—such as the story of the USNS **Comfort**, a Navy hospital ship, touted by Trump as aid to the city, that actually barred COVID patients and remained almost empty as city hospitals struggled under the strain—but it maintained its both-sides-of-the-truth way of reporting on Trump. When he announced his ban on travel from Europe, the **Times** titled its story "Trump Suspends Most Travel from Europe to Try to Limit the Virus." Gregg Gonsalves, an epidemiologist at Yale and a veteran of AIDS activism, wrote on Facebook, "What the fuck is The NY Times doing? NO ONE THINKS THIS POLICY HAS ANYTHING TO DO WITH PUBLIC HEALTH." (The paper appeared to have changed the headline online subsequently.) Three weeks later, the **Times** had the following headline: "Trump Suggests Lack of Testing Is No Longer a Problem. Governors Disagree." Gonsalves tweeted, "This is journalistic malpractice. . . . Next: Trump says earth flat, scientists say otherwise." One of the authors of the story, Jonathan Martin, responded, "You're picking the wrong fight, move along." The paper's position seemed to be that its institutional habits should not be challenged, internally or externally, because the **Times** would outlive both the coronavirus and Trump. It is a hell of an assumption.

There have been exceptions in the mainstream media, of course—not only in the more nimble genre of podcasts but inside the venerable old institutions themselves. David Fahrenthold, a reporter with **The Washington Post**, uses a radically transparent approach to investigative reporting: he asks for tips and follow-up information on Twitter, openly corresponds with informants, and allows followers to stay abreast of his thinking and reporting. He tweeted, for example, "Update: I am still looking for 9 of the 12 sites supposedly vetted for the G-7. The White House says they were in these states, but won't say where. Let me know if you know something!" He followed up with a tweet saying, "@realDonaldTrump said the frontrunner was his own golf club in Doral, Fla. But is that the final choice? Not clear. The Doral mayor says they've still heard nothing." The approach is not only a strikingly effective method of crowdsourcing—Fahrenthold won a Pulitzer for his reporting on Trump's charities—but it also revolutionizes the relationship between a journalist and his readers. Fahrenthold positions himself on the side of the readers: together, they are digging into Trump's business. The relationship between the journalist and the president is explicitly adversarial, and the relationship between the journalist and the readers is one of actual, observable cooperation. Most American journalists and editors would agree that this is as it should be—the journalists are working on behalf of the public, and their relationship with power should not be overly cozy—but in reality, the tone of neutrality, authority, and restraint that legacy publications adopt has a way of shifting the journalist away from the public and toward the person in power, making them act more like go-betweens than representatives of one side and one side only. That makes the media ill-equipped to resist the autocrat's project of coming to dominate the communications sphere.

There is a larger problem with where journalists stand in relationship to power and the public, and this is that most American journalists have been trained to think that they stand nowhere. All traditional media organizations forbid political activism and campaign contributions among news staff, and some news reporters abstain even from voting. Until recently, legacy media held that journalists should not write about the struggles of their own social groups—that African American reporters shouldn't write about civil rights, LGBT people shouldn't write about the LGBT movement, and disabled people shouldn't cover disability issues. (And basically, yes, straight white men should write about everything, which was indeed largely the case for most of journalism history.) Rosen has criticized this conceit as the "view from nowhere." The habit is so strong that many, indeed probably most, traditionally trained journalists—though they do in fact have political views—would have trouble writing a story or crafting a radio report in a way that reflected a view from where they actually stand. This culture, perhaps even more than the institutional inertia of old media behemoths, helps explain why podcasts have been able to adopt an estranged view of Trumpism while more traditional media have struggled: to cover Trumpism as a system, journalists have to position themselves clearly—and critically—outside that system.

16.

HOW POLITICS DIES

What was lost first, and almost impercep-
tibly, was substantive political discussion.
Countries look to their political leaders to
articulate who they are as a people, what
future they are building, what hopes,
dreams, and ideals unite them and make
them a political community. In the Trump
era, there is no past and no future, no
history and no vision—only the anxious
present. There can be no hopes, dreams,
and ideals where there is no shared
reality; and there is no political community
where there is only the self-obsessed and

endlessly self-referential president. One did not notice the disappearance of political speech immediately—it was like an object that, by the time one realizes it is gone, has been absent for some time.

In 2019, Trump delivered a Fourth of July address that in the earlier days of his administration might have been described as "presidential." Commentators noted that Trump didn't use the opportunity to attack the Democratic Party, to issue explicit campaign slogans, or, it would appear, to make any impromptu additions (with the possible exception of one moment, when he claimed that American troops commandeered enemy airports during the Revolutionary War). The president was so disciplined on the occasion of the republic's two hundred and forty-third birthday that Vox called his speech "inoffensive." **Slate** gave the speech credit for being "not a complete authoritarian nightmare." The **Times** noted that Trump called for unity, in a gesture uncharacteristic of his "divisive presidency." The word "tame" popped up in different outlets, including Talking Points Memo, which concluded that "the whole thing was pretty standard."

The celebration itself was in fact anything but standard. After two and a half years, Trump got what he had first said he wanted for his inauguration: a military parade, complete with flyovers. But against this background, Trump delivered one of his less explicitly offensive speeches—unless, that is, one considered its place in the tradition of presidential Fourth of July addresses.

Trump's most recent predecessors had presided over Fourth of July naturalization ceremonies. A rhetorical link between the holiday and immigration had long seemed unbreakable. During his last Independence Day as president, Bill Clinton chose to speak in New York Harbor, against the backdrop of Ellis Island and the Statue of Liberty. "Perhaps more than any other nation in all history, we have drawn our strength and spirit from people from other lands," he said. "On this Fourth of July, standing in the shadow of Lady Liberty, we must resolve never to close the golden door behind us and always, not only to welcome people to our borders but to welcome people into our hearts." In a much-criticized series of Independence Day events in 1986, President Reagan lit the torch of the Statue of Liberty and noted the swearing in of twenty-seven thousand new citizens across the country. He also referred to the "immigrant story" of his then new Supreme Court nominee, Antonin Scalia.

That immigrant story was, of course, the story the Trump administration has abandoned. Trump's American story was the story of struggle, "the epic tale of a great nation whose people have risked everything for what they know is right," as he said in the address. Over the course of forty-seven minutes, Trump enumerated American military conquests and the branches of the U.S. armed forces. A quick listing of civilian achievement—medical discoveries, cultural accomplishments, civil rights advancements, and space exploration—was thrown in at the beginning of the speech, but the master narrative Trump proposed was one of wars and victories, punctuated by the roar of airplane engines for flyovers and the music of each branch of the armed forces.

The narrative was also one of fear. Trump spoke like the leader of a country under siege. The president and the people who joined him onstage stood in a fortress of their own, a clear protective enclosure that, streaked with rain, made for an incongruously melancholy sight, as though the audience had been watching them through a veil of tears.

Trump extolled the strength and battle-readiness of American troops but named no current threat. He promised only to strike fear into the hearts of America's enemies. His intended audience, however, knew who the enemy was. North Korea or China could go from enemy to partner to friend on a whim, but there was one enemy whom Trump had consistently, obsessively described as an existential threat: the immigrant.

Two days before the July Fourth celebration, the Department of Homeland Security's inspector general issued an urgent report on the conditions in migrant detention facilities in the Rio Grande Valley. Photographs in the report showed children and adults in crowded cages. Other pictures showed people in extremely crowded holding rooms raising up signs in windows, apparently attempting to attract the attention of government inspectors. The document reported "serious overcrowding" and prolonged detention that violated federal guidelines. Children had no access to showers and hadn't been provided with hot meals. At one facility, the report said, adults were held in standing-room-only conditions. "Most single adults had not had a shower . . . despite several being held for as long as a month," the report said. A diet of bologna sandwiches had made some of the detainees sick. The report left no doubt that "concentration camps" was an accurate term for the facilities it described. On the eve of Independence Day, the media reported the story, and it took its place among other stories, other headlines—as the part of American life that it had become.

The president responded in a series of tweets in which he blamed the Democrats and the immigrants themselves. "If Illegal Immigrants are unhappy with the conditions in the quickly built or refitted detentions centers, just tell them not to come. All problems solved!" he tweeted. Most of Trump's tweeting day, though, was spent on other issues: railing against the Supreme Court's decision not to allow a citizenship question on the census, for example, and hyping expectations for his Fourth of July extravaganza. In the Trumpian universe, immigrants posed a superhuman threat but were themselves of subhuman significance. He also habitually dismissed documented facts. In Trump's reality, it was not just that the administration refused to be held accountable for running concentration camps; it was that the camps, and the suffering in them, did not exist.

The July Fourth celebration, inspired in part by Trump's visit to France during Bastille Day festivities in 2017 and informed by his affinity for the saber-rattling tyrants of the world, was a high point in the president's battle to command reality. With the possible exception of rain streaks, the pictures from the rally were his image of himself and the country. Following his speech, Trump kept retweeting photographs of his own limo leaving the White House, of fighter jets flying, of the red stage and a strange cross-like formation of red elevated platforms, and of himself speaking. In these pictures, Trump was the supreme ruler of the mightiest military empire in the history of the world, and his people were with him in the public square. Nothing else existed.

In addition to not mentioning immigrants, Trump omitted mention of the complexity of the American project. Until he came to office, Republican and Democratic presidents regularly reminded the American public that the country's democracy was a work in progress, that its guiding principles were a set of abstract ideals that continued to be reinterpreted.

"This union of corrected wrongs and expanded rights has brought the blessings of liberty to the two hundred and fifteen million Americans, but the struggle for life, liberty, and the pursuit of happiness is never truly won," President Gerald Ford said on July 4, 1976.

> Each generation of Americans, indeed of all humanity, must strive to achieve these aspirations anew. Liberty is a living flame to be fed, not dead ashes to be revered, even in a Bicentennial Year. It is fitting that we ask ourselves hard questions even on a glorious day like today. Are the institutions under which we live working the way they should? Are the foundations laid in 1776 and 1789 still strong enough and sound enough to resist the tremors of our times? Are our God-given rights secure, our hard-won liberties protected?

Forty years later, in a much more casual celebration on the White House lawn, President Obama said, "On a day like this, we celebrate, we have fun, we marvel at everything that's been done before, but we also have to recommit ourselves to making sure that everybody in this country is free; that everybody has opportunity; that everybody gets a fair shot; that we look after all of our veterans when they come home; that we look after our military families and give them a fair shake; that every child has a good education."

In less than three years, the crudeness of the tweets, the speed of the news cycle, the blatant quality of the lies, and the brutality of official rhetoric had dulled American senses so much that Trump has successfully reframed America, stripping it of its ideals, dumbing it down, and reducing it to a nation at war against people who want to join it. That is what was passing for "inoffensive," "tame," and "standard."

Once again, Trump was making a quantum leap from a running start. For half a century—since John F. Kennedy's presidency—the role of ideals in American political rhetoric had been decreasing. With the exceptions of Reagan and, to a much lesser extent, Obama, American presidents had come to define leadership in terms of competence, expertise, and technical prowess rather than ideals and ideas. The end of the Cold War—the presumed end of the world struggle of Communist and liberal-democratic ideologies—had relegated arguments about ideals to the margins. During the 2016 presidential campaign, Democrats ran the quintessential technocratic candidate, Hillary Clinton, on a platform of competence, while Bernie Sanders—the Democratic contender who insisted on approaching politics as an open-ended conversation rather than a battle of résumés—was mocked by the Democratic Party leadership and often covered with a sort of bemused condescension by the media. American political conversation had become a space free from imagination and aspiration. Rather than talk about the future, we talked about policy; rather than talk about what's right and just, we talked about what's realistic and lawful; rather than discuss values, we discussed strategies. It was this dull, neutral, largely hollow space that Trump so easily filled with his crudeness, cruelty, and lies.

The leader or leaders who will help American politics heal after Trump will need to re-embrace the language of ideals—and hope. The longer Trumpism lasts, however, the harder that path will be, because of the damage Trump is inflicting on political language.

When the time for recovery comes, as it inevitably will, we will need to do the work of rebuilding a sense of shared reality. For journalists, the task is much bigger than returning to an imagined state of normalcy before Trump, or even than deciding to retire some words and rehabilitate others. A new focus on using words intentionally will not be a matter for usage manuals but rather will require that journalists accept a responsibility that anodyne headlines, equivocal statements, and the style of extreme restraint have helped avoid. To state directly what they are seeing, journalists will have to reveal where they stand. To tell stories that situate the current moment in history, journalists will have to acknowledge that the media is inherently a political actor and decisions journalists make—which words to use and which stories to tell—are political decisions. And to make these decisions, journalists, too, will need to abandon the idea that politics is the province of technocrats—and accept their responsibility for shaping and facilitating the political conversation citizens must have in a democracy.

In their relationship to the next president, journalists will have to reassert their position as representatives of the American people, guarantors of the people's right to know. Journalists will have to do their part to rebuild the expectation that statements made by the president have immediate meaning. Meaning is distinct from consequences: Trump's tweets and tantrums have consequences, but their meaning is often secondary to their tone, hard to discern, or downright [unintelligible]. Political speech—that is, speech intended to find common ground across difference, to negotiate the rules of living together in society—is speech that, on the one hand, brings reality into focus and, on the other, activates the imagination. The job of revitalizing the language of politics will fall primarily to political leaders. It will be the job of journalists to embody and enforce the expectation of meaning. It will also be the job of journalists to create a communications sphere in which people feel not like spectators to a disaster that defies understanding but like participants in creating a common future with their fellow citizens. This is the fundamental project of democracy, and the reason it requires media.

Part Three

WHO IS "US"?

17.

A WHITE MALE SUPREMACIST PRESIDENCY

Seven months into Trump's presidency, a sense familiar from election night returned: **this** could not be happening. White supremacists held a series of demonstrations in Charlottesville, Virginia, to protest the removal of a Confederate statue. When the gatherings grew violent, Governor Terry McAuliffe declared a state of emergency. Several hours later, one of the protesters rammed his car into a crowd of counterprotesters, killing thirty-two-year-old Heather Heyer and injuring at least nineteen others.

Trump responded from his golf club in Bedminster, New Jersey:

> We condemn in the strongest possible terms this egregious display of hatred, bigotry and violence, on many sides. On many sides. It's been going on for a long time in our country. Not Donald Trump, not Barack Obama. This has been going on for a long, long time.

He was equating the "many sides" of a demonstration during which protesters had worn Nazi and KKK insignia and shouted Nazi slogans, such as "Blood and Soil," a rallying cry from Hitler's Germany. Even Republican politicians responded to Trump's reaction with swift outrage. "The Nazis, the KKK and white supremacists are repulsive and evil, and all of us have a moral obligation to speak out against the lies, bigotry, anti-Semitism, and hatred that they propagate," former presidential candidate Senator Ted Cruz said in a statement. Another primary opponent of Trump's, Senator

Marco Rubio, tweeted, "Very important for the nation to hear @potus describe events in Charlottesville for what they are, a terror attack by #whitesupremacists." One after another, members of the president's Manufacturing Council resigned in protest. Most Americans had probably never heard of the Manufacturing Council, but these departures seemed to confirm the sense that this—if nothing else, then this—had to be the end of the Trump presidency. Surely a man who drew an equivalency between the KKK and neo-Nazis on the one hand and their opponents on the other could not be president. Even more simply, a man who did not recoil in horror at the sight of a woman being murdered for protesting racism, in the middle of a crowd, on a clear afternoon in an American city in 2017—a man who did not convey that his heart was broken and his mind could know no peace, a man who showed no emotion in response to this event—surely could not be president of the United States.

But he was. Nothing else happened. The

prominent Republicans' protest did not extend beyond their initial tweeted statements. Trump dissolved the Manufacturing Council. The presidency went on. This **was** the presidency: a white male supremacist presidency.

18.

"THROW OFF THE MASK OF HYPOCRISY"

Every political project requires a definition of "us," the community of people it aims to unite and protect. This is true of both democratic and antidemocratic projects, it is true of nationalist and imperialist projects, and it is true, too, of autocratic attempts, though they are fundamentally antipolitical. Precisely because an autocratic attempt is the opposite of politics, it demands a narrowing definition of "us," in opposition to an ever greater and more frightening "them." Where Obama's rhetoric was expansive—an ongoing effort to create a narrative that included all Americans—Trump's rhetoric is exclusionary. Trump never tires of reminding us that not everyone can be an American or deserves to be seen as an American, and that even people who have thought of themselves as Americans—culturally, socially, politically, and legally—can be declared not-American, un-American, or anti-American. Trump's America is like Trump: white, male, straight, besieged, aggressive. His campaign had promised to return his constituents to an imaginary past in which their jobs and daughters were safe from brown-skinned immigrants, in which the threat of what Trump called "radical Islamic terrorism" was vanquished or had never existed, in which white people did not have to treat African Americans as equals, women didn't meddle in politics, gay people didn't advertise their sexual orientation, and transgender people didn't exist.

Trump promised to reverse history and rewrite the American story. His electoral opponent campaigned on the story of America as a multicultural society, a society where the arc of history bends toward ever greater inclusiveness, a country that can surprise itself by being even better—more generous, more imaginative, more just— than it believes itself to be. This was the country that had awakened in November 2008 to discover that it was capable of electing a black president. This was a country with the aspiration of improving further, in a world where acceptance of difference was posited as a value. Trump promised to do more than to reverse this period of progress: he promised to change the narrative, to assign a different set of values to the American story. This prospect was offered as a balm to Trump supporters who felt injured by the culture of inclusion—slighted by affirmative action, forced into contortions by political correctness, and generally sidelined by a society that used to belong to them. The promise is, You no longer have to pretend.

But Trump promised more than that: he promised that as a country we would no longer have to pretend to be better than we are—and that those who resisted this new call to ugliness would be marginalized. In February 2018, the U.S. Citizenship and Immigration Services, the federal agency that handles visas, green cards, and naturalization, revised its mission statement. It had begun, "USCIS secures America's promise as a nation of immigrants." The phrase "nation of immigrants," which generations of Americans had learned as children, was, like most national myths and more than some, a lie: the United States was a settler colonialist nation whose economy was rooted in the enslavement of Africans forcibly brought to its shores. The new statement dropped the phrase altogether. This had nothing to do with correcting the record—it was part of the Trumpian project to redefine America in nationalist, nativist terms. The old mission statement put forth the agency's function as "granting immigration and citizenship benefits, promoting an awareness and understanding of citizenship, and ensuring the integrity of our immigration system."

The new statement defined it as "administer[ing] the nation's lawful immigration system . . . while protecting Americans, securing the homeland, and honoring our values." The new statement, in other words, made it clear that **immigrants** and **Americans** are two distinct groups that exist in opposition to each other. Immigrants, it indicated, are not Americans, now or in the future. Americans need to be protected from immigrants. This was a radical narrowing of the definition of "us." It was also an act of closing the community of "us" to those not already included in it.

If the United States was not a nation of immigrants and immigrants were not Americans in the making, then Americans must be defined by birth—and, one suspected, by ethnicity: blood and soil. Later in 2018, Trump began talking, insistently, of revoking birthright citizenship. "We are the only country in the world where a person comes in and has a baby and the baby is essentially a citizen of the United States for eighty-five years with all of those benefits.

It's ridiculous. And it has to end." Trump was lying: the United States is by no means the only country that grants birthright citizenship. He was lying, too, when he promised to repeal birthright citizenship by executive order: he lacked the power to cancel the Fourteenth Amendment. But he was effectively communicating that his America was a nation closed to outsiders and newcomers. In January 2018, when Trump referred to immigrants from Haiti and African states as coming from "shithole countries," the White House followed up with a statement saying, "Certain Washington politicians choose to fight for foreign countries, but President Trump will always fight for the American people." A racist remark was framed as an effort to protect "us."

In June 2018, the administration formed a task force to identify people who had lied on their citizenship applications and denaturalize them. These were, by definition, people who had not committed any other infraction that might have put them on the USCIS radar. They were otherwise law-abiding citizens, all of whom had lived in the country for many years (a prerequisite for naturalization), who were to be ferreted out, denaturalized, and deported.

These actions—the excision of "nation of immigrants," the threat to revoke birthright citizenship, and the denaturalization task force—were not as dramatic or as immediately consequential as some of Trump's other attacks on immigrants, such as the Muslim travel ban or the separation of families, but they showed how broad a front he had opened against immigrants. Trump, who in other areas had a way of lashing out, flailing, and withdrawing, was pursuing a sustained and consistent strategy on immigration. It had probably been articulated by someone else—someone actually capable of articulating a policy agenda—but it fit Trump's spontaneously expressed desires and his instincts. It fit his concept of America. In it, a part of the population—native-born straight men of white European descent, like Trump himself—were the nation. Everyone else was an interloper.

Israeli philosopher Moshe Halbertal has written that a moral life demands overcoming the natural human tendency to "self-privilege." People feel most comfortable and secure in a closed circle of "us," but we also realize that broadening that circle to include others makes us better people. This understanding underpins the aspirational narrative of American politics. For most of its history, U.S. immigration policy had represented an attempt to negotiate the dueling demands of moral ambition and fear of the other. On the one hand, the country proclaimed itself a nation of immigrants and adopted the Statue of Liberty, with Emma Lazarus's sonnet "The New Colossus" on its base, as its symbol. "Give me your tired, your poor, your huddled masses yearning to be free, the wretched refuse of your teeming shore" were words of aspiration. On the other hand, the country enforced racist immigration policies, created quotas, and harshly punished those who sought to make their home on its shores without submitting to onerous and arbitrary procedures.

Hypocrisy in politics, as infuriating and damaging as it can be, serves the function of reiterating aspirational values. But the Trump administration has no moral ambition. Indeed, Trump's appeal to his voters lay in large part in the implicit call to "throw off the mask of hypocrisy," as Hannah Arendt once described part of the appeal of fascism. In August 2019, acting director of USCIS Ken Cuccinelli was asked by an NPR reporter whether "The New Colossus" remained the basis of the American ethos. Cuccinelli offered to revise the poem to fit the age: "Give me your tired and your poor—who can stand on their own two feet and who will not become a public charge." He wasn't kidding—he was calling things as the Trump administration saw them. And even this wasn't the full story. Some people do come to the United States armed with evidence that they "can stand on their own two feet"; these are applicants for HB-1 visas, reserved for skilled workers and used mostly by high-tech companies. In April 2017, Trump signed an unusually detailed executive order called "Buy American and Hire American," directing heads of federal agencies to devise new protectionist practices. U.S. Citizenship and Immigration Services issued new policy guidelines, and the rate of denials of HB-1 visas soon quadrupled. The vast majority of HB-1 visa applicants came from India. Many of those whose applications were denied under the new rules were renewal applicants who had been living, working, and paying taxes in the country for years; now they had to sell their houses, pull their children out of school, and leave the United States.

19.

THE ANTIPOLITICS OF FEAR

In the absence of moral ambition, fear comes to the fore: the fear of the other and the fear "we" want to instill in the other. A week into his presidency, Trump signed an executive order titled "Enhancing Public Safety in the Interior of the United States." As its premise it claimed, counterfactually if vaguely, that "many aliens who illegally enter the United States and those who overstay or otherwise violate the terms of their visas present a significant threat to national security and public safety"; in reality, immigrants of all categories commit crimes at lower rates than U.S. citizens. The order directed the relevant agencies to deport any immigrants who had been charged with crimes or "in the judgment of an immigration officer, otherwise pose a risk to public safety or national security." The immediate function of the order was to revoke the Obama-era policy of de-prioritizing the deportation of people who had not committed any crimes in the United States (even with that policy in place, the Obama administration had deported a record number of people, laying the groundwork for Trump's policies): the order launched the era of indiscriminate deportations. The order also led to the formation of the Victims of Immigration Crime Engagement Office (VOICE). "Criminal aliens routinely victimize Americans and other legal residents," wrote Secretary of Homeland Security John Kelly in a February 2017 memo establishing VOICE. He ordered that any funds that were being used for advocacy on behalf of "illegal aliens" be redirected to this office, which Trump, in his first address to Congress, promised would "give voice" to victims who had been "ignored by our media and silenced by special interests."

The denaturalization task force, the ICE raids, the redefinition of the mission of the USCIS, the threat of revoking birthright citizenship, and, most of all, the incessant talk of "protecting" the American people from intruders served to send the message that "they" will never become "us"—that Trump had reversed history and shrunk the circle of "us." In September 2017, he delivered his first speech to the General Assembly of the United Nations. He announced, "In foreign affairs, we are renewing [the] founding principle of sovereignty. . . . As president of the United States, I will always put America first. . . . As long as I hold this office, I will defend America's interests above all else." For the leader of the world's most powerful country, the sovereignty of which was by no stretch of the imagination questioned, challenged, or undermined, these were strange words. These were strange things to say, too, on the floor of an organization created to foster cooperation among nations. But Trump was saying that he viewed cooperation as a fundamentally suspect proposition. "We can no longer be taken advantage of, or enter into a one-sided deal where the United States gets nothing in return," he said. Trump used the word "sovereign" or "sovereignty" twenty-one times in the speech. The following year, when he addressed the assembly again, he said the word ten times. In 2019, he was down to five utterances of "sovereign," but his message had been honed. "The future does not belong to globalists," he said, using a term the alt-right had turned into an anti-Semitic slur. "The future belongs to patriots. The future belongs to sovereign and independent nations."

No longer a nation of immigrants, Trump's America was also no longer a country founded on a set of abstract ideals. Though the din of his own presidency kept drowning him out, Trump was announcing repeatedly that his America was a sovereign, isolationist nation-state, where a nation-state—a country built around a shared ethnic, cultural, and linguistic heritage—had never existed.

———

Washington people cycle in and out of government. When one party's best minds are serving in the administration, their counterparts from the other party work in think tanks; then they switch. The inertia of this routine continued into the Trump administration, even though it drew many of its people from outside the usual circles. In late April 2019, at a security conference in Washington, a former State Department policy director, Anne-Marie Slaughter, interviewed the then current one, Kiron Skinner. In their introductory banter, both women noted that it was remarkable that two State Department policy directors were speaking to each other and that both were women. They didn't mention it, but the audience saw that one of them, Skinner, is an African American woman. Three days earlier Trump had doubled down on his characterization of the neo-Nazis who had marched in Charlottesville as "very fine people," and one's brain could break trying to grasp the meaning of this woman's status and presence.

The ensuing discussion was conducted in the moderately accessible policy jargon that is typical of such conversations. Except this time the familiar language, which usually feels sticky and overburdened, had the opposite quality: it sounded hollow, like the words meant nothing. The chasm between what the words might have meant to one interlocutor and what they meant when spoken by the other was so vast that it was as though the words were no longer part of a recognizable language.

A large part of Skinner's job was listening to what the president says and trying to make sense of it. She said as much. "The president provides the hunches and instincts," she said, "and it's my job, and that of Secretary Pompeo, to turn those hunches and instincts into hypotheses." She called the hypotheses the "Trump Doctrine" and the "Pompeo

Corollary." Slaughter, logically, asked what the Trump Doctrine was. "That's a tough one," Skinner responded, without a hint of irony. "It is, in a kind of broad way, a set of pillars that address twenty-first-century realities."

The pillars were: the "return to national sovereignty," as she put it; national interest; reciprocity in international relations and trade; "burden sharing," particularly in defense; and "new regional partnerships" for what she described as "particular crises." These were fancy bureaucratic terms designed to camouflage exceedingly simple concepts.

"If I can summarize," Slaughter suggested, "the Trump Doctrine is 'The United States is a sovereign nation guided by its national interest—we'll do for you if you'll do for us.'"

Skinner confirmed that Slaughter's understanding was correct. Then she described this primitive approach to international relations the way an art critic might talk about naïve art. "Donald Trump, who probably has not studied international relations extensively, and who has been a successful businessman, but who did study at Penn," said Skinner (who was educated at Spelman College and Harvard), had reignited debate "on some concepts that we thought were settled." He had forced the foreign-policy establishment to revisit "first principles"—most important, to debate the meaning of national sovereignty. Skinner did not elaborate on the substance of the debate, and she could not have if she tried. Trump's "hunches and instincts" were more like grunts and rages that reflected the full extent of his perception of the world: it is us against the other, everyone is out to get us, and the only expression of power is aggression. Trump's speech was destructive in affect and intent. Saying that his utterances had reignited a theoretical debate was like saying that someone who has carpet-bombed your city has turned your fellow citizens into builders again: technically it's true, but morally and intellectually it is a lie.

It came time for Slaughter to ask about

the Pompeo Corollary. Skinner seemed almost surprised to have to answer the question. "The Pompeo Corollary," she said, "is trying to find the diplomatic angle in all aspects of what the President is attempting to do—in security, society, the economy, energy, and the international system, and in each of those, looking at, what's the role of diplomacy?" she said. In other words, she was saying, the available minds at the State Department were tasked with inventing passably diplomatic approaches that could plausibly be connected to the president's utterances. "We are working on that, and it's a lot of fun!" Skinner said. No one, including Skinner, seemed to smile. But once the floor was opened to questions, everyone was very polite, as though they were having an actual substantive conversation with a key government official. It was not the first time most of the participants had been polite when they might have preferred not to be. In a sense, their behavior was hypocritical. But this was the opposite of the political hypocrisy in which they had been trained: they were not collectively pretending to hold lofty ideals and formulate policy accordingly; they were collectively putting a face of normalcy and acceptability onto naked hatred and aggression.

20.

CONFRONTING CIVIL SOCIETY

When Trump announced his candidacy for president in June 2015, he made a lot of promises. He promised to bring back jobs and lower the national debt. He promised to end the Common Core curriculum and repeal the Affordable Care Act. He promised to pull out of the Iran nuclear deal signed by Obama and revitalize the U.S. military. He promised to rebuild infrastructure and mentioned a Trump hotel under construction in Washington, D.C. He promised, of course, to make America great again. A speech had been drafted for him, but he ad-libbed continuously, and this may be why he returned to the topic of immigration in every section of the talk. Near the start of his announcement, he said:

> When Mexico sends its people, they're not sending their best. They're not sending you. They're not sending you. They're sending people that have lots of problems, and they're bringing those problems with us [sic]. They're bringing drugs. They're bringing crime. They're rapists. And some, I assume, are good people.
>
> But I speak to border guards and they tell us what we're getting. And it only makes common sense. It only makes common sense. They're sending us not the right people.
>
> It's coming from more than Mexico. It's coming from all over South and Latin America, and it's coming probably—probably—from the Middle East. But we don't know. Because we have no protection and we have no competence, we don't know what's

happening. And it's got to stop and it's got to stop fast.

Much later in the speech, Trump pledged:

I would build a great wall, and nobody builds walls better than me, believe me, and I'll build them very inexpensively, I will build a great, great wall on our southern border. And I will have Mexico pay for that wall.

He added, "I will immediately terminate President Obama's illegal executive order on immigration, immediately." He was referring to Deferred Action for Childhood Arrivals, or DACA, a program that granted stays of deportation to some of the people who had been brought to the United States as children. Finally, he said, "Nobody would be tougher on ISIS than Donald Trump. Nobody." Later in the year, he called for "a total and complete shutdown of Muslims entering the United States until our country's representatives can figure out what is going on." As the election grew closer, he bore down on that promise but also attached some more official-sounding wording to it: it was now "extreme vetting."

The Wall and the Muslim ban became the litmus tests of Trumpism. For Trump's supporters, his willingness and ability to deliver on these radical promises would be proof of his commitment to a kind of politics a wealthy divorced secular businessman from New York who used to be a Democrat and has been married to two immigrants might not be expected to embrace. Because these promises went to identity—both Trump's and his voters'—they were ultimately more important than what he said about jobs, the deficit, or infrastructure, and what he delivered on those fronts. Writing for the anti-immigrant think tank Center for Immigration Studies, political scientist Stanley Renshon said, "Immigration is not 'just another issue.' It is a basic foundation of American political, economic, social, and cultural life, and increasing worries reflect growing public appreciation of that fact."

No fan of Trump, this right-wing intellectual credited him with "opening the floodgates" of the immigration debate in the presidential campaign. Sticking to his promises of the Muslim ban and the Wall positioned Trump as a radical, a speaker of forbidden truths, whom someone like Renshon would see as useful. Most important, it reflected Trump's deep instinctual understanding of the world as a strange and hostile place where one needed to live in a fortress.

The Wall and the Muslim ban would also serve as tests of civil society's ability to resist Trump. If Trump was to be successful in his autocratic attempt, he would need to trample civil society—from grassroots activist organizations to professional civil society groups such as the American Civil Liberties Union: the activists who would march for the rights of immigrants, the aid workers who would provide direct services to them, and the lawyers who would fight for their legal rights. A confrontation like this had never occurred before. No American president had staged an autocratic attempt—and no other country's civil society was as vast and varied, as well funded, and as separate from the state as American civil society. In post-Communist countries such as Hungary or Russia, civil society was weak, quite new, and dependent on foreign donors for much of its funding—and this made it relatively easy to crush or co-opt. In Western-style liberal democracies such as Italy or Israel, civil society was intertwined with political parties and dependent on the state for some of its funding—and this made it relatively easy to intimidate and marginalize. In the United States, civil society appeared uniquely well equipped to resist a bully like Trump.

On January 27, 2017—a week after taking office—Trump signed Executive Order 13769, headlined "Protecting the Nation from Foreign Terrorist Entry into the United States." It banned entry for citizens of seven majority-Muslim countries: Iran, Iraq, Libya, Somalia, Sudan, Syria, and Yemen. It went into effect immediately, stranding people at airports both in the United States and overseas, separating families, and disrupting numerous lives. America protested. Activists and ordinary people went to JFK International Airport in New York, Dulles in Washington, DC, LAX in Los Angeles, and airports in other American cities to demonstrate against the new policy. Volunteer lawyers and interpreters went to the airports as well, while other lawyers immediately filed challenges to the new law in courts across the country. Within a day, several courts stayed the presidential order. Their decisions were based on a number of different legal arguments, but a dominant one was the constitutional prohibition on religious discrimination.

It was a textbook triumph of civil society: grassroots activists and professional advocates working in concert, as though by prior arrangement (there had indeed been some planning on the part of immigrant rights groups that anticipated the order, but much of the protest was spontaneous), the groundswell crystallizing public opinion and spurring the courts to act quickly and decisively. The system worked as it should.

But the system is not designed to deal with a president like Trump—a bad-faith actor, one who rejects the possibility that his power should be limited by institution or tradition. Trump deals with the courts, the law, and society the way a New York real-estate developer would deal with city hall and the neighbors—by pushing stubbornly ahead and looking for loopholes. He dealt with the travel ban the way a building owner might deal with being denied a construction permit: he shifted a few things around and filed again. Even before the government had exhausted its appeals on the first travel ban, on March 6, Trump signed a new executive order with the same title. He had dropped Iraq from the list of countries, provided a delay in implementation, and exempted people who already had travel authorization. Then he issued a Twitter tirade against what he saw as a watering-down of his travel ban. The new order was again stayed by the courts, though the Supreme Court eventually allowed part of it to stand. But the Trump administration tried again in September

2017, with Presidential Proclamation 9645, "Enhancing Vetting Capabilities and Processes for Detecting Attempted Entry Into the United States by Terrorists or Other Public-Safety Threats." Now Chad, North Korea, and Venezuela had been added to the list, perhaps to shed the appearance of a "Muslim ban." By this time, protests had subsided and public attention had shifted to other issues. The president prevailed. He had worn down the opposition and worked around the courts. Both civil society and the judiciary function on the assumption that they are partners in an ongoing negotiation, in which arguments can be settled, at least for a period of time; Trump sees any attempt at negotiation as an affront to his power—something that needs to be quashed at any cost.

Trump deployed the same blunt-force strategy as he pursued the Wall. Early on in his presidency, when many observers wanted to push the Wall out of their minds, dismissing it as so much campaign hot air, the administration solicited bids and designs and commissioned prototypes. Seven were built in the San Diego area in the fall of 2017. Trump then went to Congress to ask for eighteen billion dollars in funding, over ten years, for the construction of the Wall. By late 2018, demands for Wall funding exploded into an all-out conflict between the president and Congress, precipitating a government shutdown. Trump threatened to declare a national emergency in order to commandeer the funding.

In January 2019, Trump gave his first televised Oval Office address—to campaign for Wall funding. He spoke about the dangerous immigrant criminals again, claiming falsely that "day after day, precious lives are cut short by those who have violated our borders." He enumerated crimes—stabbings, rapes, and beatings—and demanded, "How much more American blood must we shed before Congress does its job?"

Congressional Democratic leaders appeared on television screens next, to give their rebuttal. Both the Speaker of the House, Nancy Pelosi, and the Senate minority leader, Chuck Schumer, stressed that they broadly agreed with the president on the need for border security. The disagreement, they claimed, concerned only the best way to accomplish it. Pelosi proposed new technology, more personnel, and the vague measure of "more innovation to detect unauthorized crossings." She said that bipartisan legislation rejected by Trump would fund the government and "smart, effective border-security solutions," and claimed that "we all agree we need to secure our borders."

Schumer led by explicitly allying himself with the president's position. "Make no mistake," he said, "Democrats and the president both want stronger border security." The problem with the Wall, according to Schumer, was that it was expensive and ineffective. He didn't say that it was immoral. He called his disagreement with the president a "policy difference," dignifying Trump's rants and tantrums. Neither of the congressional leaders pushed back against the premise that "we" Americans needed to be protected from "them," the immigrants clamoring to cross the border. Neither mentioned that a majority of the people then trying to cross the border were exercising the right to seek asylum, which is guaranteed by international law. Neither mentioned that the promise of asylum—of a safe haven for the "wretched refuse"—had been an ideal essential to this country's self-concept.

Trump had succeeded in shifting the way the country talked about asylum. In the lead-up to the 2018 midterm elections, he had continuously conjured the specter of a "caravan" of migrants marching through Central America to Mexico, preparing to storm the U.S. border. There was indeed a large number of people making their way to the border—this was a fairly regular occurrence in Central America, where many people found it was safer and somewhat easier to make the journey in the company of others. But this time, Trump was raging about "criminal aliens," a "national emergency," an attack on the nation's sovereignty, and a threat to the "safety of every single American." He claimed that "very bad people," MS-13 gang members, and "unknown Middle Easterners" were in the group. Even a Fox News host, Shep Smith, saw fit to fact-check Trump and point out that some of his statements were unfounded. Yet the story of the procession across Honduras and Mexico served to normalize more of Trump's xenophobic anti-immigrant rhetoric.

Following Trump's lead, everyone, it seemed, took to calling the procession a "caravan." The journalist Luke O'Neil pointed out that the word's Persian roots conjured the image of "people trekking across the desert with camels (i.e., terrorists of course)." What if journalists had resisted adopting Trumpian language in this case? They might have described the procession as the spontaneous movement of thousands who were fleeing a place more than they were pursuing a destination. They might even have called it an exodus, a term and an image that would have appealed to empathy—and tapped into religious associations—rather than to fear. A December 2018 study by MIT Media Lab showed that over the course of 2018, coverage of the movement of Central Americans toward the U.S. border had shed the words "refugee" and even "immigrant" and shifted instead to "migrant." Study author Emily Boardman Ndulue wrote, "'Migrants' convey[s] individuals who are by nature itinerant, while 'refugees' impl[ies] those affected by situationally-forced migration, and 'immigrants' impl[ies] that the individuals will be entering and settling in the US. The media's adoption of the phrase 'migrant caravan' and 'migrants' is further evidence of the adoption of Trump's anti-immigrant framing and rhetoric."

More insidiously, writers, again following Trump's lead, adopted the word "deter" and its derivatives. Outlets ranging from Breitbart to the **Times** to Jezebel debated whether the administration's policies had been, or could be, effective in "deterring" asylum seekers. This question lodged itself firmly in the discourse at the height of the media's attention to the separation of children from their families at the southern border. Before 2017, the words "migrants" and "asylum" and "deterrent" appeared primarily in coverage of foreign countries. Denmark was trying to "deter" Syrian refugees from approaching its borders. Australia used the word "deterrence" a lot. Indeed, the Australian far right, aided mightily by Rupert Murdoch's media outlets, got about a decade's head start on its American counterpart in this method of talking about asylum seekers. The word "deterrence" comes from the language of crime prevention, and its use reinforces the view of asylum seekers as criminals.

By late 2018, MSNBC was asking "whether anything will deter these people." Brian Stelter, of CNN, took to Twitter to exhort the news media to show the location of the procession on a map, demonstrating that it was still many hundreds of miles from the U.S. border. His argument seemed to be that the pro-Trump media was overestimating the immediate danger posed by the asylum seekers by minimizing the distance they still had to traverse, as if the people seeking refuge were an advancing army, or a natural disaster. By implication, he and Trump did not disagree about whether the caravan presented a threat, only about its current potency.

But the people walking through Mexico were not an army or a hurricane. They were not even planning to cross the border illegally. International law guaranteed their right to seek asylum. The United States had an obligation to consider their claims. Trump did not have a moral or legal leg to stand on when he talked about deterring the asylum seekers, much less when he promised to send the military to stop them. But most of the media, across the political spectrum, were now standing right there with him. They might have been uncomfortable with some of the language that Trump used in discussing immigration, but he had still succeeded in shifting their frame.

The circle of "us" had shrunk that much.

21.

THE POWER OF MORAL AUTHORITY

Following Trump's Oval Office address on funding for the Wall—when Democratic congressional leaders responded by, in effect, accepting his framing of the issue—one Democratic politician offered a substantive answer to Trump. She did not fact-check the president, thereby amplifying his falsehoods. Nor did she accept his terms of the conversation. Speaking on **The Rachel Maddow Show**, Representative Alexandria Ocasio-Cortez of New York said:

The one thing that the president has not talked about is the fact that he has systematically engaged in the violation of international human rights on our border. He has separated children from their families. He talked about what happened the day after Christmas—on the day **of** Christmas, a child died in [Customs and Border Protection] custody. The president should not be asking for more money to an agency that has systematically violated human rights; the president should be really defending why we are funding such an agency at all. Because right now what we are seeing is death, right now what we are seeing is the violation of human rights, these children and these families are being held in what are called **hieleras**, which are basically freezing boxes that no person should be maintained in for any amount of time. . . . He is trying to restrict every form of legal immigration there is in the United States. He is fighting against family reunification, he's fighting against the diversity visa lottery. . . . This is systematic, it is wrong, and it is anti-American.

Just the summer before, twenty-eight-year-old Ocasio-Cortez had won a Democratic primary against a longtime incumbent. At the time of making this comment, she had been in office for less than a week. A year and a half later, she would similarly step forward to call things as they are, this time speaking about detention facilities for migrants. After reporters at **The New York Times** and the **El Paso Times** broke the story of deplorable conditions at a detention center near the border and more information on similar centers followed, Ocasio-Cortez secured a visit to such a facility. In a livestream, she used the term "concentration camps." The following day, she tweeted, "This administration has established concentration camps on the southern border of the United States for immigrants, where they are being brutalized with dehumanizing conditions and dying.

This is not hyperbole. It is the conclusion of expert analysis." She linked to an article in **Esquire** in which Andrea Pitzer, a historian of concentration camps, was quoted making the same assertion: that the United States has created a "concentration camp system." Pitzer argued that "mass detention of civilians without a trial" was what made the camps concentration camps.

Outrage followed. Representative Liz Cheney, of Wyoming, tweeted, "Please @AOC do us all a favor and spend just a few minutes learning some actual history. 6 million Jews were exterminated in the Holocaust. You demean their memory and disgrace yourself with comments like this." A high-pitched battle of tweets and op-eds took off down the much-traveled dead-end road of arguments about historical analogies, a virtual shouting match about the Holocaust in which the Holocaust Museum in Washington also criticized Ocasio-Cortez. As is always the case with such debates, one side argued that nothing can be as bad as the Holocaust, therefore nothing can be compared to it; the other argued that the cautionary lesson of history can be learned only by acknowledging the similarities between now and then.

But the argument was really about how we perceive history, ourselves, and ourselves in history. We learn to think of history as something that has already happened, to other people. Our own moment, filled as it is with minutiae destined to be forgotten, always looks smaller in comparison. As for history, the bigger the event, the more mythologized it becomes. The myth becomes a caricature of sorts. Hitler, or Stalin, comes to look like a two-dimensional villain—someone whom contemporaries, as we imagine them, could not have seen as a human being. The Holocaust, or the Gulag, are such monstrous events that the very idea of rendering them in any sort of gray scale seems monstrous, too. This has the effect of making them, essentially, unimaginable. In crafting the story of something that should never have been allowed to happen, we forge the story of something that could not possibly have happened. Or, to use a phrase only slightly out of context, something that can't happen here.

A logical fallacy becomes inevitable. If this can't happen, then the thing that is happening is not it. What we see in real life, or at least on television, can't possibly be the same monstrous phenomenon that we have collectively decided is unimaginable. In Russia, people who know Vladimir Putin and his inner circle will insist that they are not monsters. Yes, they have overseen assassinations, imprisonments, and wars, but they are not thoroughly terrible, these people will claim—they are not like Stalin and his henchmen. In other words, they are not the monsters of our collective historical imagination. They are today's flesh-and-blood monsters, and this makes them seem somehow less monstrous. Every time a commentator calls Trump "presidential," every time a politician accepts his terms of debate, or every time a journalist simply covers Trump's actions and statements as one would normally cover politics, the message is the same: Trump does not live up—or down—to the stature of a history-book monster. Time itself is complicit. Anything that happens here and now is normalized, not solely through the moral failure of contemporaries but simply by virtue of actually existing.

Donald Trump has played this trick on Americans many times, beginning with his very election: first, he was impossible, and then he was president. Did that mean that the impossible had happened—an extremely hard concept to absorb—or did it mean that Trump was not the catastrophe so many of us had assumed he would be? The choice between these two positions was at the root of the argument between Ocasio-Cortez and the critics of her concentration-camp comment. It was not an argument about language. Ocasio-Cortez and her opponents agreed that the term "concentration camp" referred to something so horrible as to be unimaginable. It is the choice between thinking that whatever is happening in reality is, by definition, acceptable, and thinking that some actual events in our current reality are fundamentally incompatible with our concept of ourselves—not just as Americans but as human beings—and therefore unimaginable. The latter position is immeasurably more difficult to hold—not so much because it is contentious and politically risky, but because it is cognitively strenuous. It makes one's brain implode. It places concepts—moral concepts in particular—above the simple human need to be unconflictingly present in the present. It is also the only meaningful response to Trump's attempt to redefine the nation.

Speaking from a place of moral authority—and moral aspiration—is the strategy historically adopted by dissidents in undemocratic regimes such as totalitarian Poland, apartheid South Africa, or contemporary autocratic Belarus. Trump, an attempting autocrat, intuits that moral authority poses a threat to his project. In January 2017, he unleashed a Twitter fury against Congressman John Lewis, who vowed to boycott the inauguration. "All talk, talk, talk—no action or results. Sad!" tweeted the president-elect. He continued going after the civil rights icon long after Trump's usual Twitter attention span would have run out.

Trump came across as clueless, as though he did not know who Lewis was, which district had elected him, and more important, what history he represented. But his instincts were guiding him into a confrontation that was hardly new. Autocratic power requires the degradation of moral authority—not the capture of moral high ground, not the assertion of the right to judge good and evil, but the defeat of moral principles as such. Once cynicism triumphs, wrote the dissident Václav Havel in a 1975 letter to the Communist leader of Czechoslovakia, "Everyone who still tries to resist by, for instance, refusing to adopt the principle of dissimulation as the key to survival, doubting the value of any self-fulfillment purchased at the cost of self-alienation—such a person appears to his ever more indifferent neighbors as an eccentric, a fool, a Don Quixote, and in the end is regarded inevitably with some aversion, like everyone who behaves differently from the rest and in a way which, moreover, threatens to hold up a critical mirror before their eyes." The majority then stands to applaud his humiliation.

The war on principles unleashed in the Soviet world was more successful than Havel could have imagined in 1975—long outlasting the collapse of the Soviet Union itself. His own calls for a moral politics were mocked by a significant number of his countrymen, and by an even greater number when he stepped down—all this long after the dissolution of the Eastern Bloc and the apparent defeat of the Soviet post-totalitarian system. In the Russian language today, the entire vocabulary of principles and ideals has, after decades of abuse, been relegated to disuse. Even in private conversation, Russians will frequently apologize for using words or concepts that they feel are marked with "pathos," a word that has come to connote not so much suffering as earnestness and loftiness of concept. In the public sphere, the language of "pathos" does not exist at all: a word like "democracy" can be pronounced only with a smirk.

For a number of years, perhaps since the end of the Cold War, the language of ideals and principles had been fading from American political discourse too, giving way to the language of realism and action. In his farewell speech, President Obama addressed the "work of democracy," the daily grind of change and the importance of the belief in the American experiment rather than the ideals on which the experiment is based. When he rehearsed the milestones of American history, he framed them in terms of "purpose" rather than vision, idea, or yearning. This was hardly a failure of Obama's: his language went as high as and perhaps higher than the political conversation as it has evolved over the last quarter century allowed. The groundwork for Trump's assault, his drive to debase us all, had been laid long before Obama was elected. (Another striking example of how well the soil had been tilled for Trump's project was Obama's apparently ad-libbed line:* "I reject discrimination against Muslim Americans, who are just as patriotic as we are"—he too saw Muslim Americans as not "us.") But there was Representative Lewis, who could say, as he did in his **Meet the Press** interview, "You cannot be at home with something that you feel . . . is wrong."

When Trump dismissed Lewis as "all talk, talk, talk," he was dismissing the value of moral politics in general, and in particular the basic conversation about right and wrong in which Lewis was engaging. In attacking Lewis, Trump lashed out not only against the legacy of the civil rights movement that Lewis represented but also the rhetorical history of moral protest: Lewis, like Havel, Lech Wałęsa, Andrei Sakharov, Nelson Mandela, and

---

*I deduce that the line was ad-libbed because the text speech provided by the White House on the day of the speech had the sentence ending with "Muslim Americans." The final transcript provided by the Obama Library contains the rest of the phrase: "who are just as patriotic as we are."

286

others before him, was reaching for a higher note.

That higher note is a necessary condition of vision. Havel, who conceptualized the "power of the powerless" as an entirely novel form of resistance, lived to lead his country. So did Mandela. Raw power can overtake moral authority, and perhaps today it is easier than ever before, but a determined effort to preserve ideals when they are under attack can serve as a bridge to the future.

It was this vision, and the ability to speak clearly and morally, that helped to propel Ocasio-Cortez's seemingly instant rise to national prominence—and unnerved Trump. Ocasio-Cortez and three other freshman representatives, all of them women of color—Ayana Pressley of Massachusetts and the only two Muslim women to have been elected to Congress, Rashida Tlaib of Michigan and Ilhan Omar of Minnesota—became known as the Squad, after Ocasio-Cortez used the word to caption an Instagram photo of the four. Their vocal rejection of pragmatic politics unnerved establishment Democrats, too. In July 2019, for example, all four refused to vote for a bipartisan bill that expanded funding for immigration authorities by 4.6 billion dollars without any specific requirement for changing the handling of asylum seekers—such as shutting down the concentration camps. A **New York Times** piece quoted Pelosi reprimanding them: "All these people have their public whatever and their Twitter world," she said. "But they didn't have any following. They're four people and that's how many votes they got." Ninety-one other Democrats had voted against the bill but had not been as vocal or visible in their opposition. The next day, **The Washington Post** reported that the Squad was being systematically marginalized by more-senior Democrats.

Then Trump jumped in. He tweeted, in three installments, "So interesting to see 'Progressive' Democrat Congresswomen, who originally came from countries whose governments are a complete and total catastrophe, the worst, most corrupt and inept anywhere in the world (if they even have a functioning government at all), now loudly . . . and viciously telling the people of the United States, the greatest and most powerful Nation on earth, how our government is to be run. Why don't they go back and help fix the totally broken and crime infested places from which they came. Then come back and show us how . . . it is done. These places need your help badly, you can't leave fast enough. I'm sure that Nancy Pelosi would be very happy to quickly work out free travel arrangements!" A day later, speaking to reporters at the White House, Trump reiterated this message. "As far as I'm concerned, if you hate our country, if you're not happy here, you can leave," he said. "If you're not happy in the U.S., if you're complaining all the time, you can leave. You can leave right now."

The media recognized the comments as racist. And still they fell into the rhetorical trap set by Trump. CNN pointed out that Trump was "falsely implying they weren't natural-born American citizens" and other media stressed that only one of the four women was born outside the United States—as though this mattered. One doesn't have to be a natural-born citizen to be a member of Congress, and, more important, one doesn't have to be any kind of citizen to have an opinion about the United States government. Even commentators who recognized the racism of Trump's comments unwittingly participated in policing the boundary of the narrowed circle of "us."

The Squad responded with a press conference during which Omar and Tlaib called for Trump's impeachment. Omar said, "It is time for us to stop allowing this President to make a mockery of this country." Months before Pelosi announced an impeachment inquiry, the Squad was calling for it—and framing it in explicitly moral rather than legal terms.

22.

WHO IS "US"? AND WHO ARE WE?

In the fall of 2019, American political institutions mounted their counteroffensive against Trump's autocratic attempt: congressional committees held a series of hearings and, as the legislative session wrapped up, the House of Representatives—or, rather, the Democratic majority in the House of Representatives—voted to impeach the president for abuse of power and obstruction of Congress. It followed a trajectory that had become familiar from the Russia probe and the aftermath of Charlottesville: for a brief moment, it seemed inconceivable that the Trump presidency would continue—and then both sides retreated to their previous positions, the Republican establishment closed ranks around Trump, and Trumpism continued. But in the process, both sides in this battle—Trump on the one hand and congressional Democrats on the other—chose their symbolic heroes.

House Speaker Pelosi, speaking after the impeachment vote, invoked the memory of Elijah Cummings, the chairman of the House Committee on Oversight and Reform who died in October 2019. Cummings had been an outspoken critic of Trumpism, and Trump had attacked him with the viciousness he reserves for voices of moral authority—especially those who are not white men. Pelosi quoted a statement Cummings had issued at the beginning of impeachment proceedings, just a few weeks before his death: "When the history books are written about this tumultuous era, I want them to show that I was among those in the House of Representatives who stood up to lawlessness and tyranny." She added another Cummings quote, this one from the conclusion of a February 2019 hearing at which Trump's personal lawyer Michael Cohen, then already on his way to jail, had testified. Cummings said, "When we are dancing with the angels, the question will be, did we—what did we do to make sure we kept our democracy intact?"

Pelosi said, "We did all we could, Elijah."

The hero Trump chose during the fall of his impeachment was Navy SEAL Chief Petty Officer Edward Gallagher. In the summer of 2019, Gallagher faced trial for allegedly killing an unconscious, unarmed captive in Iraq. The Navy fumbled the investigation, and at the last minute a witness who had been granted immunity testified that he, not Gallagher, had killed the young man; Gallagher was acquitted on most charges and convicted only of posing for an Instagram photo with the body of the captive and the knife he appeared to claim to have used to murder him. By this time, the case, covered extensively by Fox News, had already drawn Trump's attention; the president had tweeted his support for

Gallagher. After Gallagher was acquitted, Trump congratulated him by tweet. He then intervened to reverse the Navy's decision to discharge Gallagher without honors—once again demonstrating that the commander in chief can issue orders by tweet. Trump also reinstated Gallagher's rank and pay, and stripped the prosecutors in the case of their Navy medals. Ultimately, the struggle over Gallagher's fate cost the secretary of the Navy, Richard Spencer, his job.

Gallagher had been turned in by members of his own platoon. At the end of 2019, **The New York Times** published a trove of investigators' video interviews with men who had served with him. They characterized him as "freaking evil," someone who "was perfectly okay with killing anybody that was moving," intentionally targeted women and children, and "just wants to kill anybody he can." Meanwhile, thanks to Trump's intervention, Gallagher left the service on his own terms and launched a career as an Instagram influencer, a peddler of sportswear and Trumpian ideas. Trump hosted Gallagher at his residence in Mar-a-Lago, continued to praise him as a hero, and floated the possibility of having him speak at the 2020 Republican convention. Gallagher embodied the essence of the presidency: raw, unchecked power, contempt for rules, laws, and norms, and an unbridled desire to act out of hatred.

Historian Greg Grandin has argued that Trumpism is the culmination of the devolution of American imperialism. In a 2019 book, Grandin wrote that to justify its colonial and postcolonial mission, the United States had created the myth of a goodness it embodied—and brought to those it colonized and policed.

It not only conveyed the idea that the country was moving forward but promised that the brutality involved in moving forward would be transformed into something noble. Frontier expansionism would break every paradox, reconcile every contradiction between, say, ideals and interests, virtue and ambition. Extend the sphere, and you will ensure peace, protect individual freedom, and dilute factionalism; you will create a curious, buoyant, resourceful people in thrall to no received doctrine, transcend regionalism, spread prosperity, and move beyond racism. As horizons broaden, so will our love for the world's people. As boundaries widen, so will our tolerance, the realization that humanity is our country. There was no problem caused by expansion that couldn't be solved by more expansion. War-bred trauma could be rolled over into the next war; poverty would be alleviated by more growth.

Grandin diagnosed the Trump era as a kind of fundamental recoiling. Not only is Trumpism isolationist, but it rejects even the myths that were used to justify expansionism. All that America had worked to make bigger, more complicated, more varied, would now get smaller and simpler.

Trump's America is an America that is contracting, keeping ever more people out, both geographically—by expelling and rejecting immigrants—and politically—by rejecting and marginalizing nonwhite, non-straight, non-male people. It is not that war abroad is impossible under Trump—indeed, his isolationist rhetoric notwithstanding, war is likely because Trump craves the adulation it can bring a leader. But Trump wages war the way he governs—by performative gesture, by dropping the Mother of All Bombs on Afghanistan or, in January 2020, launching a drone strike at an Iraqi airport in order to kill Iranian military leader Qasem Soleimani. When Trump announced that Soleimani was killed to prevent planned attacks on Americans, he was probably lying, as he has lied about most things; there seemed to be no evidence of such plots. Trump was not the first president to use lies to justify starting a war—George W. Bush's administration did this in 2003, when its secretary of state, Colin Powell, told the United Nations that Iraq had weapons of mass destruction—but he might have been the first president to frame an act of war abroad solely as self-defense. "Soleimani was plotting imminent and sinister attacks on American diplomats and military personnel, but we caught him in the act and terminated him," said the president. He made no pretense of promoting democracy or even of policing the world: he seemed to see himself as a king barricaded in his castle, with thousands of soldiers in the battlement, the sights of their rifles trained on potential intruders. Trump's is a war triggered by the sense of inhabiting a contracting space rather than an expansive empire.

The inexorable logic of contraction has dictated that Trump reverse the course of politics both in ways consistent with his apparent values—his long history of racist statements, his proud misogyny—and in ways that appeared to contradict his previous beliefs. A week and a half before the 2016 election, at a campaign event in Colorado, Trump became the first Republican presidential candidate in history to hold up a rainbow flag. He held it upside down, though the lettering on the flag—a hastily scrawled "LGBTs for Trump"—appeared right side up. The awkward spectacle seemed symbolic of the moment. The gains made by the LGBT movement over the preceding few years—with same-sex marriage becoming the law of the land, gay and lesbian and transgender people serving openly in the military, and, most important, a tectonic shift in public opinion—had, it seemed, made this moment inevitable.

But Trump also said that he opposed the Supreme Court decision legalizing same-sex marriage, and pledged to appoint justices who would reverse it. He chose one of the country's most notoriously antigay politicians to be his running mate. In February 2017, the administration rescinded protections allowing transgender students to use the bathrooms of their choice. In May, Trump signed an executive order directing his attorney general to support and defend so-called religious-freedom laws, which lay out legal grounds for discriminating against LGBT people. In July, Trump tweeted out a ban on transgender service members. In September, the Justice Department filed a Supreme Court brief in support of a Colorado baker who refused to make a cake for a same-sex wedding (the court would go on to punt the case). In October, a year after Trump had stood up holding a rainbow flag, Attorney General Jeff Sessions issued detailed guidelines based on Trump's religious-freedom executive order and, separately, instructed U.S. attorneys to stop interpreting federal law as protecting transgender employees from discrimination on the basis of sex. In October 2019, when the Supreme Court heard two cases on employment discrimination against gay and transgender people, the solicitor general argued that the Civil Rights Act of 1964 did not protect people from discrimination on the basis of sexual orientation—that such discrimination was and should continue to be legal.

The logic of the Trump presidency in the context of American politics made these attacks on LGBT people inevitable: the support Trump had drawn from the evangelical right had bound him to an antigay agenda. But the greater logic at play was the logic of narrowing the circle of "us." Trump got elected on the promise of a return to an imaginary past—a time we don't remember because it never actually was, but one when America was a kind of great that Trump has promised to restore. Trump shares this brand of nostalgia with Putin, who has spent the last seven years talking about Russian "traditional values," with Viktor Orbán, who has warned LGBT people against becoming "provocative," and with any number of European populists who promise a return to a mythical "traditional" past.

With few exceptions, countries that have grown less democratic in recent years have drawn a battle line on the issue of LGBT rights. Moscow has banned Pride parades and the "propaganda of non-traditional sexual relations," while Chechnya—technically a region of Russia—has undertaken a campaign to purge itself of queers. In Recep Tayyip Erdoğan's Turkey, water cannons were used to disperse an Istanbul Pride parade. Narendra Modi's India has recriminalized homosexuality. In Egypt, where gays experienced new freedoms in the brief interlude of democracy after the 2011 revolution, they are now, under Abdel Fattah el-Sisi's dictatorship, subjected to constant harassment and surveillance, and hundreds have been arrested.

In the early twenty-first century, LGBT people in the popular imagination in many countries became a stand-in for all that is new and all that is frightening about the future. Will the future be populated by people who have no identifiable gender? Will our children become people with whom we have no common ground? Will there be no place for us? Trump has a knack for speaking directly to these anxieties. Trump's campaign ran on the word "again," the promises to "take back" a sense of safety and "bring back" a simpler time. When he pledged to build the Wall or to fight a variety of nonexistent crime waves—urban, immigrant—he was promising to shield Americans from the strange, the unknown, the unpredictable. Queers can serve as convenient shorthand. By tweeting that he had decided to ban transgender people from the military, Trump showed that he is the autocrat that he was elected to be: he can control people by issuing an order. The order juxtaposed the military—the symbol of Americans' security—with transgender people, who make so many Americans feel so anxious. To Trump's voters, it signaled that life was returning to the way they imagined it once was: comfortable, familiar, and lived among people who were like them.

———

A president's most visible actions are tangible: executive orders, regulations, and the positions the administration takes in the courts. In his first three years in office, Trump fundamentally reshaped immigration by effectively closing the country to asylum seekers from Latin America and refugees from the rest of the world, by severely cutting the number of people who can get work visas, by instituting the travel ban, and, more broadly, by creating an atmosphere of fear and uncertainty that functions as the ultimate deterrent to people who might seek entry or legal status in the country. The effect of his administration's policies on LGBT Americans has been structurally similar: signal rollbacks in policy have created the expectation of bigger and worse things to come. The exclusion of immigrants and LGBT people from "us" is, however, only the jutting, explicit tip of the Trumpian promise. The broader logic of the contraction is racist, and it too shows in both rhetoric—such as Trump's reaction to Charlottesville and the particular viciousness he unleashes on nonwhite political opponents—and in policy. The Justice Department went to court to defend state voting laws that would kick thousands off the rolls—disproportionately affecting people of color. The Justice Department under Jeff Sessions also reversed its decades-old stance on the consideration of race in college admissions. The administration's unrelenting attack on the Affordable Care Act allowed hundreds of thousands to be stripped of insurance or become underinsured. This was only the most visible and best-publicized part of the attack on what remained of the American welfare state, as when rule changes deprived as many as three million people of food stamps. Where it comes to the poor—those who cannot "stand on their own two feet" and who need the welfare state—Trumpism treats them with the same disdain as it does the "wretched refuse" from other shores. Trump's lone legislative accomplishment—tax reform— plainly benefited the rich and hurt the poor, also once again disproportionately affecting people of color. Deregulation that reversed years of progress on air pollution and resulted in thousands more deaths a year also hit the poor—people who are more likely to live in polluted neighborhoods and less likely to have access to help when disasters drastically increase pollution.

As Trump's policies have created a moat around the shrunken circle of "us," his speech has invited—though a better word may be "incited"—his supporters to patrol the borders of this new, smaller American society. Trump's campaign promise of a return to the imaginary past was largely a promise to transport Americans to a time when racism, misogyny, and xenophobia were mainstream attitudes. More than that: it was the promise of a new history in which a greater inclusivity not only had not happened but would never happen. In this story, Archie Bunker, the comically racist, sexist, and xenophobic protagonist of the 1970s sitcom **All in the Family**, is not the clueless old man who will have to cede his house and his country to new times and new, different people—in the Trump script, he owns the place, and he is not going anywhere. He is Edward Gallagher, who has had his status upgraded from criminal to hero and who posts a picture of himself wearing a wife-beater emblazoned with an American flag and holding a coffee mug inscribed with the words "I love it when I wake up in the morning and Donald Trump is president." From his bully pulpit in the White House and at rallies, Trump calls out to the worst in his people. He models and molds the language of the time. Speaking on immigration, he referred to members of the gang MS-13 as "animals." When he was criticized, he said it again and again. "I called them 'animals' the other day and I was met with rebuke," he said. "They said, 'they're people.' They're not people. They're animals. We have to be very, very tough." Dehumanizing people so blatantly is not alien to American public discourse—it was a hallmark of the way the George W. Bush administration talked about terrorists—but Trump uses this weapon more widely and with ever more gusto, inviting his supporters to join him in demonizing the Other.

Hate crimes in the United States surged following the 2016 election. Three political scientists from Texas compared hate-crime statistics from counties where Trump had held campaign rallies to demographically similar counties where rallies were not held—and concluded that Trump rallies were correlated with a 226 percent rise in hate crimes. Two other researchers, Griffin Edwards and Stephen Rushin, professors of business and law, respectively, hypothesized that "it was not just Trump's inflammatory rhetoric throughout the political campaign that caused hate crimes to increase. Rather, we argue that it may have been Trump's subsequent election as President of the United States that validated this rhetoric in the eyes of perpetrators and fueled the hate crime surge." A third group—three political scientists at the University of Massachusetts at Amherst—analyzed survey data from the 2016 election to try to settle the question of which played a greater role in bringing voters to Trump: economic anxiety or racist and sexist attitudes. Their conclusion: "We find that while economic considerations were an important part of the story, racial attitudes and sexism were much more strongly related to support for Trump." Trump, they found, had tapped into some white voters' feeling of being newly marginalized and aggrieved. He also won votes by denigrating his opponent, insulting female reporters, and even as a result of the release of a videotape in which he bragged about sexually assaulting women. Together, these studies paint a portrait of Trumpism: racist and sexist resentment given voice by Trump and affirmed by his election leads to greater violence against the growing number of people whom Trumpism defines out of American personhood.

The hate crimes of the Trump era have included: Charlottesville in August 2017; the October 2018 shooting at the Tree of Life synagogue in Pittsburgh, where eleven people were killed on Refugee Shabbat, a nationwide event initiated by the Hebrew Immigrant Aid Society, by a man who had posted online screeds such as "HIAS likes to bring invaders in that kill our people"; and the August 2019 shooting at a Walmart in El Paso, Texas, where a white supremacist killed twenty-two people, most of them Latino. The hate crimes also include attacks on mosques or Islamic centers in almost every state in the Union; several thousand anti-Semitic incidents; and violent crimes against transgender people, especially transgender women of color, at least twenty-two of whom were murdered in 2019.

Many people have advocated using the term "domestic terrorism" to describe the acts of people like the Pittsburgh and El Paso shooters, or the man who stabbed five people during a December 2019 Hanukkah celebration in Monsey, New York, but this term is misleading: it implies that the violence exists in opposition to the rule of law imposed by the state. In fact, these crimes are violence delegated by the American president in much the same way that Putin delegates attacks on his political opponents, Duterte delegates the killing of drug users, and Netanyahu delegates to Israeli settlers violence against Palestinians. Trump delegates by incitement and reward. In August 2017, for example, he pardoned Joe Arpaio, an Arizona sheriff who faced charges over his practice of hunting down immigrants in order to turn them over to the immigration authorities. Trump pardoned him before he could face trial, and announced the decision in a tweet: "I am pleased to inform you that I have just granted a full Pardon to 85 year old American patriot Sheriff Joe Arpaio. He kept Arizona safe!" Two years later, he not only pardoned Gallagher but celebrated him as a hero.

Then came the coronavirus, which Trump no sooner began taking seriously than he started calling the "Chinese virus." The World Health Organization, which chose the name COVID-19 for the disease caused by the new virus, had adopted a specific policy of not naming epidemics for the geographic regions where they were first identified—in order to avoid fomenting prejudice and discrimination. But in late March 2020, the United States derailed a G-7 statement on the coronavirus by insisting that the document refer to it as the "Wuhan Virus." A close-up photograph of Trump's briefing notes showed that the word "corona" had been crossed out and replaced with "Chinese." It was at this point that hate crimes against Asian Americans skyrocketed.

Much as Trump might have feared that an epidemic would hurt his chances for reelection, much as he evidently wanted to other the virus and avoid being associated with a public health disaster, COVID-19 was the perfect disease for the Trump era. All over the world, it fueled fear of the Other and prompted the closing of borders. In the United States, Trump rapidly progressed from pointing the finger at China to blaming Europe to inciting fear of New Yorkers. The fear spawned, or exposed, dozens, perhaps hundreds, of mini Trumps. The governors of Florida and Rhode Island deployed the National Guard to ferret out New Yorkers and other visitors from out of state. Rhode Island posted "R.I. Residents Only" signs on its golf courses and stationed police to monitor them. Residents of Cape Cod and the nearby islands petitioned the governor of Massachusetts to close the bridges—a move that would have shut them off from most supplies and from garbage removal but, they seemed to imagine, would keep them safe from the coronavirus. In each case, the officials and local activists claimed, among other things, that hospitals would be unable to handle the strain if outsiders added to the local patient load. Other arguments were conceivable—that every New Yorker who temporarily moved to a less densely populated area, for example, was perhaps breaking the chain of contagion; that the population as a whole might be better served if people could redistribute themselves to areas with lower demand for hospital beds—but it was impossible to make these arguments now. Three years of Trumpism had extinguished whatever remained in American politics of the language of solidarity or the idea of public welfare. In an ultimate expression of micro-Trumpism, a New York City co-op board expelled a New Hampshire doctor who had answered the call of city hospitals asking for help; he was staying in his brother's apartment, helping save the lives of New Yorkers—but to his brother's neighbors, he was outside the circle of "us."

SURVIVING AUTOCRACY

———

In Bálint Magyar's terminology, we are at the stage of an autocratic attempt—an attempt that may still be rebuffed and reversed by institutional means. The impeachment process in Congress was an attempt at such a reversal. Its failure demonstrated that, just as Magyar has written, a monopoly on political power—having both the executive branch and the Senate in Republican hands—can enable autocracy. The next chance at reversing the autocratic attempt of Trumpism will probably come in November 2020, at the polls. To succeed at reversing the autocratic attempt—and to hold on to that victory in the face of what is certain to be massive and possibly violent backlash—we will have to do more than vote, and more than campaign. We will have to engage both formal and informal political institutions, and we will have to understand anew why these institutions exist.

The country that elected Trump was a country that had laid the groundwork for his presidency. It was a country that, during a world refugee crisis of unprecedented proportions, was deporting more people than it was resettling—and was resettling proportionately fewer people than Canada, or any of the countries of Europe. It was a country that, even as it continued to tell a story of itself as a "nation of immigrants," grew more fearful of the outside world, more isolationist, and more resentful with every passing year. It was a country that dismantled its welfare state and enabled a small group of white men to accumulate ever more wealth and power. It was a country that had but a memory of moral aspiration and now viewed government like a management company—as though efficiency and competence were the supreme and sufficient qualities for which one looked in a leader. In other words, it was a country that had already begun to damage itself in the way that Trumpism exacerbated. He preyed on the fear, he weaponized the hatred, and he filled the void left by the lack of vision.

To reverse Trump's autocratic attempt, we

will have to abandon the idea of returning to an imaginary pre-Trump normalcy when American institutions functioned as they should. Instead, we have to recall that what undergirds the Congress and the courts, the media and civil society, is the belief that this can be a country of all its people. Moral aspiration forms the foundation of these institutions. Yes, moral aspiration has been used as a cover for hypocrisy and a justification for violence, but it is moral aspiration nonetheless. It will now need to be reinvented. That reinvention is likely a job for the people who are the opposites of Trump in every way: political figures of powerful moral authority that comes in part from lives lived outside Trump's circle of "us," like the late Elijah Cummings or the ailing John Lewis, but also the women of the Squad. Most media and political experts have described the new generation of insurgent politicians—of whom the Squad are the most visible representatives—in terms of leftist politics, and have discussed the need for the Democratic Party to move left to attract more and younger voters. But the key distinction of this new crop of politicians is not that they hold left-of-center policy positions—though many of them do. What makes them different from the last couple of generations of American politicians is that they come to the public not only with policy proposals but with a vision of a different politics, a different life, and a different society that may be possible in the future. Distinct as their visions may be from one another, all focus on dignity rather than power, equality rather than wealth, and solidarity rather than competition. These new ways of thinking about politics have not yet bubbled up into mainstream consciousness: the Democratic Party and most media still discuss the vote in terms of policy proposals, solutions, and, of course, fund-raising and electability, however they measure it. But what will make Trump's opponent successful—if he can indeed be successful—is the ability to counter his simple promise of returning to an "us" from a white male supremacist past with a vision of who we are that is more complicated, offers fewer certainties, but is also more inspiring to more Americans—a vision of America as it could be.

The poet Langston Hughes described this vision—and the need for this vision—with absolute precision in 1936 in his poem "Let America Be America Again." It ended with the following lines:

> O, yes,
> I say it plain,
> America never was America to me,
> And yet I swear this oath—
> America will be!
>
> Out of the rack and ruin of our gangster
>   death,
> The rape and rot of graft, and stealth,
>   and lies,
> We, the people, must redeem
> The land, the mines, the plants, the
>   rivers.
> The mountains and the endless plain—

WHO IS "US"?

All, all the stretch of these great green
    states—
And make America again!

In our times, this would be an audacious
slogan.

EPILOGUE

The coronavirus pandemic, like all crises, is fundamentally political—it raises the question of how we live together, how we choose to govern and be governed, how we think of who we are, and whom we include in this "we." But first, the pandemic destroyed us.

The coronavirus, combined with the Trump administration's disastrous response, dealt the economy the biggest sudden hit in memory. Hundreds of thousands lost their jobs in just the first week of the American stage of the pandemic; millions followed. Inequalities in wealth, opportunity, and access to health care instantly became even more glaring than they had been a few weeks earlier.

The social fabric was torn in unprecedented ways, with school closings, the widespread shift to working from home, social distancing, and sheltering in place. Where we used to share dozens of experiences a day with friends, acquaintances, and strangers—riding the subway, working in an office, standing in line for takeout, going to a concert, eating at a restaurant, chatting with an Uber driver—many of us were reduced to sharing only isolation and the fear of chance encounters, if either of those could be said to be shared. Other people became the source of danger; proximity inspired fear.

The political system, frayed as it was, came under unprecedented stress. The Supreme Court delayed cases. The Justice Department sought extreme powers, such as the right for judges to detain people indefinitely without trial. The administration and its allies used the crisis to push through a more extreme version of its agenda, including further environmental deregulation, the suspension of affirmative action, and, in several states, the closing of abortion clinics. The election campaign entered a state of suspended animation. The borders were effectively closed. At the local level, quarantine measures stopped town council, school board, and community meetings.

It was as if the virus and the president were working in concert. Not only did the pandemic cripple the existing political system, it demanded that Trump govern in precisely the manner to which he aspired: unilaterally, decisively, with few checks on his power—and with the eyes of the nation riveted to him. And though he had little interest in understanding the problem; though he was reluctant to use his executive power actually to fight the pandemic; though he was inconsistent and apparently incapable of staying on point, showing empathy, or comprehending the gravity of the situation—he still got to be the center of attention, he still got to show that he was in charge, and he got to watch his approval ratings climb.

In **The Origins of Totalitarianism**, Hannah Arendt identified a key precondition: "Only where great masses are superfluous or can be spared without disastrous results of depopulation is totalitarian rule, as distinguished from a totalitarian movement, at all possible." She was writing about state terror, which is possible only when a regime is willing to sacrifice millions of its own people. A pandemic also exerts terror. Effective terror is random; terror has been achieved when every person in the population has a credible fear of suffering and dying. COVID-19 was not unleashed by the state under the cover of ideology, but it has functioned like terror. Trump did not deploy the virus, but he was positioned to reap its reward: a population gripped by terror created extraordinary opportunities for him as he continued to grope his way to autocratic rule.*

Another friend of the autocrat, counterintuitively, is a tanking economy and a scarcity environment. For three years, Trump had seen a strong economy as his ultimate argument and best campaign asset. As the economy took a dive the likes of which had not been seen in recorded history, Trump scrambled to salvage what the economy had always meant to him: a brutal and broken oligarchy. In the process, he condemned a majority of Americans to economic hardship—and as many as a third to unemployment. He may inadvertently have created perfect conditions for autocratic consolidation. The inability to plan, to have the certainty of being able to feed

---

*Totalitarianism is a subcategory of autocracy. I am not arguing that Trump is building a totalitarian regime, but that he is an aspiring autocrat functioning in a world that has seen a number of totalitarian regimes. Arendt's insights are helpful in highlighting some of the features of Trumpism.

one's family today and tomorrow, produces more anxiety and fear of change. Arendt wrote about the ways in which totalitarian regimes instrumentalize instability while at the same time dangling the promise of stability. No matter what happens, Trump continues to claim that our economy is the strongest and we are the best-prepared and best-protected country—and if the history of totalitarian societies is any indication, this hypnotic insistence may work in a time of extreme anxiety.

The anxiety also propelled the popularity of New York governor Andrew Cuomo, whose own daily coronavirus briefings projected the confidence, empathy, and decisiveness Trump's so clearly lacked. A Jezebel writer waxed romantic: "I need Cuomo's measured bullying, his love of circumventing the federal government"—a sort of authoritarianism with a human face, or, at best, government as competent management. But if Trumpism has taught us anything, it's that mere competence—no matter how many lives it may save in a time of crisis—cannot defeat the promise of the return to an imaginary past. For the brief moment of a virtual Trump–Cuomo stand-off, two visions of the past competed: the romantic Trumpian one against Cuomo's implied promise of a return to a time of efficient technocratic government.

We relate to the virus, in some ways, as we relate to Trump. We yearn desperately to return to a time of imagined normalcy, before Trump and before the coronavirus. But we can heal only by looking forward—perhaps to a life that will be slower, more environmentally responsible and less materially comfortable, but also more clearly rooted in mutual aid and the understanding of our fundamental equality and interdependence. Now that the pandemic, aided by Trump, has stripped our politics and our society to the bare basics, the question facing Americans is, What do we want our future to look like? Will we, as we did after 9/11, sacrifice civil liberties and human rights? Will we, as we did in response to the financial crisis of 2008, create even greater wealth inequality? Will we, in other words, choose solutions that exacerbate the root problems? In 2020, that would mean forfeiting more freedoms, accepting ever greater inequality, and reelecting Trump. Or will we commit ourselves to reinvention?

**April 2020
New York City / Falmouth, Massachusetts**

ACKNOWLEDGMENTS

I am, as ever, grateful to my agent, Elyse Cheney, who, after twenty years and ten books together, is more of a guardian angel. This book would not have been possible without the support of the New America Foundation, where I was a fellow in 2019, and the Civitella Ranieri Foundation, where I was a director's guest in August 2019. It also would not have been possible without the help, faith, and guidance of several editors. Hugh Eakin at **The New York Review of Books** edited and published the original "Autocracy: Rules for Survival" essay; he apparently believed I was in a position to comment on U.S. politics. David Remnick invited me to join the staff at **The New Yorker**, where Jessica Winter has been helping me think and write more clearly

ACKNOWLEDGMENTS

for almost three years. Rebecca Saletan at Riverhead guided me through several drafts of this book until I finally found the voice and the distance from which the story needed to be told. And no one read more iterations of this book and gave me more unsparing advice and loving encouragement than Julia Loktev.

NOTES

PROLOGUE

xiii **about the pandemic:** "Read President Trump's Speech on Coronavirus Pandemic: Full Transcript," **The New York Times,** March 11, 2020. https://www .nytimes.com/2020/03/11/us/poli tics/trump-coronavirus-speech.html.

xiii **the genetic code of the virus:** Lisa Schnirring, "China Releases Genetic Data on New Coronavirus, Now Deadly," CIDRAP News, January 11, 2020. http://www.cidrap .umn.edu/news-perspective/2020/01 /china-releases-genetic-data-new-coro navirus-now-deadly.

xiv **wasted most of that time:** Lori Dajose, "The Tip of the Iceberg: Virologist David Ho (BS '74) Speaks About COVID-19," Caltech.edu, March 20, 2020. https://www.caltech .edu/about/news/tip-iceberg-virolo gist-david-ho-bs-74-speaks-about -covid-19?fbclid=IwAR3smTvmGi NmAOAOsNEq8ecFae0EIy1kG pjUq2H7D34pHrDksPV5NLc6Src.

xiv **had been kept secret:** Aram Roston and Marisa Taylor, "Exclusive: White House Told Federal Health Agency to Classify Coronavirus Deliberations—Sources." Reuters, March 11, 2020. https://www .reuters.com/article/us-health-corona virus-secrecy-exclusive/exclusive -white-house-told-federal-health -agency-to-classify-coronavirus-delib erations-sources-idUSKBN20Y2LM.

xiv **first American deaths occurred:** Riley Beggin, "First Coronavirus Death in the US Reported in Washington State," Vox, March 1, 2020. https://

www.vox.com/science-and-health
/2020/2/29/21159055/coronavirus
-death-us-south-korea-cases.

xv **"he did fine"**: Ian Schwartz, "Don Lemon Blows Up on John Kasich for Not Hating Trump's Coronavirus Address: 'I Thought He Did Fine,'" RealClear Politics, March 11, 2020. https://www.realclearpolitics.com /video/2020/03/11/don_lemon _blows_up_on_john_kasich_for _not_hating_trumps_coronavirus_ad dress_i_thought_he_did_fine.html.

xvi **"No, I don't take responsibility"**: James Fallows, "2020 Time Capsule #3: 'I Don't Take Responsibility at All.'" **The Atlantic**, March 13, 2020. https:// www.theatlantic.com/notes/2020/03 /2020-time-capsule-3-i-dont-take-re sponsibility-at-all/608005/.

xvi **He would tell governors**: Jordan Fabian, "Trump Told Governors to Buy Own Virus Supplies, Then Outbid Them," Bloomberg, March 19, 2020. https://www.bloomberg.com/news/ar

ticles/2020-03-19/trump-told-gover
nors-to-buy-own-virus-supplies-then
-outbid-them.

xvi **virtues of untested drugs:** Jessica McDonald, "Trump Hypes Potential COVID-19 Drugs, but Evidence So Far Is Slim," FactCheck.org, March 25, 2020. https://www.fact check.org/2020/03/trump-hypes-po tential-covid-19-drugs-but-evidence -so-far-is-slim/.

xvi **rushed to use:** Associated Press in Phoenix, Arizona, "Arizona Man Dies After Attempting to Take Trump Coronavirus 'Cure,'" **The Guardian**, March 24, 2020. https://www.the guardian.com/world/2020/mar/24 /coronavirus-cure-kills-man-after -trump-touts-chloroquine-phos phate.

xvi **He would resist calls:** Salvador Rizzo, "Is Trump Using the Defense Production Act?" **The Washington Post**, March 25, 2020. https://www.wash ingtonpost.com/politics/2020/03/25

/is-trump-using-defense-production
-act/.

xvii **approve of Trump's response:** Aaron
Blake, "Trump's Positive Coronavirus Polls," **The Washington Post**,
March 25, 2020. https://www.wash-
ingtonpost.com/politics/2020/03/25
/trumps-positive-coronavirus-polls/.

CHAPTER 1.
WHAT DO WE CALL IT?

3 **William B. Taylor, Jr., testified:** John
Cassidy, "Why Ambassador William
Taylor's Testimony Was So Damaging to Trump," **The New Yorker**,
October 23, 2019. https://www.new
yorker.com/news/our-columnists/why
-ambassador-william-taylors-testi
mony-was-so-damaging-to-trump\.

4 **House Republicans stormed:** Toluse
Olorunnipa, Josh Dawsey, and Mike
DeBonis, "Republicans Storm Closed-
Door Impeachment Hearing as Es-
calating Ukraine Scandal Threatens

Trump," **The Washington Post**, October 23, 2019. https://www.washingtonpost.com/politics/republicans-storm-closed-door-impeachment-hearing-as-escalating-ukraine-scandal-threatens-trump/2019/10/23/29877c06-f5a5-11e9-8cf0-4cc99f74d127_story.html.

4   **attorney William Consovoy argued:** Ann E. Marimow and Jonathan O'Connell, "In Court Hearing, Trump Lawyer Argues a Sitting President Would Be Immune from Prosecution Even if He Were to Shoot Someone," **The Washington Post**, October 23, 2019. https://www.washingtonpost.com/local/legal-issues/ny-based-appeals-court-to-decide-whether-manhattan-da-can-get-trumps-tax-returns/2019/10/22/8c491346-ef6e-11e9-8693-f487e46784aa_story.html.

4   **launched a criminal probe:** Katie Brenner and Adam Goldman, "Justice Dept. Is Said to Open Criminal Inquiry into Its Own Russia Investigation," **The New**

York Times, October 24, 2019. https://
www.nytimes.com/2019/10/24/us
/politics/john-durham-criminal-in
vestigation.html.

4 **found in contempt of court:** Erica L.
Green and Stacy Cowley, "Betsy DeVos
Is Held in Contempt over Judge's
Order on Loan Collection," **The
New York Times**, October 24, 2019.
https://www.nytimes.com/2019/10
/24/us/politics/education-dept-loan
-repayments-corinthian.html.

5 **"exceedingly rare judicial rebuke":**
Michael Stratford, "DeVos Held in
Contempt for Violating Judge's Order
on Student Loans," **Politico**, October 24, 2019. https://www.politico
.com/news/2019/10/24/judge-holds
-betsy-devos-in-contempt-057012.

8 **autocratic attempt, autocratic break-
through:** Bálint Magyar and Bálint
Madlovics, **The Anatomy of Post
-Communist Regimes: A Conceptual
Framework**, prepublication manu-
script, Fall 2019.

CHAPTER 2.
WAITING FOR THE
REICHSTAG FIRE

10 "Yesterday, before votes": Sarah Larimer, "Here Are Obama's Remarks Following Trump's Win," **The Washington Post**, November 9, 2016. https://www.washingtonpost.com /politics/2016/live-updates/gen eral-election/real-time-updates-on -the-2016-election-voting-and-race -results/here-are-obamas-remarks-fol lowing-trumps-win/.

12 "American civil religion": Sanford Levinson, **Constitutional Faith** (Princeton, NJ: Princeton University Press, 1988).

17 Sedition Act of 1918 "the most repressive": Geoffrey R. Stone, **Perilous Times: Free Speech in Wartime from the Sedition Act of 1798 to the War on Terrorism** (New York: W. W. Norton, 2004), 185.

CHAPTER 3.
THE STYROFOAM PRESIDENT

25 **In his opening remarks:** Coral Davenport, "Scott Pruitt, Testifying to Lead E.P.A., Criticizes Environmental Rules," **The New York Times**, January 18, 2017. https://www.nytimes.com/2017/01/18/us/politics/scott-pruitt-testifying-to-lead-epa-criticizes-environmental-rules.html.

25 **Puzder withdrew his nomination:** Yuki Noguchi, "Trump Labor Nominee Andrew Puzder Withdraws, First Cabinet Pick to Fall," NPR, February 15, 2017. https://www.npr.org/2017/02/15/515425370/trump-labor-pick-andrew-puzders-nomination-appears-in-jeopardy?t=1565543183922\.

26 **a "conventional candidate":** Jim Puzzanghera, "Trump Labor Nominee Acosta Frustrates Democrats by

Dodging Questions at Confirmation Hearing," **Los Angeles Times**, March 22, 2017. https://www.latimes .com/business/la-fi-acosta-labor-hear ing-20170322-story.html.

26 **promised to abolish:** Brad Plumer, "Rick Perry Once Wanted to Abolish the Energy Department. Trump Picked Him to Run It," Vox, December 13, 2016. https://www.vox.com/energy -and-environment/2016/12/13/1393 6210/rick-perry-energy-department -trump\.

27 **betrayed an utter lack of famil- iarity:** Rebecca Mead, "The Betsy DeVos Confirmation Debacle," **The New Yorker**, February 7, 2017. https://www.newyorker.com/news /daily-comment/the-betsy-devos-con firmation-debacle\.

27 **ProPublica compiled a list:** Eric Umansky and Marcelo Rochabrun, "5 Trump Cabinet Members Who've Made False Statements to Congress," ProPublica, March 2, 2017. https://

www.propublica.org/article/five
-trump-cabinet-members-made
-false-statements-to-congress.

27 **DeVos also appeared to have cribbed:**
Mike DeBonis and Emma Brown,
"DeVos Questionnaire Appears to Include Passages from Uncited Sources,"
The Washington Post, January 31,
2017. https://www.washingtonpost
.com/powerpost/devos-questionnaire
-appears-to-include-passages-from-un
cited-sources/2017/01/31/50577dec
-e7be-11e6-b82f-687d6e6a3e7c
_story.html.

28 **As president-elect, Trump opted:**
Rebecca Savransky, "Trump on Intelligence Briefings: 'I Get It When
I Need It,'" **The Hill**, December 11,
2016. https://thehill.com/homenews
/campaign/309840-trump-on-in
telligence-briefings-i-get-it-when-i
-need-it.

33 **the D.C. National Guard lost his job:**
Colin Dwyer, "D.C. National Guard
Commander Told to Step Down on

Inauguration Day," NPR, January 12, 2017. https://www.npr.org/sections/thetwo-way/2017/01/13/509704620/d-c-national-guard-commander-told-to-step-down-on-inauguration-day.

35 **an exact copy:** Amy B. Wang and Tim Carman, "Trump's Inaugural Cake Was Commissioned to Look Exactly Like Obama's, Baker Says," **The Washington Post**, January 22, 2017. https://www.washingtonpost.com/news/food/wp/2017/01/21/trump-had-a-huge-luxurious-inauguration-cake-was-it-plagiarized/.

36 **she was "honored to witness":** Valerie Strauss, "Historic—or 'Historical'—Inauguration? DeVos Tweets the Wrong One, Deletes It, Then Blames Staff," **The Washington Post**, January 21, 2017. https://www.washingtonpost.com/news/answer-sheet/wp/2017/01/20/historic-or-historical-inauguration-devos-the-next-education-secretary-tweets-the-wrong-one/.

36 **diagnosed with the novel coronavirus:**

Tom McCarthy and Ed Pilkington, "The Missing Six Weeks: How Trump Failed the Biggest Test of His Life," **The Guardian**, March 28, 2020. https://www.theguardian.com/us-news/2020/mar/28/trump-coronavirus-politics-us-health-disaster?fbclid=IwAR3J3SP-JcINtoKJipmv_eRGK0Q0Yl1vqDxaBnDueq8RWVFS6BjFe5y27v0.

36 **he was warned:** Shane Harris, Greg Miller, Josh Dawsey, and Ellen Nakashima, "U.S. Intelligence Reports from January and February Warned About a Likely Pandemic," **The Washington Post**, March 20, 2020. https://www.washingtonpost.com/national-security/us-intelligence-reports-from-january-and-february-warned-about-a-likely-pandemic/2020/03/20/299d8cda-6ad5-11ea-b5f1-a5a804158597_story.html.

37 **writing in The Wall Street Journal:** Luciana Borio and Scott Gottlieb, "Act Now to Prevent an American

Epidemic," **The Wall Street Journal**, January 28, 2020. https://www.wsj .com/articles/act-now-to-prevent-an -american-epidemic-11580255335.

37 **coronavirus as a "hoax"**: Oliver Milman, "Seven of Donald Trump's Most Misleading Coronavirus Claims," **The Guardian**, March 31, 2020. https://www.theguardian.com /us-news/2020/mar/28/trump-co ronavirus-misleading-claims.

37 **"It's going to be just fine"**: Matthew J. Belvedere, "Trump Says He Trusts China's Xi on Coronavirus and the US Has It 'Totally Under Control,'" CNBC, January 22, 2020. https:// www.cnbc.com/2020/01/22/trump -on-coronavirus-from-china-we-have -it-totally-under-control.html.

37 **"I like this stuff"**: "Trump on Coro- navirus: 'People Are Really Surprised I Understand This Stuff,'" BBC News, March 9, 2020. https://www.bbc.com /news/av/world-us-canada-51761 880/trump-on-coronavirus-people

-are-really-surprised-i-understand
-this-stuff.

37 **try to correct Trump:** Maggie Haberman, "Trump Has Given Unusual
Leeway to Fauci, but Aides Say He's
Losing His Patience," **The New York
Times**, March 23, 2020. https://www
.nytimes.com/2020/03/23/us/poli
tics/coronavirus-trump-fauci.html.

38 **at great personal risk:** Katie Benner
and Michael D. Shear, "After Threats,
Anthony Fauci to Receive Enhanced
Personal Security," **The New York
Times**, April 1, 2020. https://www
.nytimes.com/2020/04/01/us/poli
tics/coronavirus-fauci-security.html.

38 **at great cost to her reputation:** Noah
Weiland and Maggie Haberman, "For
Dr. Deborah Birx, Urging Calm Has
Come with Heavy Criticism," **The New
York Times**, March 27, 2020. https://
www.nytimes.com/2020/03/27/us
/politics/deborah-birx-coronavirus
.html.

38 **as a "wartime president":** Gaby Orr

and Lara Seligman, "Trump Team's New Mission: Defend the 'Wartime President,'" **Politico**, March 19, 2020. https://www.politico.com/news/2020 /03/19/trump-wartime-president -coronavirus-136892.

CHAPTER 4.
WE COULD CALL IT A KAKISTOCRACY

40 **On the day Trump assumed office:** Burgess Everett, "Trump Set to Take Office Without Most of His Cabinet," **Politico**, January 17, 2017. https://www.politico.com/story/2017 /01/trump-senate-confirmations-slog -233726.

40 **only thirty-four out of seven hundred:** Tal Kopan, "Trump Administration Lags in Filling Key Posts," CNN, February 17, 2017. https:// edition.cnn.com/2017/02/17 /politics/donald-trump-administra tion-slow-appointments/.

40 **he had even reportedly hoped:** Brooke Seipel, "Trump Team Wanted Tanks, Missile Launchers in Parade: Report," **The Hill**, January 19, 2017. https://thehill.com/blogs/blog -briefing-room/news/315184-trump -team-wanted-tanks-missile-launch ers-in-parade-report.

41 **mayor Rudy Giuliani before finally announcing:** Josh Dawsey and Louis Nelson, "Trump Taps Tillerson for Secretary of State," **Politico**, December 13, 2016. https://www.poli tico.com/blogs/donald-trump-admin istration/2016/12/trump-to-name-se cretary-of-state-pick-tuesday-232544.

41 **a slate of executive orders:** Josh Keller, Adam Pearce, and Wilson Andrews, "Tracking Trump's Agenda, Step by Step," **The New York Times**, updated October 1, 2018. https:// www.nytimes.com/interactive/2017 /us/politics/trump-agenda-tracker .html?_r=0&module=inline.

42 **The presidential workday:** Glenn

Thrush and Maggie Haberman, "Trump and Staff Rethink Tactics After Stumbles," **The New York Times**, February 5, 2017. https://www.nytimes.com/2017/02/05/us/politics/trump-white-house-aides-strategy.html?partner=rss&emc=rss&smid=tw-nytpolitics&smtyp=cur&_r=0.

42 **spurred by "random inputs"**: Peter Baker, "Trump's Impulses Now Carry the Force of the Presidency," **The New York Times**, January 25, 2017. https://www.nytimes.com/2017/01/25/us/politics/donald-trump-presidency.html?smid=tw-nytimes&smtyp=cur&_r=0.

45 **at best his phone call delayed**: Tom Chiarella and James Lynch, "The Last Shift: What Really Happened to Those Carrier Jobs That Trump Saved," **Popular Mechanics**, May 15, 2018. https://www.popularmechanics.com/technology/infrastructure/a20066498/carrier-factory-donald-trump-jobs/.

46 **he reportedly asked**: Media Matters

Staff, "MSNBC's Joe Scarborough: Trump Asked Three Times in an Hour Briefing, 'Why Can't We Use Nuclear Weapons?'" Media Matters for America, August 3, 2016. https://www.mediamatters.org/don ald-trump/msnbcs-joe-scarborough -trump-asked-three-times-hour-brief ing-why-cant-we-use-nuclear.

47 **being president was proving harder:** Stephen J. Adler, Jeff Mason, and Steve Holland, "Exclusive: Trump Says He Thought Being President Would Be Easier Than His Old Life," Reuters, April 27, 2017. https://www.reuters .com/article/us-usa-trump-100days -idUSKBN17U0CA.

48 **"domestic political errand"** . . . **"We had all kinds":** Amber Phillips, "'He Was Being Involved in a Domestic Political Errand': Fiona Hill's Take on Gordon Sondland, Annotated," **The Washington Post**, November 21, 2019. https://www.washingtonpost .com/politics/2019/11/21/he-was-be

ing-involved-domestic-political-er
rand-fiona-hills-take-gordon-sond
land-annotated/.

50 **John Bolton either quit or was
fired:** Peter Baker, "Trump Ousts
John Bolton as National Security
Adviser," **The New York Times**,
September 10, 2019. https://www.ny
times.com/2019/09/10/us/politics
/john-bolton-national-security-advis
er-trump.html.

50 **character assassination by rumor:**
Washington Post Staff, "Transcript:
Marie Yovanovitch's Nov. 15 Testimony in Front of the House Intelligence Committee," **The Washington
Post**, November 16, 2019. https://
www.washingtonpost.com/pol
itics/2019/11/16/transcript-marie-yo
vanovitchs-nov-testimony-front-house
-intelligence-committee/.

50 **game of diplomacy-by-racket:** Kyle
Cheney, "'I Have Learned Many
Things': Kurt Volker Revises Ukraine
Testimony," **Politico**, November 19,

2019. https://www.washingtonpost.com/politics/white-house-lawyer-moved-transcript-of-trump-call-to-classified-server-after-ukraine-adviser-raised-alarms/2019/10/30/ba0fbdb6-fb4e-11e9-8190-6be4deb56e01_story.html.

51 **helped cover up the effort:** Carol D. Leonnig, Tom Hamburger, and Greg Miller, "White House Lawyer Moved Transcript of Trump Call to Classified Server After Ukraine Adviser Raised Alarms," **The Washington Post**, October 30, 2019. https://www.washingtonpost.com/politics/white-house-lawyer-moved-transcript-of-trump-call-to-classified-server-after-ukraine-adviser-raised-alarms/2019/10/30/ba0fbdb6-fb4e-11e9-8190-6be4deb56e01_story.html.

51 **it was held up:** Robert P. Baird, "What Went Wrong with Coronavirus Testing in the U.S.," **The New Yorker**, March 16, 2020. https://www.new

yorker.com/news/news-desk/what
-went-wrong-with-coronavirus-test
ing-in-the-us.

CHAPTER 5.
WE COULD CALL IT
CORRUPTION

53 **a forty-five-minute interview:** "Donald Trump's New York Times Interview: Full Transcript," **The New York Times**, November 23, 2016. https://www.nytimes.com/2016/11/23/us/politics/trump-new-york-times-interview-transcript.html.

55 **Ivanka took an office:** Sara Murray and Daniella Diaz, "Roles for Ivanka Trump, Jared Kushner Come into Focus," CNN Politics, December 15, 2016. https://edition.cnn.com/2016/12/14/politics/ivanka-trump-white-house-office-of-the-first-family/.

55 **moved to the West Wing:** Annie Karni, "Ivanka Trump Set to Get West Wing Office as Role Expands,"

Politico, March 20, 2017. https://
secure.politico.com/story/2017/03
/ivanka-trump-white-house-236273.

55 **She joined her father in a meeting:** Will
Worley, "Donald Trump Daughter
Ivanka Pictured in Meeting with Japanese Prime Minister Shinzo Abe," **The
Independent**, November 18, 2016.
https://www.independent.co.uk/news
/people/ivanka-trump-meeting-don
ald-trump-japanese-prime-minister
-shinzo-abe-a7424191.html.

55 **then a meeting with German chancellor:** Anna Iovine, "Photo of Ivanka
Trump and Angela Merkel Raises
Eyebrows," Aol.com, March 20, 2017.
https://www.aol.com/article/news
/2017/03/20/photo-of-ivanka-trump
-and-angela-merkel-raises-eyebrows
/21903159/.

55 **a meeting of G20 leaders:** Abby
Phillip, "Ivanka Trump Takes Fa-
ther's Seat at G-20 Leaders' Table in
Break from Diplomatic Protocol,"
The Washington Post, July 8, 2017.

https://www.washingtonpost.com/pol
itics/ivanka-trump-takes-fathers-seat
-at-g-20-leaders-table-in-break-from
-diplomatic-protocol/2017/07/08/f8
eabe8a-63ea-11e7-a6c7-f769fa1d56
91_story.html.

55 **The Office of Government Ethics disagreed:** Walter M. Shaub, Jr., Director,
United States Office of Government
Ethics, to Senators Elizabeth Warren
and Thomas Carper, April 25, 2017.
https://www.warren.senate.gov/files
/documents/2017_05_01OGE_Re
sponse_Ivanka.pdf. U.S. Senate News-
room, press release, "Warren and
Carper Receive Response from OGE
on Ethical Concerns Raised by Ivanka
Trump's White House Role," May 1,
2017. https://www.warren.senate.gov
/oversight/letters/warren-and-carper-re
ceive-response-from-oge-on-ethical
-concerns-raised-by-ivanka-trump-and
-039s-white-house-role.

56 **Trump made the announcement:**

Jonathan Lemire, "What Was in Those Folders at Donald Trump's Press Conference?" **The Boston Globe**, January 12, 2017. https://www.boston globe.com/news/politics/2017/01 /12/what-was-those-folders-donald -trump-press-conference/BVq5qgR jAKk2rpICgQEOTN/story.html.

56 "a very serious disappointment": Brooke Seipel, "Outgoing Ethics Director: Ethics Program 'A Very Serious Disappointment in the WH,'" **The Hill**, July 7, 2017. https://thehill.com /homenews/news/341080-outgoing -ethics-director-ethics-program-a-very -serious-disappointment-in-the-wh.

57 **Nordstrom dropped Ivanka's foot-wear line:** Rachel Abrams, "Nordstrom Drops Ivanka Trump Brand from Its Stores," **The New York Times**, February 2, 2017. https:// www.nytimes.com/2017/02/02/busi ness/nordstrom-ivanka-trump.html ?module=inline.

NOTES

57 **"My daughter Ivanka"**: Richard W. Painter, "The Lesson of Nordstrom: Do Business with the Trumps or Else," **The New York Times**, February 9, 2017. https://www.nytimes .com/2017/02/09/opinion/the-les son-of-nordstrom-do-business-with -the-trumps-or-else.html?mwrsm =Facebook.

57 **"Go buy Ivanka's stuff"**: Richard Perez-Pena and Rachel Abrams, "Kellyanne Conway Promotes Ivanka Trump Brand, Raising Ethics Concerns," **The New York Times**, February 9, 2017. https://www.nytimes .com/2017/02/09/us/politics/kelly anne-conway-ivanka-trump-ethics .html.

58 **Melania got a settlement:** Owen Bowcott and Holly Watt, "Melania Trump Accepts Daily Mail Damages and Apology in Libel Case," **The Guardian**, April 12, 2017. https://www.the guardian.com/us-news/2017/apr/12

/melania-trump-accepts-damages-and
-apology-from-daily-mail.

59 **the couple remained beneficiaries:**
Jesse Drucker, Eric Lipton, and Maggie
Haberman, "Ivanka Trump and Jared
Kushner Still Benefiting from Business Empire, Filings Show," **The New
York Times**, March 31, 2017. https://
www.nytimes.com/2017/03/31/us
/politics/ivanka-trump-and-jared
-kushner-still-benefiting-from-busi
ness-empire-filings-show.html?emc
=edit_na_20170331&nl=breaking
-news&nlid=60539443&ref=cta
&_r=0.

59 **The Republican National Committee held:** Sam Stein, "The RNC
Is Hosting Its Christmas Party This
Year at Donald Trump's Hotel," **The
Huffington Post**, December 7, 2016.
https://www.huffpost.com/entry/rnc
-donald-trump-party_n_5848cf6ee4
b0f9723d003c70.

59 **Lobbyists for the Saudi Arabian**

government: David A. Fahrenthold and Jonathan O'Connell, "Saudi-Funded Lobbyist Paid for 500 Rooms at Trump's Hotel After 2016 Election," **The Washington Post**, December 5, 2018. https://www.washington post.com/politics/saudi-funded-lobby ist-paid-for-500-rooms-at-trumps -hotel-after-2016-election/2018/12 /05/29603a64-f417-11e8-bc79-6860 4ed88993_story.html.

60 **Zelensky said that during his last visit:** Aaron Blake, "The Full, Rough Transcript of Trump's Call with Ukraine President, Annotated," **The Washington Post**, September 25, 2019. https://www.washingtonpost.com/pol itics/2019/09/25/rough-transcript -trumps-call-with-ukraines-president -annotated/.

60 **produced more allegations of conflicts:** Bill Allison, Jennifer Dlouhy, Anna Edney, Christopher Flavelle, David Kocieniewski, Caleb Melby, Zachary R. Mider, Shahien Nasiripour,

Ari Natter, and David Voreacos, "Trump Team's Conflicts and Scandals: An Interactive Guide," Bloomberg, updated March 14, 2019. https://www.bloomberg.com/graphics/trump-administration-conflicts/.

60 **DeVos was an investor:** "U.S. Office of Government Ethics Report for Betsy DeVos," uploaded to SCRIBD by Josh White. https://www.scribd.com/document/337104757/U-S-Office-of-Government-Ethics-Report-for-Betsy-DeVos.

60 **an investor in gas and steel companies:** Matt Jarzemsky, "Wilbur Ross's Next Big Bet: Oil and Gas," **The Wall Street Journal**, August 20, 2016. https://www.wsj.com/articles/wilbur-rosss-next-big-bet-oil-and-gas-1471690803.

60 **Mick Mulvaney received tens of thousands:** Alan Rappeport, "Payday Rules Relax on Trump's Watch After Lobbying by Lenders," **The New York Times**, February 2, 2018. https://

www.nytimes.com/2018/02/02/us/politics/payday-lenders-lobbying-regulations.html.

60 **Tillerson was in Saudi Arabia:** Hanna Trudo, "Tillerson Hails 'Historic Moment' in U.S.-Saudi Relations," **Politico**, May 20, 2017. https://www.politico.com/story/2017/05/20/rex-tillerson-saudi-arabia-arms-deal-investment-historic-moment-238637.

60 **that country signed a major deal:** "ExxonMobil and SABIC Sign Agreement for Next Phase of Proposed U.S. Petrochemical Project," Exxon-Mobil News, May 20, 2017. https://news.exxonmobil.com/press-release/exxonmobil-and-sabic-sign-agreement-next-phase-proposed-us-petrochemical-project.

60 **Kushner personally brokered:** Mark Landler, Eric Schmitt, and Matt Apuzzo, "$110 Billion Weapons Sale to Saudis Has Jared Kushner's Personal Touch," **The New York Times**, May 18, 2017. https://www.nytimes

.com/2017/05/18/world/middleeast
/jared-kushner-saudi-arabia-arms-deal
-lockheed.html.

61 **Pruitt:** Emily Holden, Anthony
Adragna, and Alex Guillen, "Pruitt Spent
over $105,000 on First-Class Flights,"
Politico, March 20, 2018. https://
www.politico.com/story/2018/03/20
/pruitt-epa-first-class-flights-430700.

61 **Interior Secretary Ryan Zinke:** Ben
Lefebvre, "Zinke Brought Security
Team to Vacation in Turkey and
Greece, Records Show," March 21,
2018. https://www.politico.com/story
/2018/03/21/zinke-security-team-per
sonal-vacation-429302.

61 **Mnuchin:** Victoria Guida, "Mnuchin's
Plane Travel Cost Taxpayers $1 Mil-
lion, Documents Show," **Politico**,
March 15, 2018. https://www.polit
ico.com/story/2018/03/15/steven-
mnuchin-plane-travel-cost-421176.

61 **Carson attempted to order:** Jon Swaine
and Ben Jacobs, "US Official: I Was
Demoted for Rejecting Ben Carson's

Costly Office Revamp," The Guardian, February 27, 2018. https://www.theguardian.com/us-news/2018/feb/27/hud-ben-carson-office-redecoration-trump-appointee.

62 **Officials tried to persuade:** Katrin Bennhold and David E. Sanger, "U.S. Offered 'Large Sum' to German Company for Access to Coronavirus Vaccine Research, German Officials Say," The New York Times, March 15, 2020. https://www.nytimes.com/2020/03/15/world/europe/cornonavirus-vaccine-us-germany.html.

62 **bid against one another:** Sarah Mervosh and Katie Rogers, "Governors Fight Back Against Coronavirus Chaos: 'It's Like Being on Ebay with 50 Other States,'" The New York Times, March 31, 2020. https://www.nytimes.com/2020/03/31/us/governors-trump-coronavirus.html.

62 **gave Jared Kushner broad authority:** Adam Cancryn and Dan Diamond, "Behind the Scenes, Kushner Takes

Charge of Coronavirus Response," **Politico**, April 1, 2020. https://www.politico.com/news/2020/04/01/jared-kushner-coronavirus-response-160553.

CHAPTER 6.
WE COULD CALL IT
ASPIRATIONAL AUTOCRACY

69 "It is not hard to see why Trump might choose": Timothy Snyder, "Trump's Putin Fantasy," **The New York Review of Books**, April 19, 2016. https://www.nybooks.com/daily/2016/04/19/trumps-putin-fantasy/.

69 **Trump admired Putin's grip on power:** James Fallows, "Trump Time Capsule #96: 'Putin Has an 82 Percent Approval Rating!'" **The Atlantic**, September 7, 2016. https://www.theatlantic.com/notes/2016/09/trump-time-capsule-96-putin-has-an-82-percent-approval-rating/499100/.

69 "a leader far more than our president": Jacob Pramuk, "Trump: Putin

Has Been a Leader 'Far More' Than Obama," CNBC.com, September 7, 2016. https://www.cnbc.com/2016/09/07/trump-putin-has-been-a-leader-far-more-than-obama.html.

70 **"He goes in, he takes over"**: Evan McMurry, "Trump on North Korean Leader Kim Jong-un: 'You Gotta Give Him Credit,'" ABC News, January 10, 2016. https://abcnews.go.com/Politics/trump-north-korean-leader-kim-jong-gotta-give/story?id=36198345.

70 **"We fell in love"**: Philip Rucker and Josh Dawsey, "'We Fell in Love': Trump and Kim Shower Praise, Stroke Egos on Path to Nuclear Negotiations," **The Washington Post**, February 25, 2019. https://www.washingtonpost.com/politics/we-fell-in-love-trump-and-kim-shower-praise-stroke-egos-on-path-to-nuclear-negotiations/2019/02/24/46875188-3777-11e9-854a-7a14d7fec96a_story.html.

70 **Trump invited Philippine dictator:**

Reuters, "Donald Trump Invites Rodrigo Duterte to Washington," **The Guardian**, April 30, 2017. https://www.theguardian.com/us-news/2017/apr/30/donald-trump-invites-rodrigo-duterte-to-washington.

70 **lauded him for his war against drugs:** Reuters, "Donald Trump Tells Duterte: 'You're Doing a Great Job,' Philippines Claims," **The Guardian**, May 3, 2017. https://www.theguardian.com/world/2017/may/03/trump-tells-duterte-youre-doing-a-great-job-philippines-claims.

70 **an honorary gold collar:** Julia Reinstein, "What Exactly Did Trump Just Do Before the Saudi King?" BuzzFeed, May 20, 2017. https://www.buzzfeednews.com/article/juliareinstein/trump-saudi-king.

70 **was murdered inside the Saudi embassy:** "Khashoggi Killing: UN Human Rights Expert Says Saudi Arabia Is Responsible for 'Premeditated Execution,'" United Nations Human Rights,

Office of the High Commissioner, June 19, 2019. https://www.ohchr.org /EN/NewsEvents/Pages/DisplayNews .aspx?NewsID=24713&LangID=E.

70 **Trump's statement in response:** The White House, "Statement from President Donald J. Trump on Standing with Saudi Arabia," November 20, 2018. https://www.whitehouse.gov /briefings-statements/statement-presi dent-donald-j-trump-standing-saudi -arabia/.

71 **They addressed each other:** Peter Baker and Ian Fisher, "Trump Comes to Israel Citing a Palestinian Deal as Crucial," **The New York Times**, May 22, 2017. https://www.nytimes .com/2017/05/22/world/middleeast /trump-israel-visit.html.

71 **proclamation recognizing Jerusalem:** Proclamation No. 9683, 82 Fed. Reg. 236 (Dec. 11, 2017). https://www .whitehouse.gov/presidential-actions /presidential-proclamation-recogniz ing-jerusalem-capital-state-israel-relo

cating-united-states-embassy-israel-je
rusalem/.

71 **declaring that international law:**
Karen DeYoung, Steve Hendrix, and
John Hudson, "Trump Administration
Says Israel's West Bank Settlements
Do Not Violate International Law,"
The Washington Post, November 18,
2019. https://www.washingtonpost
.com/national-security/trump-admin
istration-says-israels-west-bank-settle
ments-do-not-violate-international
-law/2019/11/18/38cdbb96-0a39-11
ea-bd9d-c628fd48b3a0_story.html.

71 **"the most beautiful piece of chocolate
cake":** Tom Phillips, "Trump Told
Xi of Syria Strikes over 'Beautiful Piece
of Chocolate Cake,'" **The Guardian**,
April 12, 2017. https://www.theguar
dian.com/us-news/2017/apr/12
/trump-xi-jinping-chocolate-cake-syr
ia-strikes.

72 **making the Republican Party genuflect:** Ben Jacobs, "Republicans
Celebrate with Trump After House

Passes Tax Bill—Again," **The Guardian**, December 20, 2017. https://www.theguardian.com/us-news/2017/dec/20/republicans-plan-celebration-with-trump-after-house-passes-tax-bill-again.

72 **"Our kind Father in Heaven":** Jennifer Hansler, "Ben Carson Leads Trump Cabinet in Prayer," CNN Politics, December 20, 2017. https://www.cnn.com/2017/12/20/politics/ben-carson-prayer-cabinet-meeting/index.html.

74 **"You're up there, you've got":** Jacob Pramuk, "'Un-American' and 'Treasonous': Trump Goes After Democrats Who Didn't Clap During State of the Union," CNBC, February 5, 2018. https://www.cnbc.com/2018/02/05/trump-calls-democrats-un-american-and-treasonous.html.

76 **the White House ordered administration employees:** "Trump Orders Two Ex-White House Aides Not to Testify at House Hearing on

Tuesday," Reuters, September 16, 2019. https://www.reuters.com/article/us-usa-trump-impeachment/trump-orders-two-ex-white-house-aides-not-to-testify-at-house-hearing-on-tuesday-idUSKBN1W203Y.

77 **called to congratulate Erdoğan:** Mark Lander, "Trump Congratulates Erdogan on Turkey Vote Cementing His Rule," The New York Times, April 17, 2017. https://www.nytimes.com/2017/04/17/us/politics/trump-erdogan-turkey-referendum.html?module=inline.

77 **lauded him as an ally:** Julie Hirschfeld Davis and Mark Lander, "Trump Praises Erdogan as Ally in Terrorism Fight, Brushing Aside Tensions," The New York Times, May 16, 2017. https://www.nytimes.com/2017/05/16/world/middleeast/erdogan-turkey-trump.html?smid=tw-nytimes&smtyp=cur&_r=0&referer=https://t.co/44V37e0Bi7.

77 **The day of that visit:** Nicholas Fandos and Christopher Mele, "Erdogan Security Forces Launch 'Brutal Attack' on Washington Protesters, Officials Say," **The New York Times**, May 17, 2017. https://www.nytimes.com/2017/05/17/us/turkish-embassy-protest-dc.html.

CHAPTER 7.
WE COULD PRETEND HE IS AN ALIEN, OR CALL IT THE GOVERNMENT OF DESTRUCTION

82 now claiming that millions of immigrants: Philip Bump, "Yet Again, Trump Falsely Blames Illegal Voting for Getting Walloped in California," **The Washington Post**, July 23, 2019. https://www.washingtonpost.com/politics/2019/07/23/yet-again-trump-falsely-blames-illegal-voting-getting-walloped-california/.

82 **that Obama had had him wiretapped:**

Eugene Kiely, "Revisiting Trump's Wiretap Tweets," FactCheck.org, September 22, 2017. https://www.fact check.org/2017/09/revisiting-trumps -wiretap-tweets/.

82 **Meanwhile, Trump boasted:** Linda Qiu, "Trump Says 'No President Has Ever Cut So Many Regulations.' Not Quite," **The New York Times**, February 23, 2018. https://www.ny times.com/2018/02/23/us/politics /trump-says-no-president-has-ever-cut -so-many-regulations-not-quite.html.

83 **in the State Department either left:** Josh Rogin, "The State Department's Entire Senior Administrative Team Just Resigned," **The Washington Post**, January 26, 2017. https://www.wash ingtonpost.com/news/josh-rogin /wp/2017/01/26/the-state-depart ments-entire-senior-management -team-just-resigned/.

83 **or were fired:** Elise Labott, "Trump Administration Asks Top State Department Officials to Leave," CNN

Politics, January 27, 2017. https://
www.cnn.com/2017/01/26/politics
/top-state-department-officials-asked
-to-leave-by-trump-administration/in
dex.html.

84 **State Department briefings were
suspended:** Kevin Quealy, "'The
Lowest-Profile State Department in
45 Years,' in 2 Charts," **The New York
Times**, updated October 4, 2017.
https://www.nytimes.com/interac
tive/2017/08/01/upshot/lowest-pro
file-state-department-in-decades
.html.

84 **as were the Pentagon's briefings:**
Richard Sisk, "The Drought Is Over:
Pentagon Spokesman Holds 1st Formal Press Briefing," Military.com,
September 20, 2019. https://www
.military.com/daily-news/2019/09
/20/drought-over-pentagon-spokes
man-holds-1st-formal-press-briefing
.html.

84 **effectively discontinued briefings
too:** Karen Yourish and Jasmin C. Lee,

"The Demise of the White House Press Briefing Under Trump," **The New York Times**, updated January 28, 2019. https://www.nytimes.com/inter active/2019/01/22/us/politics/white -house-press-briefing.html.

84 **The Environmental Protection Agency exceeded:** U.S. Environmental Protection Agency, Office of Inspector General, "EPA Exceeded the Deregulatory Goals of Executive Order 13771," Report No. 19-P-0267, August 9, 2019. https://www.epa.gov/sites/production /files/2019-08/documents/_epaoig _20190809-19-p-0267.pdf.

84 **Advisory groups resigned:** Josh Zumbrun, "Donald Trump's Cabinet Won't Include Chairman of CEA," **The Wall Street Journal**, February 9, 2017. https://www.wsj.com/articles/ donald-trumps-cabinet-wont-include -chairman-of-cea-1486670755.

84 **information on climate change disappeared:** Chris Mooney and Juliet Eilperin, "EPA Website Removes

Climate Science Site from Public View After Two Decades," **The Washington Post**, April 29, 2017. https://www.washingtonpost.com/news/energy-environment/wp/2017/04/28/epa-website-removes-climate-science-site-from-public-view-after-two-decades/.

85 **asked Ben Carson about REOs:** Aaron Rupar, "Ben Carson's First Hearing Before Maxine Waters's Committee Was a Disaster," Vox, May 21, 2019. https://www.vox.com/2019/5/21/18634580/ben-carson-oreo-hearing-disaster.

85 **in 2018, NASA, Energy:** "What Trump Proposed Cutting in His 2019 Budget," **The Washington Post**, February 16, 2018. https://www.washingtonpost.com/graphics/2018/politics/trump-budget-2019/.

85 **by 2019, only Commerce:** Kate Rabinowitz and Kevin Uhrmacher, "What Trump Proposed in His 2020 Budget," **The Washington Post**, up-

dated March 12, 2019. https://www
.washingtonpost.com/graphics/2019
/politics/trump-budget-2020/.

85 **Each of the proposed budgets:** Kim
Soffen and Denise Lu, "What Trump
Cut in His Agency Budgets," **The
Washington Post**, updated May 23,
2017. https://www.washingtonpost
.com/graphics/politics/trump-presi
dential-budget-2018-proposal/?utm
_term=.baaa8747fa4e.

86 **packing the courts is packing the
courts:** Elie Mystal, "Donald Trump
and the Plot to Take Over the
Courts," **The Nation**, July 15, 2019.
https://www.thenation.com/article
/trump-mcconnel-court-judges-plot/.

87 **Trump has chosen to bypass:** Philip
Bump, "How Unusual Are Trump's
'Not-Qualified' Judicial Nominations?"
The Washington Post, December 15,
2017. https://www.washingtonpost
.com/news/politics/wp/2017/11/10
/how-unusual-are-trumps-not-quali
fied-judicial-nominations/.

CHAPTER 8.
THE DEATH OF DIGNITY

89 he even distanced himself from Trump's: Matt Ford, "Gorsuch Calls Trump's Attacks on the Judiciary 'Disheartening,'" **The Atlantic**, February 8, 2017. https://www.theatlantic.com/politics/archive/2017/02/gorsuch-trump-criticism/516102/.

89 By the measures of judicial philosophy: "What Does Kavanaugh's Paper Trail Say? Let's Ask the Experts," **The Washington Post**, August 31, 2018. https://www.washingtonpost.com/opinions/what-does-kavanaughs-paper-trail-say-lets-ask-the-experts/2018/08/31/beffd014-ad33-11e8-a8d7-0f63ab8b1370_story.html.

89 he voted with the majority: Robert Barnes, "They're Not 'Wonder Twins': Gorsuch, Kavanaugh Shift the Supreme Court, but Their Differences Are Striking," **The Washington Post**, June 29, 2019. https://www.washing

tonpost.com/politics/courts_law/they
re-not-wonder-twins-gorsuch-kava
naugh-shift-the-supreme-court-but
-their-differences-are-striking/2019
/06/28/63754902-99b6-11e9-916
d-9c61607d8190_story.html?arc404
=true.

90 **On September 27, 2018:** "Kavanaugh Hearing: Transcript," **The
Washington Post**, September 27,
2018. https://www.washingtonpost
.com/news/national/wp/2018/09/27
/kavanaugh-hearing-transcript/.

92 **"I am looking for a fair process":**
Anna North and Li Zhou, "Brett
Kavanaugh's Fox News Interview,
Explained in 5 Phrases," Vox, September 24, 2018. https://www.vox
.com/2018/9/24/17898746/brett-ka
vanaugh-fox-interview-martha-mac
callum-ford.

92 **Kavanaugh acknowledged:** Tara
Golshan, "Read: Brett Kavanaugh's
Written Testimony Denying All
Allegations of Sexual Misconduct,"

Vox, September 26, 2018. https://www.vox.com/2018/9/26/17906226/brett-kavanaugh-written-testimony-sexual-assault.

93 **Trump had called Kavanaugh:** Meg Wagner, Brian Ries, Sophie Tatum, and Paul P. Murphy, "Brett Kavanaugh and Christine Blasey Ford Testify on Sex Assault Allegations," CNN Politics, September 27, 2018. https://edition.cnn.com/politics/live-news/kavanaugh-ford-sexual-assault-hearing/h_b1504fccaafc71fb23fec31ab2885507.

93 **Kavanaugh started shouting:** CBS News, "Brett Kavanaugh's Opening Statement at Senate Hearing," YouTube, 44:38, September 27, 2018. https://www.youtube.com/watch?v=eahnOcp883k.

94 **The president enjoyed the show:** Tucker Higgins, "Trump Sticks by Kavanaugh After Day of Hearings: He 'Showed America Exactly Why I Nominated Him,'" CNBC, Sep-

tember 27, 2018. https://www.cnbc
.com/2018/09/27/trump-sticks-by-ka
vanaugh-after-day-of-hearings-he
-showed-america-exactly-why-i-nomi
nated-him.html.

95 a "female assistant": Matt Stevens, "What We Know About Rachel Mitchell, the Prosecutor Who Questioned Christine Blasey Ford," **The New York Times**, September 26, 2018. https://www.nytimes .com/2018/09/26/us/rachel-mitch ell-bio-facts.html.

95 eighty-three different complaints: "Tenth Circuit Judicial Council Issues Order on Complaints Against Justice Brett M. Kavanaugh," The United States Court of Appeals for the Tenth Circuit, December 18, 2018. https://www.ca10.uscourts.gov/ce /misconduct/kavanaugh-complaints.

95 all of those complaints were dismissed: Zoe Tillman, "All 83 Ethics Complaints Against Justice Brett Kavanaugh Have Been Dismissed for

Good," BuzzFeed News, August 2, 2019. https://www.buzzfeednews.com /article/zoetillman/ethics-complaints -dismissed-brett-kavanaugh-su preme-court.

CHAPTER 9.
MUELLER DID NOT SAVE US

97 **contrasted Mueller's old-money roots:** Marc Fisher and Sari Horwitz, "Mueller and Trump: Born to Wealth, Raised to Lead. Then, Sharply Different Choices," **The Washington Post**, February 23, 2018. https://www.wash ingtonpost.com/politics/mueller-and -trump-born-to-wealth-raised-to-lead -then-sharply-different-choices/20 18/02/22/ad50b7bc-0a99-11e8-8b0d -891602206fb7_story.html.

97 **"America's straightest arrow":** Garrett M. Graff, "What Donald Trump Needs to Know About Bob Mueller and Jim Comey," **Politico**, May 18, 2017. https://www.politico

.com/magazine/story/2017/05/18
/james-comey-trump-special-prosecu
tor-robert-mueller-fbi-215154.

98 "the other end of the spectrum":
"The Trad in Washington," **Die,
Workwear**, 2018. https://diework
wear.com/post/164343953889/the
-trad-in-washington.

98 "a throwback to an earlier regime":
Mattathias Schwartz, "Robert Mueller,
the Master of Silence," **GQ**, November 8, 2018. https://www.gq.com/story
/robert-mueller-master-of-silence.

98 a thirty-five-dollar Casio: David
Taylor, "'America's Straightest Arrow':
Robert Mueller Silent As Urgency
Mounts," **The Guardian**, November 24, 2018. https://www.theguar
dian.com/us-news/2018/nov/23/ro
bert-mueller-profile-donald-trump
-russia-investigation.

99 a sixty-nine-page report on the FBI:
American Civil Liberties Union,
"Unleashed and Unaccountable: The
FBI's Unchecked Abuse of Authority,"

September 4, 2013. https://www
.aclu.org/sites/default/files/assets
/unleashed-and-unaccountable-fbi-re
port.pdf.

100 "although more terrorist attacks were
feared": Marc Fisher and Sari Horow-
itz, "Mueller and Trump: Born to
Wealth, Raised to Lead," **The Washington Post**, February 23, 2018. https://
www.washingtonpost.com/politics
/mueller-and-trump-born-to-wealth
-raised-to-lead-then-sharply-differ
ent-choices/2018/02/22/ad50b7bc
-0a99-11e8-8b0d-891602206fb7
_story.html.

100 the story of Russian interference:
Robert S. Mueller III, "Report on
the Investigation into Russian Interference in the 2016 Presidential
Election: Volume I of II," U.S. Department of Justice, Washington, DC,
March 2019. https://www.justice.gov
/storage/report.pdf.

101 campaign manager Paul Manafort:
Spencer S. Hsu, Rachel Weiner, and

Ann E. Marimow, "Paul Manafort Sentenced to a Total of 7.5 Years in Prison for Conspiracy and Fraud, and Charged with Mortgage Fraud in N.Y.," **The Washington Post**, March 13, 2019. https://www.washingtonpost.com/local/legal-issues/paul-manafort-faces-sentencing-in-washington-in-mueller-special-counsel-case/2019/03/12/d4d55dd4-44d0-11e9-aaf8-4512a6fe3439_story.html.

101 **Trump's personal lawyer:** Devlin Barrett, "President's Former Lawyer Cohen Arrives at Prison to Serve Sentence for Tax, Campaign Finance Crimes," **The Washington Post**, May 6, 2019. https://www.washingtonpost.com/world/national-security/presidents-former-lawyer-to-report-to-prison-on-tax-campaign-finance-charges/2019/05/06/0c70f152-7002-11e9-8be0-ca575670e91c_story.html.

103 **"Finally, we concluded that in the rare case":** Robert S. Mueller III, "Report

on the Investigation into Russian Interference in the 2016 Presidential Election: Volume II of II," U.S. Department of Justice, March 2019, p. 8. https://www.justice.gov/storage /report_volume2.pdf.

105 **including the travel ban:** William Barr, "Former Attorney General: Trump Was Right to Fire Sally Yates," **The Washington Post**, February 1, 2017. https://www.washingtonpost .com/opinions/former-attorney-gen eral-trump-was-right-to-fire-sally -yates/2017/02/01/5981d890-e809-1 1e6-80c2-30e57e57e05d_story.html.

105 **decision to fire FBI director:** William Barr, "Former Attorney General: Trump Made the Right Call on Comey," **The Washington Post**, May 12, 2017. https://www.washing tonpost.com/opinions/former-attor ney-general-trump-made-the-right -call-on-comey/2017/05/12/0e8584 36-372d-11e7-b4ee-434b6d506b37 _story.html.

105 **Trump asked him to serve:** Barr, "Former Attorney General: Trump Made the Right Call on Comey."

105 **an apparently unsolicited memo:** William Barr, "Memorandum Re: Mueller's 'Obstruction' Theory," **The New York Times**, June 8, 2018. https://int.nyt.com/data/document helper/549-june-2018-barr-memo -to-doj-mue/b4c05e39318dd2d13 6b3/optimized/full.pdf#page=1.

105 **"The evidence developed":** "Read: Attorney General Barr's Letter on the Mueller Report's Principal Conclusions," **The Washington Post**, April 30, 2019. https://www .washingtonpost.com/context/read -attorney-general-barr-s-principal-con clusions-of-the-mueller-report/218b8 095-c5e3-4eab-9135-4170f5b3e87f/.

106 **"The summary letter":** "Special Counsel Mueller's Letter to Attorney General Barr," **The Washington Post**, May 1, 2019. https://www.washing tonpost.com/context/special-counsel

-mueller-s-letter-to-attorney-general
-barr/e32695eb-c379-4696-845a-1b4
5ad32fff1/.

108 **It fell to junior Democrats:** Aaron
Rupar, "New Congress Member Creates Stir by Saying of Trump: 'We're
Going to Impeach This Mother-
fucker!'" Vox, January 4, 2019. https://
www.vox.com/policy-and-politics/20
19/1/4/18168157/rashida-tlaib
-trump-impeachment-motherfucker.

108 **supporters of impeachment grew
slowly:** Justin McCarthy, "Congress
Approval, Support for Impeaching
Trump Both Up," Gallup, October 16, 2019. https://news.gallup.com
/poll/267491/congress-approval-sup
port-impeaching-trump.aspx.

CHAPTER 10.
INSTITUTIONS HAVE NOT
SAVED US

110 **"The President must be held accountable":** John Cassidy, "Nancy

Pelosi Finally Goes All In on Impeachment," **The New Yorker**, September 24, 2019. https://www.newyorker.com/news/our-columnists/nancy-pelosi-finally-goes-all-in-on-impeachment.

111 **as paying guests to his properties:** Josh Dawsey and David A. Fahrenthold, "Near the Airport, Ample Parking: Why Trump Says His Florida Golf Club Should Host the Next G-7," **The Washington Post**, August 26, 2019. https://www.washingtonpost.com/politics/trump-sings-the-praises-of-his-resort-in-florida-as-g-7-host-for-2020/2019/08/26/17409c1e-c7ea-11e9-8067-196d9f17af68_story.html.

112 **The incident that the whistleblower chose to report:** "Document: Read the Whistle-Blower Complaint," **The New York Times**, September 26, 2019. https://www.nytimes.com/interactive/2019/09/26/us/politics/whistle-blower-complaint.html.

CHAPTER 11.
WORDS HAVE MEANING, OR
THEY OUGHT TO

120 "system of national cooperation": "How Viktor Orban Hollowed Out Hungary's Democracy," **The Economist**, August 29, 2019. https://www .economist.com/briefing/2019/08/29 /how-viktor-orban-hollowed-out-hun garys-democracy.

121 "It represents an honorable goal": "Prime Minister Viktor Orbán's Speech at the 29th Bálványos Summer Open University and Student Camp," Abouthungary.hu, July 30, 2018. http://abouthungary.hu/speeches-and -remarks/prime-minister-viktor-or bans-speech-at-the-29th-balvanyos -summer-open-university-and-stu dent-camp/.

122 "You know, we have a guest": Dara Lind, "Donald Trump's Feud with the Cast of Hamilton, Explained," Vox, November 21, 2016. https://

www.vox.com/policy-and-politics /2016/11/21/13699046/trump-hamil ton-pence-apologize.

125 **Trump performed the same trick:** Donald J. Trump (@realDonald Trump), "The Greatest Witch Hunt In American History!" Twitter, October 31, 2019, 11:31 a.m. https:// twitter.com/realdonaldtrump/status /1189927952168996865?lang=en.

125 **"witch hunt," which he repeatedly claimed:** Donald J. Trump (@real Don aldTrump), "A total WITCH HUNT with massive conflicts of interest!" Twitter, March 19, 2018, 9:07 a.m. https://twitter.com/realdonald trump/status/975720503997620224 ?lang=en.

125 **was being carried out:** Donald J. Trump (@realDonaldTrump), "This is the single greatest witch hunt of a politician in American history!" Twitter, March 18, 2017, 7:52 a.m. https:// twitter.com/realdonaldtrump/status /865173176854204416?lang=en.

126 flipped the term "fake news": Donald J. Trump (@realDonaldTrump), "The FAKE NEWS media (failing @ny times, @NBCNews, @ABC, @CBS, @CNN) is not my enemy, it is the enemy of the American People!" Twitter, February 17, 2017, 4:48 p.m. https://twitter.com/realdonaldtrump/status/832708293516632065?lang=en.

126 Macedonian teenagers: Saska Cvetkovska, Aubrey Belford, Craig Silverman, and J. Lester Feder, "The Secret Players Behind Macedonia's Fake News Sites," Organized Crime and Corruption Reporting Project, July 18, 2018. https://www.occrp.org/en/spooksandspin/the-secret-players-behind-macedonias-fake-news-sites.

127 Trump called NATO "obsolete": Michael R. Gordon and Nirak Chokshi, "Trump Criticizes NATO and Hopes for 'Good Deals' with Russia," The New York Times, January 15, 2017. https://www.nytimes

.com/2017/01/15/world/europe/don ald-trump-nato.html?module=inline.

127 **others continued to debate:** "Of Course NATO Is Obsolete," **The American Conservative**, February 28, 2018. https://www.theamericanconser vative.com/articles/of-course-nato-is -obsolete/.

127 **maintain that it was:** Christian Whiton, "NATO Is Obsolete," **National Interest**, July 6, 2018. https:// nationalinterest.org/feature/nato-ob solete-25167.

128 **"Number one, there's great":** "Transcript of AP Interview with Trump," Associated Press, April 23, 2017. https://apnews.com/c810d7de280a4 7e88848b0ac74690c83.

131 **"Broadly speaking, postmodernist arguments":** Michiko Kakutani, **The Death of Truth: Notes on Falsehood in the Age of Trump** (New York: Tim Duggan Books, 2018), 47–48.

133 **"We know from experience":** Hannah

Arendt, **The Promise of Politics**, ed. Jerome Kohn (New York: Schocken Books, 2007), 128.

CHAPTER 12.
THE POWER LIE

140 The official Twitter account of the National Park Service retweeted: reported on **The Verge**, January 20, 2017, https://www.theverge.com/2017/1/20/14341882/national-park-service-twitter-account-anti-trump-messages-inauguration.

140 **Trump took time away:** Graham Kates, "Email: Trump 'Directly Involved' in Post-Inauguration Hunt for Rogue Tweeter," CBS News, May 2, 2017. https://www.cbsnews.com/news/trump-rogue-nps-twitter-account/.

141 **He attacked the television networks:** "Remarks by President Trump and Vice President Pence at CIA Headquarters," The White House, January 21, 2017. https://www.white

house.gov/briefings-statements/re marks-president-trump-vice-president -pence-cia-headquarters/.

142 **"We want to play for you"**: Reena Flores, "Sean Spicer Slams Media over Inauguration Crowd Coverage," CBS News, January 21, 2017. https://www .cbsnews.com/news/sean-spicer-me dia-coverage-inauguration-crowd/.

142 **declined to air the press conference live**: Brian Steinberg, "CNN Declines to Air White House Press Conference Live,"Variety,January21,2017.https:// variety.com/2017/tv/news/cnn-white -house-press-conference-sean-spicer -donald-trump-1201966230/.

142 **"Why put him out there"**: "Meet the Press 01/22/17," NBC News, January 1, 2017. https://www.nbcnews .com/meet-the-press/meet-press-01 -22-17-n710491.

148 **Comey said that it wasn't true**: Michael S. Schmidt and Michael D. Shear, "Comey Asks Justice Dept. to Reject Trump's Wiretapping Claim,"

The New York Times, March 5, 2017. https://www.nytimes.com/2017/03 /05/us/politics/trump-seeks-inquiry -into-allegations-that-obama-tapped -his-phones.html.

148 **When, in the fall of 2019, he lied:** Tara Law and Gina Martinez, "NOAA Disputes Its Own Experts, Siding with President Trump over Hurricane Dorian and Alabama. Here's a Full Timeline of the Controversy," **Time**, September 8, 2019. https://time.com /5671606/trump-hurricane-dorian-al abama/.

149 **the United States was prepared:** "Remarks by President Trump After Meeting with Republican Sena- tors," The White House, March 10, 2020. https://www.whitehouse.gov /briefings-statements/remarks-presi dent-trump-meeting-republican-sen ators-2/?utm_source=link&utm_me dium=header.

149 **promised quickly to triumph:** Nolan D. McCaskill, "Trump Predicts

Victory over Coronavirus 'Much Sooner' Than Expected," **Politico**, March 22, 2020. https://www.politico.com/news/2020/03/22/trump-predicts-victory-coronavirus-143459.

149 **had the necessary equipment:** "Coronavirus: Trump Says US in Good Shape to Meet 'Peak,'" BBC News, March 31, 2020. https://www.bbc.com/news/world-us-canada-52101321.

149 **had access to tests:** Noah Weiland, "Anyone Who Wants a Coronavirus Test Can Have One, Trump Says. Not Quite, Says His Administration," **The New York Times**, March 7, 2020. https://www.nytimes.com/2020/03/07/us/politics/trump-coronavirus-messaging.html.

149 **promised health and wealth:** Jim Tankersley, Maggie Haberman, and Roni Caryn Rabin, "Trump Considers Reopening Economy, over Health Experts' Objections," **The New York Times**, March 23, 2020. https://www

.nytimes.com/2020/03/23/business /trump-coronavirus-economy.html.

149 **"I mean it's story after story"**: "Remarks by President Trump in Press Conference," The White House, February 16, 2017. https://www.white house.gov/briefings-statements/re marks-president-trump-press-confer ence/.

151 **Trump re-created Putin's script**: Michelle Ye Hee Lee, "All of the White House's Conflicting Explanations for Comey's Firing: A Timeline," **The Washington Post**, May 12, 2017. https://www.washingtonpost.com /news/fact-checker/wp/2017/05/12 /all-of-the-white-houses-conflict ing-explanations-for-comeys-firing -a-timeline/.

152 **"felt it was a pandemic"**: Katie Rogers, "Trump Now Claims He Always Knew the Coronavirus Would Be a Pandemic," **The New York Times**, March 17, 2020. https://www.ny

times.com/2020/03/17/us/politics/trump-coronavirus.html.

152 **then changed his mind:** Michael D. Shear, "Trump Extends Social Distancing Guidelines Through End of April," **The New York Times**, March 29, 2020. https://www.nytimes.com/2020/03/29/us/politics/trump-coronavirus-guidelines.html.

CHAPTER 13.
THE TWEET TRAP

156 **Jay Rosen's definition, journalism:** Jay Rosen, "The 'Awayness' Problem," **Columbia Journalism Review**, September/October 2013. https://archives.cjr.org/cover_story/the_awayness_problem.php.

158 **Columbia Journalism Review found:** Yochai Benkler, Robert Faris, Hal Roberts, and Ethan Zuckerman, "Study: Breitbart-Led Right-Wing Media Ecosystem Altered

Broader Media Agenda," **Columbia Journalism Review**, March 3, 2017. https://www.cjr.org/analysis/breitbart -media-trump-harvard-study.php.

160 **tracked Trump's lies:** Glenn Kessler, Salvador Rizzo, and Meg Kelly, "President Trump Has Made 12,019 False or Misleading Claims Over 928 Days," **The Washington Post**, August 12, 2019. https://www.washingtonpost .com/politics/2019/08/12/president -trump-has-made-false-or-mislead ing-claims-over-days/.

162 **Rachel Maddow proclaimed:** Maxwell Strachan, "Rachel Maddow Stopped Covering Trump's Tweets, and Her Ratings Soared," **Huffington Post**, March 13, 2017. https:// www.huffpost.com/entry/rachel-mad dow-stopped-covering-trumps-tweets -and-her-ratings-soared_n_58c6c5b 3e4b0ed71826e4248.

162 **"like a silent movie":** Maddow Blog (@MaddowBlog), "Maddow: Better to Treat Trump Regime Like a Silent

Movie #ActionsSpeakLouderThan Words http://snpy.tv/2klcsfe," Twitter, February 6, 2017, 9:22 p.m. https://twitter.com/maddowblog/status/8287 91015981015042.

162 **after Trump tweeted:** Donald J. Trump (@realDonaldTrump), "After consultation with my Generals and military experts, please be advised that the United States Government will not accept or allow. . . ." Twitter, July 26, 2017, 8:55 a.m. https://twitter.com/realdonaldtrump/status/890193981585444864.

162 **a ban on transgender people:** Donald J. Trump (@realDonald Trump), ". . . . Transgender individu-als to serve in any capacity in the U.S. Military. Our military must be focused on decisive and overwhelming. . . .," Twitter, July 26, 2017, 9:04 a.m. https://twitter.com/realdonaldtrump/status/890196164313833472.

163 **More fact-checking followed:** Anya van Wagtendonk, "Trump 'Ordered'

US Companies out of China. Despite Claiming Otherwise, He Can't Do That," Vox, August 2, 2019. https://www.vox.com/2019/8/24/20830954/trade-war-donald-trump-china-hereby-order-us-companies-tariffs-economic-powers-act-1977.

163 **it appeared that:** Keith Bradsher and Alan Rappeport, "Trump Ordered U.S. Companies to Leave China. Is That Possible?" **The New York Times**, August 24, 2019. https://www.nytimes.com/2019/08/24/business/trump-china-trade.html.

164 **"Why is the NFL":** Donald J. Trump (@realDonaldTrump), "Why is the NFL getting massive tax breaks while at the same time disrespecting our Anthem, Flag and Country? Change tax law!" Twitter, October 10, 2017, 6:13 a.m. https://twitter.com/realDonaldTrump/status/917694644481413120.

164 **"It is about time":** Donald J. Trump (@realDonaldTrump), "It is about

time that Roger Goodell of the NFL is finally demanding that all players STAND for our great National Anthem-RESPECT OUR COUNTRY," Twitter, October 11, 2017, 6:47 a.m. https://twitter.com/realDonald Trump/status/918065431939829760.

164 **"to see why so much"**: Donald J. Trump (@realDonaldTrump), "Why Isn't the Senate Intel Committee looking into the Fake News Networks in OUR country to see why so much of our news is just made up-FAKE!" Twitter, October 5, 2017, 6:59 a.m. https:// twitter.com/realDonaldTrump/status /915894251967385600.

164 **"With all of the Fake News"**: Donald J. Trump (@realDonaldTrump), "With all of the Fake News coming out of NBC and the Networks, at what point is it appropriate to challenge their License? Bad for country!" Twitter, October 11, 2017, 9:55 a.m. https:// twitter.com/realDonaldTrump/status /918112884630093825.

165 **The New York Times reminded its readers:** Peter Baker and Cecilia Kang, "Trump Threatens NBC over Nuclear Weapons Report," **The New York Times**, October 11, 2017. https://www.nytimes.com/2017/10/11/us/politics/trump-nbc-fcc-broadcast-license.html?hp&action=click&pgtype=Homepage&clickSource=story-heading&module=first-column-region&region=top-news&WT.nav=top-news.

166 **Trump's Justice Department scuttled:** "Report: Trump Directed Adviser to Pressure DOJ to Block Merger," CNN Business, March 4, 2019. https://www.cnn.com/videos/business/2019/03/04/trump-att-time-warner-merger-phillip-dnt-lead-vpx.cnn.

**CHAPTER 14.
NORMALIZATION IS
(ALMOST) UNAVOIDABLE**

169 **Trump addressed a joint session:** "Remarks by President Trump in Joint Ad-

dress to Congress," The White House, February 28, 2017. https://www.white house.gov/briefings-statements/re marks-president-trump-joint-address-congress/.

169 **"He became president":** Jason Kurtz, "Van Jones on Trump: 'He Became President of the United States in That Moment, Period,'" CNN Politics, March 1, 2017. https://edition .cnn.com/2017/03/01/politics/van -jones-trump-congress-speech-be came-the-president-in-that-moment -cnntv/index.html.

171 **"filled with inaccuracies":** Glenn Kessler and Michelle Ye Hee Lee, "Fact-checking President Trump's Address to Congress," **The Washington Post**, February 28, 2017. https://www.washingtonpost.com /news/fact-checker/wp/2017/02/28 /fact-checking-president-trumps-ad dress-to-congress/.

172 **"I think Donald Trump became":** Mark Hensch, "CNN Host: 'Donald

Trump Became President' Last Night,"
The Hill, April 7, 2017. https://thehill
.com/homenews/administration/327
779-cnn-host-donald-trump-became
-president-last-night.

173 **"We want everyone to listen":** Michael
Oreskes, "NPR Editor: Our Job Is to
Give You the Facts, Not Tell You What
to Think," NPR, September 15, 2016.
https://www.npr.org/sections/npr-ex
tra/2016/09/15/494122407/npr-ed
itor-our-job-is-to-give-you-the-facts
-not-tell-you-what-to-think?utm_me
dium=RSS&utm_campaign=stories
fromnpr.

175 **Reporter Mary Louise Kelly:** Richard
Gonzales, "NPR and the Word 'Liar':
Intent Is Key," NPR, January 25, 2017.
https://www.npr.org/sections/thetwo
-way/2017/01/25/511503605/npr
-and-the-l-word-intent-is-key.

176 **Oreskes was forced to leave:** Sydney
Ember, "Michael Oreskes Quits NPR
amid Sexual Harassment Accusations,"
The New York Times, November 1,

2017. https://www.nytimes.com/2017
/11/01/business/media/mike-oreskes
-npr-sexual-harassment.html.

178 **"To be clear: NPR"**: Elizabeth Jensen, "'Racist,' Not 'Racially Charged': NPR's Thinking on Labeling the President's Tweets," NPR, July 23, 2019. https://www.npr.org/sections/public editor/2019/07/23/744412665/racist -not-racially-charged-npr-s-thinking -on-labeling-the-president-s-tweets.

179 **"Little Rocket Man"**: "Trump: I'll Handle 'Little Rocket Man' Kim Jong-un—video," **Guardian News**, September 23, 2017. https://www.you tube.com/watch?v=ETNKAQGq8Ts.

179 **"I too have a Nuclear Button"**: Peter Baker and Michael Tackett, "Trump Says His 'Nuclear Button' Is 'Much Bigger' Than North Korea's," **The New York Times**, January 2, 2018. https:// www.nytimes.com/2018/01/02/us /politics/trump-tweet-north-korea .html.

179 **get the Nobel Peace Prize**: Simon

Denyer, "Trump Isn't the Only One Wanting a Nobel. Kim Does Too, Report Says," **The Washington Post**, February 27, 2019. https://www.washingtonpost.com/world/2019/02/27/trump-isnt-only-one-wanting-nobel-kim-does-too-report-says/.

180 **"the all-time-in-history"**: David Rohde, "Why Did Donald Trump Welcome American Prisoners Home on Live TV?," **The New Yorker**, May 18, 2018. https://www.newyorker.com/news/daily-comment/why-did-donald-trump-welcome-american-prisoners-home-on-live-tv.

180 **issued a press release:** The White House, press release, "What You Need To Know About The President's Victory For The World By Freeing Three Brave Americans," May 10, 2018. https://www.whitehouse.gov/articles/need-know-presidents-victory-world-freeing-three-brave-americans/.

180 **about his television ratings:** Chris Cillizza, "The Deep Leadership Flaw

Revealed by Trump Touting His Coronavirus Press Conference Ratings," CNN Politics, March 30, 2020. https://www.cnn.com/2020/03/30/politics/donald-trump-coronavirus-daily-briefing-white-house/index.html?et_rid=1824108704&s_campaign=fastforward:newsletter.

180 "number one on Facebook": CBS News (@CBSNews), "President Trump: 'Did You Know I Was Number One on Facebook? I Just Found Out I'm Number One on Facebook. I Thought That Was Very Nice, for Whatever It Means,'" Twitter, April 1, 2020, 6:13 p.m. https://twitter.com/cbsnews/status/1245474437568348160.

180 "Based on the tremendous anger": "Read: President Donald Trump's letter to Kim Jong Un Canceling the Summit," CNN Politics, May 24, 2018. https://edition.cnn.com/2018/05/24/politics/donald-trump-letter-kim-jong-un/index.html.

181 a thoughtful analysis: Michael

Barbaro, "Listen to 'The Daily': 'Dear Mr. Chairman . . .'" **The New York Times**, May 25, 2018. https://www .nytimes.com/2018/05/25/podcasts /the-daily/trump-north-korea-sum mit.html.

181 **The Wall Street Journal reported:** Vivian Salama, Rebecca Ballhaus, Andrew Restuccia, and Michael C. Bender, "President Trump Eyes a New Real-Estate Purchase: Greenland," **The Washington Post**, August 16, 2019. https://www.wsj.com/articles/trump -eyes-a-new-real-estate-purchase -greenland-11565904223.

182 **confirmed his interest and tweeted:** Lauren Gambino, "Trump Tweets Image of Enormous Trump Tower on Greenland," **The Guardian**, August 19, 2019. https://www.theguard ian.com/world/2019/aug/19/trump -greenland-tower.

182 **The Danish prime minister:** Matthew Robinson, "Trump Cancels Denmark Visit After PM Rejects Greenland

Sale," **The Times**, August 21, 2019. https://www.thetimes.co.uk/article /trump-cancels-denmark-visit-after -pm-rejects-greenland-sale-28xp3drzx.

183 **wrote a piece explaining:** Anne Applebaum, "Why, Actually, Do We Need Denmark?," **The Washington Post**, August 23, 2019. https://www .washingtonpost.com/opinions/glo bal-opinions/why-actually-do-we -need-denmark/2019/08/23/cf9224 40-c5ba-11e9-b72f-b31dfaa77212 _story.html.

184 **"very stable genius":** Donald J. Trump (@realDonaldTrump), ". . . . to Pres- ident of the United States (on my first try). I think that would qualify as not smart, but genius. . . . and a very stable genius at that!" Twitter, January 6, 2018, 7:30 a.m. https:// twitter.com/realDonaldTrump/sta tus/949619270631256064.

184 **"Certain violations of the social compact":** Judith Herman, **Trauma and Recovery: The Aftermath of**

Violence—From Domestic Abuse to Political Terror (New York: Basic Books, 2015).

CHAPTER 15.
RESISTING TRUMP'S WAR ON THE MEDIA

188 "Some people in the press": "Trump Backs Off White House Press Room Move, Wants Staff to Choose Access," Newsweek, January 18, 2017. https://www.newsweek.com/donald-trump-press-white-house-press-room-white-house-white-house-daily-544222.

189 "I want you to quote this": Michael M. Grynbaum, "Trump Strategist Stephen Bannon Says Media Should 'Keep Its Mouth Shut,'" The New York Times, January 26, 2017. https://www.nytimes.com/2017/01/26/business/media/stephen-bannon-trump-news-media.html.

189 Trump seized the phrase: Tom Kludt, "Trump Echoes Bannon: Media Is

'Opposition Party,'" CNN Business, January 27, 2017. https://money.cnn .com/2017/01/27/media/opposi tion-party-media-donald-trump /index.html?sr=fbCNN012717op position-party-media-donald-trump 1043PMVODtopVideo&linkId =33868769&fbclid=IwAR3_AIM Wj6gSXAPpiuzjSyS3xpdFv-qTakbiP BrSVpxpHi1Zr8UaF7JJg_s.

189 **"the enemy of the American people":** Michael M. Grynbaum, "Trump Calls the News Media the 'Enemy of the American People,'" **The New York Times**, February 17, 2017. https:// www.nytimes.com/2017/02/17/busi ness/trump-calls-the-news-media-the -enemy-of-the-people.html.

190 **had held press conferences:** "Presidential News Conferences," The American Presidency Project. https:// www.presidency.ucsb.edu/statistics /data/presidential-news-conferences\.

190 **the so-called protective pool:** National Press Club, "National Press

Organizations Direct Letter to President-elect Trump," Cision, November 16, 2016. https://www.prnews wire.com/news-releases/national -press-organizations-direct-letter -to-president-elect-trump-3003643 09.html.

190 **became extinct in stages:** Karen Yourish and Jasmine C. Lee, "The Demise of the White House Press Briefing Under Trump," **The New York Times**, January 28, 2019. https://www.ny times.com/interactive/2019/01/22 /us/politics/white-house-press-brief ing.html.

191 **"Why don't you act":** John Bowden, "Trump Clashes with Reporter During Coronavirus Briefing: 'Be Nice,'" **The Hill**, March 29, 2020. https:// thehill.com/homenews/administra tion/490093-trump-gets-in-back -and-forth-with-reporter-during-coro navirus.

192 **Grisham gave her first media interview:** Tim Hains, "WH Press

Secretary Stephanie Grisham Blasts Scaramucci in First TV Interview: 'His Feelings Seem to Be Hurt,'" Real Clear Politics, August 15, 2019. https://www.realclearpolitics.com/video/2019/08/15/wh_press_secretary_stephanie_grisham_blasts_scaramucci_in_first_tv_interview_his_feelings_seem_to_be_hurt.html.

192 **Sanders began by saying:** Masha Gessen, "The Degrading Ritual of Sarah Huckabee Sanders's Pre-Thanksgiving Press Briefing," **The New Yorker**, November 21, 2017. https://www.newyorker.com/news/our-columnists/degrading-ritual-sarah-huckabee-sanders-pre-thanksgiving-press-briefing.

201 **the White House suspended:** Joshua Rothman, "The White House's Video of Jim Acosta Shows How Crude Political Manipulation Can Be," **The New Yorker**, November 8, 2018. https://www.newyorker.com/news/current/the-white-houses-video-of-jim-acos

ta-shows-how-crude-political-manip
ulation-can-be.

202 **argued for a boycott:** Jane Merrick, "The Entire White House Press Corps Should Walk Out and Stop Indulging This Bully," CNN Opinion, November 8, 2018. https://edi tion.cnn.com/2018/11/08/opinions /the-white-house-press-corps-should -walk-out-opinion-intl/index.html.

202 **In response to the ruling:** Paul Farhi, "White House Imposes New Rules on Reporters' Credentials, Raising Concerns About Access," **The Washington Post**, May 8, 2019. https://www.wash ingtonpost.com/lifestyle/style/white -house-imposes-new-rules-on-re porters-credentials-raising-concerns -about-access/2019/05/08/793dc4 04-71dd-11e9-9eb4-0828f5389013 _story.html.

205 **"Look: they can't visit":** Jay Rosen, "Send the Interns," Press Think, January 22, 2017. http://pressthink .org/2017/01/send-the-interns/.

206 **Gitlin analyzed a Times story:**
Todd Gitlin, "The Times Still Pulls
Its Punches: Why Is the Leadership of
the 'Opposition Party' Still Mincing
Words?," **Salon**, March 30, 2017.
https://www.salon.com/2017/03
/30/the-times-still-pulls-its-punches
-why-is-the-leadership-of-the-oppo
sition-party-still-mincing-words
_partner/.

208 **paper carried the headline:** Gabriel
Snyder, "Times Public Editor: The
Readers Versus the Masthead," **Columbia Journalism Review**, August 6,
2019. https://www.cjr.org/public_ed
itor/nyt-headline-trump-mass-shoot
ings.php.

208 **It misrepresented the substance:**
Campbell Robertson, Mitch Smith,
and Rick Rojas, "The Aftermath of
Shootings in Ohio and Texas," **The New
York Times**, August 5, 2019. https://
www.nytimes.com/2019/08/05/us
/mass-shootings.html.

209 **a crisis that Baquet addressed:** Ashley

Feinberg, "The New York Times Unites vs. Twitter," **Slate**, August 15, 2019. https://slate.com/news-and-politics/2019/08/new-york-times-meeting-transcript.html.

212 **"We have to remember"**: Morgan Phillips, "NY Times Staffers Speak to CNN About Internal Tensions: 'We Are Not F—ing Part of the Resistance,'" Mediaite, August 14, 2019. https://www.mediaite.com/news/ny-times-staffers-speak-to-cnn-about-internal-tensions-we-are-not-f-ing-part-of-the-resistance/.

212 **story of the USNS Comfort**: Michael Schwirtz, "The 1,000-Bed Comfort Was Supposed to Aid New York. It Has 20 Patients," **The New York Times**, April 2, 2020. https://www.nytimes.com/2020/04/02/nyregion/ny-coronavirus-usns-comfort.html.

213 **"Trump Suggests Lack of Testing"**: Jonathan Martin, Maggie Haberman, and Mike Baker, "Trump Suggests Lack of Testing Is No Longer a Problem.

Governors Disagree," **The New York Times**, March 30, 2020. https://www
.nytimes.com/2020/03/30/us/politics
/trump-governors-coronavirus-test
ing.html?searchResultPosition=2.

213 **"This is journalistic malpractice":**
Gregg Gonsalves (@Gregggonsalves),
"This Is Journalistic Malpractice. If
We Don't Have Scale-Up of Test-
ing, We Will Be in Lock-Down for
Months & Months. There Is No
Debate on This, Why Frame It Like
There Is One? Next: Trump Says
Earth Flat, Scientists Say Other-
wise. @jmartNYT & @maggieNYT,"
Twitter, March 31, 2020, 8:21 a.m.
https://twitter.com/gregggonsalves
/status/1244962905617031170.

213 **"You're picking the wrong":** Jonathan Martin (@jmartNYT), "you're
picking the wrong fight, move along,"
Twitter, March 31, 2020, 9:21 a.m.
https://twitter.com/jmartNYT/status
/1244975910350192640.

216 **All traditional media organizations:**

SPJ Ethics Committee, "Political Involvement," Society of Professional Journalists, accessed January 9, 2020. https://www.spj.org/ethics-papers -politics.asp.

216 **some news reporters abstain:** Anna Clark, "Political Journalists on Why They Do—or Don't—Vote in the Primaries," **Columbia Journalism Review**, March 11, 2016. https://www .cjr.org/united_states_project/politi cal_reporters_primary_voting.php.

CHAPTER 16.
HOW POLITICS DIES

219 **called his speech "inoffensive":** Aaron Rupar, "Trump's 'Salute to America' Speech Wasn't as Bad as Some Feared. But It Was Still Weird," Vox, July 4, 2019. https://www.vox .com/2019/7/4/20682674/trump-sa lute-to-america-speech-recap.

219 **"not a complete authoritarian**

nightmare": Joshua Keating, "Donald Trump's 'Salute to America' Was Not a Complete Authoritarian Nightmare," **Slate**, July 4, 2019. https://slate .com/news-and-politics/2019/07 /trumps-speech-at-the-salute-to-ameri ca-was-pretty-tame.html.

219 **The Times noted that:** Michael D. Shear, "With Flyovers and Flags, Trump Plays M.C. for the Fourth," **The New York Times**, July 4, 2019. https:// www.nytimes.com/2019/07/04/us /politics/trump-4thjuly.html?action =click&module=Top%20Stories&pg type=Homepage.

220 **"the whole thing was pretty stan-dard":** Josh Marshall, "Low Energy," Talking Points Memo, July 4, 2019. https://talkingpointsmemo.com/ed blog/low-energy-5.

220 **Trump's most recent predecessors:** Jackie Calmes, "Obama Marks Fourth with New U.S. Citizens," **The New York Times**, July 4, 2012. https://

www.nytimes.com/2012/07/05/us
/politics/obama-starts-fourth-of-july
-with-new-citizens.html.

220 "Perhaps more than any other nation":
Weekly Compilation of Presidential
Documents, vol. 36, no. 26, 1585.

221 Reagan lit the torch: "Liberty Week-
end/The Statue; Notebook: Reagan
Amid 'All the Hoopla,'" The New York
Times, July 6, 1986. https://www.ny
times.com/1986/07/06/nyregion/li
berty-weekend-the-statue-notebook
-reagan-amid-all-the-hoopla.html.

223 issued an urgent report: Jennifer L.
Costello, "Management Alert—DHS
Needs to Address Dangerous Over-
crowding and Prolonged Detention of
Children and Adults in the Rio Grande
Valley," Office of Inspector General,
Department of Homeland Security,
July 2, 2019. https://int.nyt.com/data
/documenthelper/1358-ig-report-mi
grant-detention/2dd9d40be6a6b0cd
3619/optimized/full.pdf#page=1.

223 "concentration camps": Masha Gessen, "The Unimaginable Reality of American Concentration Camps," **The New Yorker**, June 21, 2019. https://www.newyorker.com/news/our-columnists/the-unimaginable-reality-of-american-concentration-camps.

225 **Trump kept retweeting photographs:** Donald J. Trump (@realDonaldTrump), Twitter video, July 4, 2019. https://twitter.com/realdonaldtrump/status/11469810845314416664?lang=en.

226 **"This union of corrected wrongs":** "Remarks of Gerald R. Ford in Philadelphia, Pennsylvania (Bicentennial Celebration)," July 4, 1976, Gerald R. Ford Presidential Library & Museum. https://www.fordlibrarymuseum.gov/library/speeches/760645.asp.

227 **"On a day like this, we celebrate":** "Remarks by the President at Fourth of July Celebration," Obama White House Archive, July 4, 2016. https://

obamawhitehouse.archives.gov/the
-press-office/2016/07/04/remarks
-president-fourth-july-celebration.

CHAPTER 17.
A WHITE MALE SUPREMACIST PRESIDENCY

236 "We condemn in the strongest": Chris Cillizza, "Donald Trump's Incredibly Unpresidential Statement on Charlottesville," CNN.com, August 13, 2017. https://www.cnn.com/2017/08/12/politics/trump-charlottesville-statement/index.html.

236 "Blood and Soil": Meg Wagner, "'Blood and Soil': Protesters Chant Nazi Slogan in Charlottesville," CNN.com, August 12, 2017. https://www.cnn.com/2017/08/12/us/charlottesville-unite-the-right-rally/index.html.

236 "The Nazis, the KKK and white supremacists": Ted Cruz (@SenTedCruz), Twitter, August 12, 2017, 9:27

p.m. https://twitter.com/SenTedCruz/status/896543609440407553\.

237 "Very important for the nation": Marco Rubio (@marcorubio), Twitter, August 12, 2017, 5:30 p.m. https://twitter.com/marcorubio/status/896483980857532416?lang=en.

238 **Trump dissolved the Manufacturing Council:** Jacob Pramuk, Patti Domm, and Kevin Breuninger, "Trump Abruptly Ends Manufacturing Council After CEOs Disband Strategic and Policy Forum," CNBC.com, August 16, 2017. https://www.cnbc.com/2017/08/16/trump-abruptly-ends-manufacturing-council-after-ceos-disband-strategy-and-policy-forum.html.

CHAPTER 18.
"THROW OFF THE MASK OF HYPOCRISY"

242 **revised its mission statement:** Ryan Devereaux, "U.S. Citizenship and

Immigration Services Will Remove 'Nation of Immigrants' from Mission Statement," theintercept.com, February 22, 2018. https://theinter cept.com/2018/02/22/u-s-citizen ship-and-immigration-services-will -remove-nation-of-immigrants-from -mission-statement/.

243 **revoking birthright citizenship:** John Cassidy, "Donald Trump Launches Operation Midterms Diversion," **The New Yorker**, October 30, 2018. https:// www.newyorker.com/news/our-col umnists/donald-trump-launches-op eration-midterms-diversion.

244 **"shithole countries":** Masha Gessen, "Trump, 'Shitholes,' and the Nature of Us," newyorker.com. January 21, 2018. https://www.newyorker.com /news/our-columnists/trump-shit holes-and-the-nature-of-us.

244 **"Certain Washington politicians":** Raj Shah, quoted in Seung Min Kim and Matthew Nussbaum, "White House Doesn't Deny Trump's 'Shithole' Immi-

gration Remark," January 11, 2018, **Politico**, https://www.politico.com/story /2018/01/11/trump-shithole-immi gration-remark-337070.

244 **a task force to identify people:** Masha Gessen, "In America, Naturalized Citizens No Longer Have an Assumption of Permanence," newyork er.com, June 18, 2018. https://www .newyorker.com/news/our-column ists/in-america-naturalized-citizens -no-longer-have-an-assumption-of -permanence.

246 **human tendency to "self-privilege":** Moshe Halbertal, **On Sacrifice** (Princeton, NJ: Princeton University Press, 2015).

247 **"throw off the mask of hypocrisy":** Hannah Arendt, **The Origins of Totalitarianism** (New York: Harcourt Brace Jovanovich, 1973), 156.

CHAPTER 19.
THE ANTIPOLITICS OF FEAR

247 **Trump signed an executive order:** "Enhancing Public Safety in the Interior of the United States," Executive Order 13768, The White House, January 25, 2017. https://www.white house.gov/presidential-actions/exec utive-order-enhancing-public-safety -interior-united-states/.

250 **the Obama administration had deported:** Department of Homeland Security, 2017 Yearbook of Immigration Statistics, Table 39. https:// www.dhs.gov/immigration-statistics /yearbook/2017/table39.

250 **"Criminal aliens routinely victimize":** John Kelly, "Enforcement of the Immigration Laws to Serve the National Interest," internal memo, US Department of Homeland Security, February 20, 2017. https://www.dhs.gov /sites/default/files/publications/17 _0220_S1_Enforcement-of-the-Im

migration-Laws-to-Serve-the-National
-Interest.pdf.

251 **"In foreign affairs, we are renewing"**:
"Remarks by President Trump to the
72nd Session of the United Nations
General Assembly," September 19,
2017. https://www.whitehouse.gov
/briefings-statements/remarks-presi
dent-trump-72nd-session-united-na
tions-general-assembly/.

252 **he said the word ten times**: "Remarks by President Trump to the
73rd Session of the United Nations
General Assembly," September 25,
2018. https://www.whitehouse.gov
/briefings-statements/remarks-presi
dent-trump-73rd-session-united-na
tions-general-assembly-new-york-ny/.

252 **"The future does not belong to
globalists"**: "Remarks by President
Trump to the 73rd Session of the
United Nations General Assembly,"
September 25, 2018.

252 **an anti-Semitic slur:** Allison Kaplan
Some, "How Did the Term 'Globalist'

Become an Anti-Semitic Slur? Blame Bannon," **Haaretz**, March 13, 2018. https://www.haaretz.com/us-news /.premium-how-did-the-term-global ist-became-an-anti-semitic-slur-blame -bannon-1.5895925.

253 **at a security conference in Washington:** Masha Gessen, "Under Trump, the Language We Use to Create Political Reality Is Crumbling," new yorker.com, April 30, 2019. https:// www.newyorker.com/news/our-col umnists/under-trump-the-language-we -use-to-create-political-reality-is -crumbling.

CHAPTER 20.
CONFRONTING CIVIL
SOCIETY

259 **When Trump announced his candidacy: Washington Post** staff, "Full Text: Donald Trump Announces a Presidential Bid," **Washington Post,**

June 16, 2015. https://www.washing
tonpost.com/news/post-politics/wp
/2015/06/16/full-text-donald-trump
-announces-a-presidential-bid/.

261 **"a total and complete shutdown of
Muslims"**: Jessica Taylor, "Trump Calls
for 'Total and Complete Shutdown
of Muslims Entering' U.S.," NPR,
December 7, 2015. https://www.npr
.org/2015/12/07/458836388/trump
-calls-for-total-and-complete-shut
down-of-muslims-entering-u-s.

262 **"extreme vetting"**: Daniel Strauss,
"Trump Defends Proposal for Muslim
Ban as Call for 'Extreme Vetting,'"
Politico, October 9, 2016. https://
www.politico.com/story/2016
/10/2016-presidential-debate-donald
-trump-muslim-ban-extreme-vet
ting-229468.

262 **"Immigration is not 'just another
issue'"**: Stanley Renshon, "Immigration in the Presidential Campaign,
Part 1," Center for Immigration

Studies, April 15, 2016. https://cis
.org/Report/Immigration-Presidential
-Campaign-Part-1.

264 **Executive Order 13769:** "Executive
Order Protecting the Nation from
Foreign Terrorist Entry into the
United States," Executive Order
13769, The White House, January 27,
2017. https://www.whitehouse.gov
/presidential-actions/executive-or
der-protecting-nation-foreign-terror
ist-entry-united-states/.

265 **Activists and ordinary people:** Lauren
Gambino, Sabrina Siddiqui, Paul
Owen, and Edward Helmore, "Thousands Protest Against Trump Travel
Ban in Cities and Airports Nationwide," **The Guardian**, January 29,
2017. https://www.theguardian.com
/us-news/2017/jan/29/protest-trump
-travel-ban-muslims-airports.

266 **a new executive order with the same
title:** "Executive Order Protecting the
Nation from Foreign Terrorist Entry
into the United States," March 6,

2017. https://www.whitehouse.gov
/presidential-actions/executive-order
-protecting-nation-foreign-terror
ist-entry-united-states-2/.

266 **a Twitter tirade:** Matt Zapolsky,
"Trump's Latest Tweets Will Probably
Hurt Effort to Restore Travel Ban,"
The Washington Post, June 15,
2017. https://www.washingtonpost
.com/world/national-security/trumps
-latest-tweets-could-hurt-effort-to-re
store-travel-ban/2017/06/05/c8eb59
40-49e8-11e7-bc1b-fddbd8359dee
_story.html.

266 **the Trump administration tried again:**
"Enhancing Vetting Capabilities and
Processes for Detecting Attempted
Entry Into the United States by Terrorists or Other Public-Safety Threats,"
Presidential Proclamation 9645, The
White House, September 24, 2017.
https://www.whitehouse.gov/presiden
tial-actions/presidential-proclama
tion-enhancing-vetting-capabilities
-processes-detecting-attempted-entry

-united-states-terrorists-public-safety
-threats/.

267 **the administration solicited bids and
designs:** Sarah Pierce, Jessica Bolter,
and Andrew Selee, "Trump's First Year
on Immigration Policy: Rhetoric vs.
Reality," Migration Policy Institute,
January 2018. https://www.migration
policy.org/research/trump-first-year
-immigration-policy-rhetoric-vs-reality.

268 **his first televised Oval Office address:** Eric Lach, "The Corrupting
Falsehoods of Trump's Oval Office
Speech," newyorker.com, January 18,
2018. https://www.newyorker.com
/news/current/the-corrupting-false
hoods-of-trumps-oval-office-speech\.

270 **a "caravan" of migrants:** Glenn
Kessler, "A Witches' Brew of Over-
the-Top Trump Attacks," **The Washington Post**, October 24, 2018. https://
www.washingtonpost.com/politics
/2018/10/24/president-trumps
-witchs-brew-over-the-top-attacks/.

271 **saw fit to fact-check Trump:** Media

Matters staff, "Shep Smith Shuts Down Fearmongering Claims About Migrant Caravan Pushed by His Fox Colleagues and Trump," Media Matters for America, October 22, 2018. https://www.mediamatters.org/fox -news/shep-smith-shuts-down-fear mongering-claims-about-migrant-car avan-pushed-his-fox-colleagues.

271 **"people trekking across the desert":** Luke O'Neil (@lukeoneil), Twitter, October 23, 2018, 8:13 a.m. https:// twitter.com/lukeoneil47/status/1054 706984832909314.

271 **A December 2018 study:** Emily Boardman Ndulue, "How the 'Migrants in the Struggle' Caravan Was Positioned as a Threat: Using Media Cloud to Track Story Origin and Framing," Media Cloud, December 13, 2018. https://mediacloud.org /news/2018/12/13/migrant-caravan.

272 **Outlets ranging from Breitbart:** Ian Hanchett, "Julian Castro: Caravan 'Proof Positive' Trump Has Been a

Total Failure on Immigration," Breitbart, October 23, 2018, https://www.breitbart.com/clips/2018/10/23/jul ian-castro-caravan-proof-positive -trump-has-been-a-total-failure -on-immigration/. Miriam Jordan, Caitlin Dickerson, and Michael D. Shear, "Trump's Plans to Deter Migrants Could Mean New 'Voluntary' Family Separations," **The New York Times**, October 22, 2018, https:// www.nytimes.com/2018/10/22/us /migrant-families-crossing-border -trump.html. Esther Wang, "An Immigration Attorney on the Migrant Caravan and Safety in Numbers: 'There Is a Level of Desperation, They Really Are Afraid,'" Jezebel, October 24, 2018, https://theslot.jezebel.com/an -immigration-attorney-on-the-mi grant-caravan-and-safe-1829916573.

273 **"whether anything will deter these people"**: Stephanie Ruhle, "Trump Administration Threatens Military Response to Migrant Caravan,"

MSNBC, October 22, 2018. http://
www.msnbc.com/stephanie-ruhle
/watch/trump-administration-threat
ens-military-response-to-migrant-car
avan-1350048835749?v=railb&.

273 **the location of the procession:** Brian
Stelter (@brianstelter), "If your news
coverage of the caravan doesn't include a map like this," Twitter, October 23, 2018, 11:16 a.m. https://
twitter.com/brianstelter/status/10547
53355237478400.

CHAPTER 21.
THE POWER OF MORAL
AUTHORITY

276 **"The one thing that the president":**
"Ocasio-Cortez Rips Trump for Systematic Attack on Immigrants," **The
Rachel Maddow Show**, MSNBC,
January 8, 2019. https://www.msnbc
.com/rachel-maddow/watch/ocasio
-cortez-rips-trump-for-systematic-at
tack-on-immigrants-1422378051711.

277 **deplorable conditions:** Simon Romero, Zolan Kanno-Young, Manny Fernandez, Daniel Borunda, Aaron Montes, and Caitlin Dickerson, "The Stuff of Nightmares: Inside the Migrant Detention Center in Clint, Texas," **El Paso Times**, July 6, 2019. https://www.elpasotimes.com/story /news/immigration/2019/07/06/bor der-patrol-el-paso-sector-migrant-de tention-center-clint-immigration/166 3750001/.

277 **"This administration has established":** Alexandria Ocasio-Cortez (@AOC), Twitter, June 18, 2019, 9:03 a.m. https://twitter.com/AOC/status /1140968240073662466.

278 **"concentration camp system":** Jack Holmes, "An Expert on Concentration Camps Says That's Exactly What the U.S. Is Running at the Border," **Esquire**, June 13, 2019. https://www.es quire.com/news-politics/a27813648 /concentration-camps-southern-border -migrant-detention-facilities-trump/.

278 **"Please @AOC"**: Liz Cheney (@Liz _Cheney), Twitter, June 18, 2019, 10:25 a.m. https://twitter.com/Liz _Cheney/status/1140988893627478018.

278 **criticized Ocasio-Cortez:** United States Holocaust Memorial Museum, press release, "Statement Regarding the Museum's Position on Holocaust Analogies," June 24, 2019. https://www.ushmm.org/information/press/press-releases/statement-regarding-the-museums-position-on-holocaust-analogies.

282 **"All talk, talk, talk"**: Donald J. Trump (@realDonaldTrump), "mention crime infested) rather than falsely complaining about the election results. All talk, talk, talk—no action or results. Sad!" Twitter, January 14, 2017, 8:07 a.m. https://twitter.com/realDonaldTrump/status/820255947956383744.

283 **"Everyone who still tries"**: Václav Havel, open letter to Dr. Husak, General Secretary of the Czechoslovak

Communist Party, April 8, 1975. http://parevo.eu/1parevo/images /PDF/01.%20Vaclav%20Havel _Open%20letter.pdf.

286 **ending with "Muslim Americans"**: "Transcript: Read the Full Transcript of President Obama's Farewell Speech," **Los Angeles Times**, January 10, 2017. https://www.latimes.com/politics /la-pol-obama-farewell-speech-tran script-20170110-story.html.

286 **"I reject"**: Barack Obama, "President Obama's Farewell Address, January 10, 2017," Barack Obama Presidential Library. https://www.obamali brary.gov/sites/default/files/uploads /documents/President%20Obamas %20Farewell%20Address%20%28 TRANSCRIPT%29.pdf.

286 **"You cannot be at home"**: Chuck Todd, Sally Bronston, and Matt Rivera, "Rep. John Lewis: 'I Don't See Trump as a Legitimate President,'" NBC News, January 13, 2017. https:// www.nbcnews.com/storyline/meet

-the-press-70-years/john-lewis-trump
-won-t-be-legitimate-president-n7
06676.

287 **became known as the Squad:** Anna
North, "How 4 Congresswomen
Came to Be Called 'the Squad,'"
Vox, July 17, 2019. https://www
.vox.com/2019/7/17/20696474
/squad-congresswomen-trump-press
ley-aoc-omar-tlaib.

288 **"All these people have":** Maureen
Dowd, "It's Nancy Pelosi's Parade,"
The New York Times, July 6, 2019.
https://www.nytimes.com/2019/07
/06/opinion/sunday/nancy-pelosi
-pride-parade.html.

288 **reported that the Squad:** Rachael
Bade and Mike DeBonis, "'Outright
Disrespectful': Four House Women
Struggle As Pelosi Isolates Them,"
The Washington Post, July 10, 2019.
https://www.washingtonpost.com
/politics/outright-disrespectful-four
-house-women-struggle-as-pelosi-iso
lates-them/2019/07/10/a33c63a8

-a33f-11e9-b7b4-95e30869bd15
_story.html.

288 "So interesting to see": Donald J.
Trump (@realDonaldTrump), Twitter, July 14, 2019, 8:27 a.m. https://
twitter.com/realDonaldTrump/sta
tus/1150381394234941448.

289 The media recognized: Michael
Luo, "Trump's Racist Tweets and
the Question of Who Belongs in
America," The New Yorker, July 15,
2019. https://www.newyorker.com
/news/our-columnists/trumps-racist
-tweets-and-the-question-of-who-be
longs-in-america.

290 "It is time for us to stop": Vivan
Ho and Joanna Walters, "Congresswomen Condemn Trump Attack:
'This Is the Agenda of White
Nationalists'—As It Happened," The
Guardian, July 15, 2019. https://
www.theguardian.com/us-news/live
/2019/jul/15/trump-news-today
-live-racist-go-back-attack-alexan
dria-ocasio-cortez-ice-raids-jeffrey-ep

stein-latest-updates?page=with:block
-5d2cf09d8f08d0b6ca531462
#block-5d2cf09d8f08d0b6ca531462.

CHAPTER 22.
WHO IS "US"? AND WHO ARE WE?

291 **voted to impeach:** Weiyi Cai, K. K. Rebecca Lai, Alicia Parlapiano, Jeremy White, and Larry Buchanan, "Impeachment Results: How Democrats and Republicans Voted," **The New York Times**, December 18, 2019. https://www.nytimes.com/interactive/2019/12/18/us/politics/trump-impeachment-vote.html.

292 **the memory of Elijah Cummings:** Jeff Barker, "'We Did All We Could, Elijah': After Trump Impeachment, Pelosi References Late Rep. Cummings," **The Baltimore Sun**, December 19, 2019. https://www.baltimoresun.com/politics/bs-md-impeachment-maryland-lawmakers-20

191218-fz4r3wijungidfieznimptqmie
-story.html.

292 **Trump had attacked him:** Tim Elfrink
and John Wagner, "Trump Lashes Out
Anew at Rep. Cummings and the 'Corrupt' City He Represents, Says Baltimore Residents Have Thanked Him,"
The Washington Post, July 30, 2019.
https://www.washingtonpost.com/na
tion/2019/07/30/he-should-investi
gate-himself-trump-echoes-fox-news
-again-lash-out-elijah-cummings/.ress

292 **"When the history books are written":** Committee on Oversight and
Reform, press release, "Chairman
Cummings Supports Impeachment,"
September 24, 2019. https://over
sight.house.gov/news/press-releases
/chairman-cummings-supports-im
peachment.

293 **"When we are dancing with the
angels":** Dan Friedman, "What Democrats Lost with Elijah Cummings'
Death," **Mother Jones**, October 17,
2019. https://www.motherjones.com

/politics/2019/10/what-democrats -lost-with-elijah-cummings-death/.

293 **The hero Trump chose:** Dave Phillips, "From the Brig to Mar-a-Lago, Former Navy SEAL Capitalizes on Newfound Fame," **The New York Times**, December 31, 2019. https:// www.nytimes.com/2019/12/31/us /navy-seals-edward-gallagher-trump .html.

293 **acquitted on most charges:** Dave Phillips, "Navy SEAL Chief Accused of War Crimes Is Found Not Guilty of Murder," **The New York Times**, July 2, 2019. https://www .nytimes.com/2019/07/02/us/navy -seal-trial-verdict.html.

293 **already drawn Trump's attention:** Navy Times Staff, "Tweeting Trump Injects White House into SEAL War Crimes Case," **Navy Times**, March 30, 2019. https://www.navytimes.com /news/your-navy/2019/03/30/tweet ing-trump-injects-white-house-into -seal-war-crimes-case/.

293 **tweeted his support:** Donald J. Trump (@realDonaldTrump), "In honor of his past service to our Country, Navy Seal #EddieGallagher will soon be moved to less restrictive confinement while he awaits his day in court. Process should move quickly! @foxand friends @RepRalphNorman," Twitter, March 30, 2019, 8:14 a.m. https://twitter.com/realDonaldTrump/status/1111965027483951105?ref_src=twsrc%5Etfw%7Ctwcamp%5Etweetembed%7Ctwterm%5E11119650274833951105&ref_url=https%3A%2F%2Fwww.navytimes.com%2Fnews%2Fyour-navy%2F2019%2F03%2F30%2Ftweeting-trump-injects-white-house-into-seal-war-crimes-case%2F.

294 **congratulated him by tweet:** Donald J. Trump (@realDonaldTrump), "Congratulations to Navy Seal Eddie Gallagher, his wonderful wife Andrea, and his entire family. You have been through much together. Glad I could help!" Twitter, July 3, 2019, 10:47 a.m.

https://twitter.com/realDonaldTrump
/status/1146430380981067777?ref
_src=twsrc%5Etfw%7Ctwcamp
%5Etweetembed%7Ctwterm%5
E1146430380981067777&ref
_url=https%3A%2F%2Fwww.ny
times.com%2F2019%2F07%2
F02%2Fus%2Fnavy-seal-trial-ver
dict.html.

294 **then intervened to reverse:** Dave Phillips, "Trump Reverses Navy Decision to Oust Edward Gallagher from SEALs," **The New York Times**, November 21, 2019. https://www.nytimes.com/2019/11/21/us/trump-seals-eddie-gallagher.html?action=click&module=RelatedLinks&pgtype=Article.

294 **reinstated Gallagher's rank:** Navy Times Staff, "Report: Trump Makes SEAL Gallagher a Chief Again," **Navy Times**, November 4, 2019. https://www.navytimes.com/news/your-navy/2019/11/04/report-trump-makes-seal-gallagher-a-chief-again/.

294 **stripped the prosecutors:** Carl Prine,

"Trump Nixes NAMs for 4 Prosecutors Tied to SEAL Case," **Navy Times**, July 31, 2019. https://www.navytimes.com/news/your-navy/2019/07/31/trump-nixes-nams-for-4-prosecutors-tied-to-seal-case/.

294 **cost the secretary:** Helene Cooper, Maggie Haberman and Dave Philipps, "Esper Demands Resignation of Navy Secretary Over SEAL Case," **The New York Times**, November 24, 2019. https://www.nytimes.com/2019/11/24/us/politics/navy-secretary-richard-spencer-resign.html.

294 **published a trove:** Dave Phillips, "Anguish and Anger from the Navy SEALs Who Turned In Edward Gallagher," **The New York Times**, December 27, 2019. https://www.nytimes.com/2019/12/27/us/navy-seals-edward-gallagher-video.html.

294 **and launched a career:** Eddie & Andrea (@eddie_and_andrea) Instagram profile. https://www.instagram.com/eddie_and_andrea/?hl=en.

294 **Trump hosted Gallagher:** Dave Phillips, "From the Brig to Mar-a-Lago, Former Navy SEAL Capitalizes on Newfound Fame," **The New York Times**, December 31, 2019. https://www.nytimes.com/2019/12/31/us/navy-seals-edward-gallagher-trump.html.

295 **"It not only conveyed the idea":** Greg Grandin, **The End of the Myth: From the Frontier to the Border Wall in the Mind of America** (New York: Metropolitan Books, 2019), 269–70.

299 **hold up a rainbow flag:** Gwynn Guilford, "Donald Trump's 'Support' of LGBT Communities in One Image," Quartz, October 31, 2016. https://qz.com/823649/donald-trump-unfurled-a-rainbow-flag-with-lgbt-written-on-it-at-a-rally-in-greeley-colorado-to-express-his-so-called-support/.

299 **But Trump also said:** Jennifer Shutt, "Trump Hopes for Reversal on Same-Sex-Marriage," **Politico**, January 31,

2016. https://www.politico.com/story /2016/01/donald-trump-iowa-cau cuses-marriage-218471.

300 **the Supreme Court heard:** Masha Gessen, "The Supreme Court Considers L.G.B.T. Rights, but Can't Stop Talking About Bathrooms," **The New Yorker**, October 9, 2019. https://www .newyorker.com/news/our-colum nists/the-supreme-court-considers -lgbt-rights-but-cant-stop-talking -about-bathrooms.

304 **The Justice Department went:** Katie Benner, "Trump's Justice Department Redefines Whose Civil Rights to Protect," **The New York Times**, September 3, 2018. https://www .nytimes.com/2018/09/03/us/politics /civil-rights-justice-department.html.

305 **allowed hundreds of thousands:** Dan Witters, "U.S. Uninsured Rate Rises to Four-Year High," Gallup, January 23, 2019. https://news.gallup.com /poll/246134/uninsured-rate-rises -four-year-high.aspx.

305 **rule changes deprived:** Catherine
Kim, "Vox Sentences: Trump's War
on Food Stamps," Vox, July 23,
2019. https://www.vox.com/vox-sen
tences/2019/7/23/20707717/vox
-sentences-trump-food-stamps-cuts.

305 **plainly benefited the rich:** Galen
Hendricks, Seth Hanlon, and Michael
Madowitz, "Trump's Corporate Tax
Cut Is Not Trickling Down," Center for American Progress, September 26, 2019. https://www.american
progress.org/issues/economy/news
/2019/09/26/475083/trumps-corpo
rate-tax-cut-not-trickling/.

305 **and resulted in thousands:** Dylan
Matthews, "Study: US Air Pollution
Deaths Increased by 9,700 a Year
from 2016 to 2018," Vox, October 24, 2019. https://www.vox.com
/future-perfect/2019/10/24/209271
03/air-pollution-study-deaths-elderly
-obama-trump.

305 **access to help when disasters:** Vivian
Ho and Mario Koran, "Laborers and

Domestic Workers Stay Behind As Thousands Flee California Wildfires," **The Guardian**, October 30, 2019. https://www.theguardian.com /us-news/2019/oct/30/california-fires -workers-kincade-easy.

307 **"I called them 'animals'"**: John Fritze, "Trump Doubles Down on Calling MS-13 Gang Members 'Animals,' Praises Rod Rosenstein," **USA Today**, May 23, 2018. https://www.usatoday .com/story/news/politics/2018/05 /23/trump-calls-ms-13-gang-mem bers-animals-praises-rod-rosenstein /638468002/.

307 **compared hate-crime statistics:** Ayal Feinberg, Regina Branton, and Valerie Martinez-Ebers, "The Trump Effect: How 2016 Campaign Rallies Explain Spikes in Hate," University of North Texas Latino/a and Mexican-American Studies. http://lmas.unt.edu /sites/lmas.unt.edu/files/lmas/Hate %20Incidents%20Spike_0.pdf.

308 **"it was not just Trump's"**: Griffin

Sims Edwards and Stephen Rushin, "The Effect of President Trump's Election on Hate Crimes," January 14, 2018; available at SSRN: https://papers.ssrn.com/sol3/papers.cfm?abstract_id=3102652.

308 **analyzed survey data:** Brian F. Schaffner, Matthew MacWilliams, and Tatishe Nteta, "Understanding White Polarization in the 2016 Vote for President: The Sobering Role of Racism and Sexism," **Political Science Quarterly** 133, 1 (Spring 2018). https://www.psqonline.org/article.cfm?IDArticle=19752.

309 **attacks on mosques:** "Anti-Muslim Activities in the United States," New America. https://www.newamerica.org/in-depth/anti-muslim-activity/.

310 **anti-Semitic incidents:** "Anti-Semitic Incidents Remained at Near-Historic Levels in 2018; Assaults Against Jews More Than Doubled," ADL, April 30, 2019. https://www.adl.org/news/press-releases/anti-semitic-incidents

-remained-at-near-historic-levels-in
-2018-assaults.

310 **twenty-two of whom were murdered:** Sarah McBride, "HRC Releases Annual Report on Epidemic of Anti-Transgender Violence," Human Rights Campaign, November 18, 2019. https://www.hrc.org/blog/hrc-releas es-annual-report-on-epidemic-of-anti -transgender-violence-2019.

310 **he pardoned Joe Arpaio:** Julie Hirschfeld Davis and Maggie Haberman, "Trump Pardons Joe Arpaio, Who Became Face of Crackdown on Illegal Immigration," **The New York Times**, August 25, 2017. https://www.nytimes.com/2017/08 /25/us/politics/joe-arpaio-trump-par don-sheriff-arizona.html.

311 **announced the decision:** Donald J. Trump (@realDonaldTrump), "I am pleased to inform you that I have just granted a full Pardon to 85 year old American patriot Sheriff Joe Arpaio.

He kept Arizona safe!" Twitter, August 25, 2017, 10:00 p.m. https://twitter.com/realDonaldTrump/status/901263061511794688?ref_src=twsrc%5Etfw%7Ctwcamp%5Etweetembed%7Ctwterm%5E901263061511794688&ref_url=https%3A%2F%2Fwww.nytimes.com%2F2017%2F08%2F25%2Fus%2Fpolitics%2Fjoe-arpaio-trump-pardon-sheriff-arizona.html.

311 **adopted a specific policy:** World Health Organization, "World Health Organization Best Practices for the Naming of New Human Infectious Diseases," May 2015. https://apps.who.int/iris/bitstream/handle/10665/163636/WHO_HSE_FOS_15.1_eng.pdf.

311 **derailed a G7 statement:** Alberto Nardelli and Alex Wickham, "The US Wanted the G7 to Release a Statement That Called Coronavirus 'The Wuhan Virus,'" BuzzFeed News,

March 25, 2020. https://www.buzz
feed.com/albertonardelli/us-g7-coro
navirus-statement-wuhan.

311 **Trump's briefing notes showed:**
"Photo Shows 'Corona' Crossed Out
and Replaced with 'Chinese' in
Trump's Briefing Notes," CNN.com,
March 19, 2020. https://www.cnn
.com/world/live-news/coronavirus
-outbreak-03-19-20-intl-hnk/h_21c6
23966aa148dbeed242de4e94943e.

312 **Hate crimes against Asian Americans
skyrocketed:** Chinese for Affirmative
Action press release, "STOP AAPI
HATE Receives over 1,100 Incident
Reports of Verbal Harassment, Shun-
ning and Physical Assault in Two
Weeks," April 3, 2020. http://www
.asianpacificpolicyandplanningcoun
cil.org/wp-content/uploads/Press_Re
lease_4_3_20.pdf.

312 **inciting fear of New Yorkers:** "Trump
Expresses Outrage at Having to 'Close
the Country' to Slow Virus," **The New
York Times**, March 24, 2020. https://

www.nytimes.com/2020/03/24
/world/coronavirus-news-live-updates
.html.

312 **The governors of Florida and Rhode
Island:** Arek Sarkissian, "DeSantis
Supports Trump's Plan to Quarantine New York," **Politico**, March 28,
2020. https://www.politico.com/states
/new-jersey/story/2020/03/28/de
santis-supports-trumps-plan-to-quar
antine-new-york-1269491; Prashant
Gopal and Brian K. Sullivan, "Rhode
Island Police to Hunt Down New
Yorkers Seeking Refuge," Bloomberg, March 27, 2020. https://
www.bloomberg.com/news/arti
cles/2020-03-27/rhode-island-police
-to-hunt-down-new-yorkers-seeking
-refuge.

312 **Rhode Island posted:** Alex Myers,
"Three Massachusetts Golfers Arrested
for Violating Rhode Island Quarantine Order," MSN.com, April 3,
2020. https://www.msn.com/en-us
/sports/golf/three-massachusetts-golf

ers-arrested-for-violating-rhode-island
-quarantine-order/ar-BB127Eqk.

312 **Residents of Cape Cod and the nearby islands petitioned:** Beth Hickman, "Close the Cape Cod Bridges" petition, Change.org. https://www.change.org /p/change-org-close-the-cape-cod -bridges?fbclid=IwAR3FSBwqSYnR fof6z3zPKCuVZFhEo-Utd5HykX 5Wy6GRcAWj_mdUMuh2HNE.

313 **a New York City co-op board expelled:** Jim Dwyer, "The Doctor Came to Save Lives. The Co-op Board Told Him to Get Lost," **The New York Times**, April 3, 2020. https://www .nytimes.com/2020/04/03/nyregion /co-op-board-coronavirus-nyc.html.

EPILOGUE

321 **millions followed:** Justin Wolfers, "The Unemployment Rate Is Probably Around 13 Percent," **The New York Times**, April 3, 2020. https://www .nytimes.com/2020/04/03/upshot/co

ronavirus-jobless-rate-great-depres
sion.html.

322 **The Supreme Court delayed cases:** Greg Stohr, "Supreme Court Postpones April Arguments; 20 Cases Delayed," Bloomberg, April 3, 2020. https://www.bloomberg.com/news/articles/2020-04-03/supreme-court-postpones-april-arguments-as-delayed-cases-hit-20.

322 **Justice Department sought extreme powers:** Betsy Woodruff Swan, "DOJ Seeks New Emergency Powers amid Coronavirus Pandemic," **Politico**, March 21, 2020. https://www.politico.com/news/2020/03/21/doj-coronavirus-emergency-powers-140023.

323 **a more extreme version of its agenda:** Samuel Bagenstos and Dahlia Lithwick, "Trump Is Already Using the Coronavirus to Push His Right-Wing Agenda," **Slate**, March 30, 2020. https://slate.com/news-and-politics/2020/03/trump-coronavirus-response-authoritarian.html.

323 **though he was reluctant:** James E. Baker, "It's High Time We Fought This Virus the American Way," **The New York Times**, April 3, 2020. https://www.nytimes.com/2020/04/03/opinion/defense-protection-act-covid.html.

324 **watch his approval ratings climb:** Jeffrey M. Jones, "President Trump's Job Approval Rating Up to 49%," Gallup, March 24, 2020. https://news.gallup.com/poll/298313/president-trump-job-approval-rating.aspx.

325 **Trump scrambled to salvage:** Michael Grunewald, "The Mega-Bailout Leaves 4 Mega-Questions," **Politico**, March 28, 2020. https://www.politico.com/news/magazine/2020/03/28/congress-coronavirus-relief-bill-152922.

325 **as many as a third to unemployment:** Dylan Matthews, "Coronavirus Could Lead to the Highest Unemployment Levels Since the Great Depression," Vox, April 1, 2020. vox.com/future

-perfect/2020/4/1/21201700/corona virus-covid-19-unemployment-rate.

326 **the anxiety also propelled:** Matt Flegenheimer, "What the 'Cuomo 2020' Fantasy Says About 2020 Reality," **The New York Times**, March 30, 2020. https://www.ny times.com/2020/03/30/us/politics /andrew-cuomo.html.

326 **"I need Cuomo's measured bullying":** Rebecca Fishbein, "Help, I Think I'm in Love with Andrew Cuomo???," Jezebel, March 19, 2020. https:// jezebel.com/help-i-think-im-in-love -with-andrew-cuomo-1842396411.

ABOUT THE AUTHOR

MASHA GESSEN is the author of eleven books, including the National Book Award–winning **The Future Is History: How Totalitarianism Reclaimed Russia** and **The Man Without a Face: The Unlikely Rise of Vladimir Putin**. A staff writer at **The New Yorker** and the recipient of numerous awards, including Guggenheim and Carnegie fellowships, Gessen lives in New York City.